American Poetry

*A*merican *P*oetry

The Rhetoric
of Its Forms

MUTLU KONUK BLASING

Yale University Press
New Haven and London

Designed by Nancy Ovedovitz and set in Perpetua type by The Composing Room of Michigan. Printed in the United States of America by BookCrafters, Inc., Chelsea, Michigan.

Permission to reprint the following material is gratefully acknowledged:

Selected poems from *The Complete Poems of Emily Dickinson,* edited by Thomas H. Johnson. © 1914, 1929, 1942 by Martha Dickinson Bianchi; © renewed 1957 by Mary L. Hampson. Reprinted by permission of Little, Brown and Company.

Selected poems from *The Poems of Emily Dickinson,* edited by Thomas H. Johnson, Cambridge, Mass.: The Belknap Press of Harvard University Press. © 1951, 1955, 1979, 1983 by The President and Fellows of Harvard College. Reprinted by permission of the publishers and of the Trustees of Amherst College.

"The Gentleman of Shalott" and "Sonnet" from *The Complete Poems, 1927–1979* by Elizabeth Bishop. © 1936, 1961, 1964 by Elizabeth Bishop. © 1983 by Alice Methfessel. Reprinted by permission of Farrar, Straus and Giroux, Inc.

"Poetry" from *The Collected Poems of Frank O'Hara* by Frank O'Hara. © 1971 by Maureen Granville-Smith. Reprinted by permission of Alfred A. Knopf, Inc.

Chapter 4 originally appeared, in somewhat different form, in *Modern Language Studies;* modified versions of chapters 6 and 9 were first published in *Contemporary Literature.* Reprinted by permission.

Library of Congress Cataloging-in-Publication Data

Blasing, Mutlu Konuk, 1944–
    American poetry–the rhetoric of its forms.
    Bibliography: p.
    Includes index.
    1. American poetry–History and criticism. 2. Literary form. I. Title.
PS303.K64 1987   811'.009   86–22395
ISBN 0–300–03793–7 (cloth)
        0–300–04607–3 (pbk.)

10   9   8   7   6   5   4   3   2

FOR RANDY

Contents

Introduction   1

Part One

One   Edgar Allan Poe, the Poet to a *T*   17
Two   T. S. Eliot and the Archaeology of Poetry   36
Three   Sylvia Plath's Black Car of Lethe   50

Part Two

Four   Ralph Waldo Emerson: Essaying the Poet   67
Five   Wallace Stevens: The Exquisite Errors of Time   84
Six   The Re-Verses of Elizabeth Bishop   101

Part Three

Seven   The Coinciding Leaves of Walt Whitman   119
Eight   Ezra Pound's Hard Currency   140
Nine   Frank O'Hara: The Speech of Poetry   156

Part Four

Ten   Emily Dickinson's Untitled Discourse   173
Eleven Hart Crane: Inscribing the Sublime   188
Twelve John Ashbery: Parodying the Paradox   200

Notes   213
Index   243

*I*ntroduction

TRADITION IN AMERICA

Poetic language, so thoroughly an embodiment of the past, is charged with the cultural memory inscribed in its conventions, forms, and traditions. Yet it begins to be heard in its American inflection only when it begins to register the loss of both the English literary tradition and the political and meta-physical assumptions underwriting the very idea of a legitimate historical authority.

Recent studies of American poetry have tended to approach this historical discontinuity with a metaphoric evasion, substituting Emerson for the lost "father" and instituting him as a literary and spiritual authority. Emerson has become a poetic father figure, the source of all conceivable traditions of American poetry. Poets as different as Walt Whitman and Emily Dickinson, Robert Frost and Hart Crane, Robert Lowell and Charles Olson, and anyone and everyone else we can name have been traced back to Emerson. "Why he stands so much at the center [of "our lives and our literature"] may always be a mystery, but who else can stand in his place?" asks Harold Bloom, an outspoken proponent of an Emersonian poetic history.[1] Bloom exempts Emerson from any "anxiety of influence": "Emerson denounced all influence as pernicious, and his involuntary disciples have fought so bitterly against influence that they have all become one version or another of their brilliantly scattered, ever metamorphic father."[2] The "involuntary disciples" include, in this immediate context, Whitman, Dickinson, Stevens, Crane, Ammons, Ashbery, Frost, and Pound. And anyone who has not become an "involuntary disciple"—Eliot, for example—has failed to be a strong poet.[3]

I have made Bloom my "representative man" partly because of his exceptional willingness to bracket his master theory of literary determinism in order to make room for Emerson and to allow for one Orphic beginning.[4] For his reading of Emerson is, in fact, representative:[5] Emerson has become the privileged center of American poetic history—a center that, in Jacques Derrida's terms, itself remains "beyond the reach of play."[6] For American literary history to be legitimate, it appears to need a father who stands outside history, mysteriously successful in repudiating the past, practically self-created, and not even primarily a poet.

I start with the assumption that no one need stand in Emerson's place. Applying the model of a dynastic tradition to American poetry evades the theoretical issues raised by its dispossession and further confuses its history by forcing widely different poets to fit within the limits of Emerson's poetic. It confuses even the issue of what poetic influence might mean, since Emerson's dynastic position is granted him on the basis of his prose; the "father" who "did contain multitudes of his descendants" and "sang" "so magnificently," sang, after all, in prose.[7] I would like to view the field of American poetry cleared of the centering figure of Emerson and to see how it might take shape without this "brave ghostly father," who has become the ghost of the brave father still presiding "in the same figure like the king that's dead."[8]

The liberation of American poets from a dynastic, central authority—whether metaphysical, political, or historical—is also a liberation from the very metaphysics and politics of centrality. It inaugurates an originally dispossessed poetry that is always explicitly conscious of the discontinuity between language and the presences it would name. Literary tradition substitutes historical continuity for the discontinuity of rhetoric and nature. American poetry begins by questioning such an authorized and authorizing history, and American poets have consciously searched for strategies of self-authorization by appealing to the nature of rhetoric, to the possibilities of rhetoric to authorize itself. Writing that works within a tradition centers outside itself; American poets' unprecedented position of having to provide self-authorization moves their center, in Derrida's terms, inside the play of rhetoric, into the play of language.

The historical dispossession—or liberation, depending on one's point of view—of American poetry from the English tradition has made the historical crisis that romanticism represents particularly acute for American poets. Romantic self-consciousness questions itself within a tradition—indeed, by playing off against it. While such rhetorical resources are not available to American poets, other and wider choices are, for they have been able to choose their traditions and to question the forms and conventions, as well as the metaphysics, of representation.

Poe, Emerson, Whitman, and Dickinson are the first American poets to show, in the formal shape of their work, a conscious engagement with the problem of the discontinuity between English literary history and American political, cultural, and intellectual history. The strategies by which these poets authorize their work are substantially different, and I propose that their different solutions are generic models that operate throughout American poetic history. By decentering the Emersonian "tradition" and tracing the evolution of these four generic models, I hope to provide a way of distinguishing different species of modernism. At the same time, such a generic history would suggest an alternative to the predominantly eclectic readings of contemporary poetry by providing a way of sorting out the varieties of postmodern poetry and poetics.

Since historical continuity has never been crucial to the development of American poetry, approaching it with more than one paradigm might give us a new perspective on the field and reveal new lines of relationships to help us reassess some of our major poets and traditions. My dissenting typology may not be the inevitable one; but a monolithic line of descent, with Emerson as the "archaic" father, is not a viable model for the American tradition.

FOUR TROPES

This book is a formalist study of a historical field, a synchronic typing of a diachronic subject. I propose a typology of the generic rhetorics of American poetry. To define the generic rhetoric of a poem, I suggest that a poem has two axes. Its linguistic and formal features—its syntax as well as its meter, rhythm, rhymes, and other features that make for its phonic shape—constitute its formal axis. This axis comprises all the substitutions and displacements that have to do with the signifier. The figuration of the poem—its imagery, tone, and meaning—constitutes its referential axis,[9] the system of substitutions and displacements that have to do with the referent.

The formal and referential axes of a poem—its "nature" and its "discourse"—may be related by a limited number of structuring tropes. Here, *trope* designates a basic structure of literary symbolism that organizes a poem intratextually (determining the relation between its "form" and "content"), intertextually (guiding a poem's relation to literary forms, conventions, and predecessors), and extratextually (shaping a poem's relation to "reality"). Intratextually, the central structural trope figures a specific conception of linguistic and literary representation, designating the relation between the verbal sign and the signified, grammar and rhetoric, the poem's formal axis and its meaning. Extratextually, the central trope proposes a specific relation between the poem as a whole and the non-verbal "reality" or "experience."

Thus a trope substitutes both words for words—or an extra-ordinary sense of a word for its ordinary sense—and the fictive for the real. Here I am following Scaliger's comprehensive definition, which "implies that no literary process can occur without continually using tropes, and conversely that the process of transmuting reality into art is also the process which creates the trope."[10] A structural understanding of tropes covers rhetoric as figuration and as persuasion—in Bloom's terms, as "signification" and as "meaning." For the aporia/link between these two conceptions of rhetoric can itself be figured on the model of a specific structural trope.[11] A structural trope, then, defines a particular relation between sound and sense, proper and transposed meanings, word and thing. Further, different relationships between the formal and referential axes of a poem imply different metaphysics—different conceptions of how the "seen" universe relates to the "unseen," how form relates to force.

Since Aristotle's *Poetics,* poetic theory has distinguished four basic tropes—what Kenneth Burke calls the four "master tropes."[12] These are metaphor, metonymy, synecdoche, and irony. *Metaphor,* used not generically but specifically, designates a trope that works with analogies to reveal resemblances. It is "a trope of transference in which an unknown or imperfectly known is clarified, defined, described in terms of a known."[13] Hence this trope can claim cognitive value yet avoid reductive equivalencies, proposing only "adequate" representations.[14] The analogical or "proportional" trope works with not a two- but a four-part relationship, again as analyzed by Aristotle: the metaphor from analogy "is possible whenever there are four terms so related that the second (B) is to the first (A), as the fourth (D) to the third (C); for one may then metaphorically put D in lieu of B, and B in lieu of D."[15] Thus metaphoric representations propose likenesses while maintaining an awareness of dissimilarities.

By contrast, *metonymy* or "change of name" has only a two-part structure, substituting one word for another, part for part, species for species. Under metonymy we might list substitutions of name for thing, container for contained, "modifier for modified, symbol for thing symbolized."[16] Metonymy is a strategy of reducing the intangible to the tangible, the immaterial to material proofs, manifestations, signs;[17] metonymic substitution thus tends toward emblematic symbolism and formalism.

Synecdoche or "taking together" substitutes either part for whole *or* whole for part, thereby identifying quantity and quality, microcosm and macrocosm. In Burke's words, synecdoche refers to substitutions that "imply an integral relationship, a relationship of convertibility, between the two terms." While metonymic "reduction" allows only for a one-way substitution of quantity for quality, effect for cause, or part for whole, synecdoche works with a two-way or duplex conversion and can substitute quality for quantity, cause for effect, genus for species; it is, in Hayden White's term, an "integrative" trope.[18]

Finally, *irony* (*eironeia* or "dissimulation") expresses two meanings simultaneously, at once affirming and denying the proposed relationship. The dialectical structure of the ironic trope is that of paradox and points up the discontinuous relationship of symbol to the thing symbolized, whether word or thing. Distinct from both verbal and dramatic irony,[19] this dialogical structure deconstructs the process of meaning itself. According to Burke, irony is a "'perspective of perspectives,'" and "none of the participating 'sub-perspectives' can be treated as either precisely right or precisely wrong." Irony is thus polyphonous and consciously comments on the nature of linguistic substitution and questions the generation of meaning through such deviant means.[20] White observes that while the first three tropes are "naive," implying faith in the capacity of language to grasp the nature of things in figurative terms, the trope of irony is "metatropological": it uses figurative language self-consciously, in order to question its claims to knowledge or truth.[21]

These four master tropes, which designate different conceptions and strategies of representation, also seem to underlie the medieval idea of four levels of textual interpretation. According to this schema, which is the origin of literary criticism, a given Biblical passage has four senses, and reading a text at four levels entails four different theories of how its rhetoric functions and of what relation it bears to extratextual experience. The first or "literal" sense of a text, as defined by Dante, "does not go beyond the strict limits of the letter"; the "literal," "historical," or "carnal" meaning is the simple narration, the basis on which the other levels rest. The second sense is the "allegorical" or "typological" meaning, and this level of interpretation draws out the New Testament truths prefigured in Old Testament passages, which are the "types" for the Christian "anti-types" that fulfill them. The "tropological" or "moral" meaning is the third level of sense and interpretation and shows the moral truth or doctrine of the same passage as it applies to the present. The "spiritual" or "anagogic" fourth level, which is "above the senses," concerns mystical truth, and interpretation refers the passage to Christian eschatology.[22]

This classification assumes that there are four levels of symbolism—four possible ways the signifier may relate to the signified, or text to meaning. In *Anatomy of Criticism,* Northrop Frye expands the implications of this medieval schema for literary criticism and suggests that each of the four levels or phases of symbolism has "a particularly close relationship to a certain kind of literature, and to a certain type of critical procedure as well." According to Frye, the literal level, when applied to literary works rather than Bible stories, must be understood to refer to the linguistic and literal shape of a poem.[23] In these terms, primarily literal readings and texts are self-conscious re-creations of "naive" forms of literalism—of readings at face value and of naively representational texts. The trope of irony structures the literal phase: "The literary structure is ironic because 'what it says' is always different in kind or degree from 'what it means.'"[24]

The analogical phase, by contrast, presupposes "an analogy of proportion between the poem and the nature which it imitates." Now, Frye suggests, "the poem is not natural in form, but it relates itself naturally to nature, and so, to quote Sidney . . . , 'doth grow in effect a second nature.'"[25] Structured by the trope of metaphor, the analogical phase proposes correspondences or resemblances between the signifier and the referent, between the textual and existential spheres. It suggests that A is *as* B, the poem is *as* the world.

Unlike the analogical model, the allegorical model of figuring poetic language proposes that the signifier stands for or metonymically represents the signified according to guidelines spelled out by tradition or history. The signified, tenor, or subject is prior to and has no natural relationship to the signifier, vehicle, or text that comes after and represents it according to convention. While on the literal level the signifier is purely itself, here it is an emblem or an allegorical marker for what it signifies. In what Frye terms this "archetypal" phase, a poem is an imitation of other poems.[26]

At the anagogic or fourth level, the signifier and the signified meet in an apocalyptic identity, and poetic structures are believed to coincide with the structure of the universe. The integrative trope of synecdoche underwrites anagogic identifications, proposing that A *is* B, the text *is* the world. Now the symbol is a "monad," and "literature imitates the total dream of man."[27] Thus the schema of four levels of textual interpretation resolves itself into four theories of symbolic meaning or the four master tropes. The accompanying chart summarizes these correspondences.

Trope	*Poetic strategy*	*Relation between signifier and referent, vehicle and tenor*
metonymy	allegory	consequence; expression; reduction
metaphor	analogy	resemblance; correspondence
synecdoche	anagogy	identity; isomorphism
irony	literalism	difference; dissemblance; anomaly

Any given poem subscribes to a particular conception of linguistic meaning, with its attendant metaphysical and epistemological implications and formal or practical directives. It derives its authority or confers on itself the status of "poem" by appealing to a particular trope, a particular structural model of how its language means or claims to offer knowledge of the world. Thus a poem may claim authority by proposing to present or express reality metonymically; to resemble and adequately represent it; to be identical with it; or to make it up.

A structural trope is a deep structure that figures the rhetorical strategy authorizing a given poetic. The intratextual functions of tropes are quite distinct, and all poets make use of a variety of such figures. Yet each of the master tropes appears to privilege particular rhetorical figures and schemes and to exhibit certain generic tendencies. Metonymic thinking tends to dramatic representations, personifications, allegorical reductions, and emblematic symbolism, and it relies on conventional schemes such as rhyme, repetition, alliteration, and so on, with none of the metaphoric poem's desire to naturalize such devices. Metamorphic thinking inclines to analogies and similes and exploits formal features for their cognitive analogies. Synecdochic thinking favors puns and metamorphic identifications, nonhierarchical and all-inclusive epical forms, and rhythms and cadences based on speech, emphasizing the natural and physiological rather than the conventional patterns of words. Ironic thinking stresses literal structures and uses such discontinuous figures and syntactic forms as catachreses, paradoxes, oxymorons, mixed metaphors, litotes, and hyperboles. The ironic poem offers a "sentimental"—in Schiller's sense of "self-conscious"—representation of the "naive" modes of the other tropes.[28] A given trope thus implies specific generic, rhetorical, and formal tendencies.

FOUR TYPES OF AMERICAN POETRY

The four structural tropes may be used to differentiate the poetic strategies of the nineteenth-century poets Poe, Emerson, Whitman, and Dickinson; in the twentieth century, American poets have continued to appeal to the same rhetorical models for their authority.

To begin with, Poe is an allegorical poet, who maintains an irreducible difference between experience and representation. Allegory's internal belatedness—of the representation in relation to the model, of the signifier in relation to the signified—mirrors a historical or intertextual belatedness, so that Poe and subsequent allegorical poets like T. S. Eliot and Sylvia Plath find themselves subject to the "forgetfulness" of poetic forms, emblems, conventions, and tradition. Within the retrospective framework of allegorical thinking, the text is an always belated representation of a prior presence, source, or truth. This reductive rhetoric tends to be accompanied by a reductive formalism; and an esthetic of method, of creating effects by manipulating formal stimuli, only reaffirms the barrier between the mind and nature, the soul and the body, the spirit and the letter of language. Such expressionism is a symptom of a dualistic metaphysics, an absolute split between force and form, which renders the body of the poem an imprisoning mechanism. And the poets in this mode often strike out at the body—their own bodies or their poems, the body of nature or of literature—to punish it for violating the soul, whether Poe's "angelic" imagination caught in the machinery and machinations of form, Eliot's "individual talent" stifled by the genius of "tradition," or Plath's "pure acetylene virgin" carried off by the "black car of Lethe."

Emerson's poetic strategy rests on analogy: he regards language as representing our perceptions of correspondences between the mind and nature. For Emerson, the metaphoric figuration and formal balances of poetry embody the analogies between the orders of nature and the mind. His conception of poetic form as an embodiment of divine and natural law enables him both to center an originally deviating rhetoric of figuration and to use traditional forms, without necessarily subscribing to their historical authority or to the literary history that validates them. His is a metaphorical or tropological rather than a metonymic or typological use of tradition: the past is not a binding precedent but is "morally" applicable to the present, for the literary structures that tradition validates have analogies in natural and social orders. Thus Emerson makes possible a poetry that neither serves, rejects, nor subverts poetic precedents, conventions, and forms. Like Emerson, Wallace Stevens and Elizabeth Bishop also consider poetry to be, in Stevens's terms, the "strange rhetoric" of the resemblance between the processes of thought and nature. They regard poetic forms as fundamental structures, whose very conventionality argues their naturalness—given the matrix of resemblances—and choose conventional forms naturally and of necessity. Working with the four-part structure of analogy, they define poetic language as the language of unlikely likenesses or diachronic identity; thus they see the temporal and spatial displacements that poetic form and rhetoric effect as speaking centrally for a human nature, whose "strange truth" *is* rhetoric. Such an understanding of metaphor internalizes the discontinuity of rhetoric and presence and makes for a connection, if eccentric, between the mind and nature, the spirit and the letter. The central/eccentric language of the Emersonian poet marries, in the moral law of a human nature, the fateful law of nature and the transcendent law of the spirit; it measures an existential and rhetorical ground where fate and freedom meet.

Anagogy proposes a coincidence of textual and existential experience, figurative and literal language, poetic and natural form. This rhetoric authorizes Whitman and other anagogic poets like Ezra Pound and Frank O'Hara. Their language aspires, in Whitman's words, to a *"perfect transparent clearness sanity, and health,"* and such a *"divine style"* not only disdains the substitutions and deferrals of similes and analogies but rejects all ordained, hierarchical forms. In such poetry, traditional forms and meters give way to free verse, transparent superimpositions or identities replace allegorical equivalencies, and actual metamorphoses replace metaphoric resemblances. Breaking down the distinction between form and content, these poets use the collage method and epic forms, in which disorder and order, accident and design, multiplicity and unity, formlessness and form, a quantitative "all" and a qualitative "All" coincide. The synecdochic conversion of quantity and quality guides a compositional method where relationships of contiguity and those of similarity coincide,[29] so that prose and poetry are points on a continuum rather than opposites.

Dickinson's rhetoric of irony emphasizes the differentiation of the very categories of subjective and objective realms, mental and natural experience. The subversive literal play of her language points up the necessary deviation of the signifier from its referent and thus dismantles the rhetoric of the Logos, the identity of word and thing that anagogy upholds. She recognizes only an articulating and disarticulating syntax—the process whereby letters, syllables, words, and sentences add up to a mind and a world. Dickinson's literalism is the obverse of Whitman's anagogy. She would agree that form and force, the letter and the spirit of language, are interchangeable; however, she regards poetic language not as the identity of these two axes of meaning but as the ground of their very differentiation. Dickinson and such poets as Hart Crane and John Ashbery devise anomalous structures. Shifting from figurative to literal senses, from semantic ambiguities to syntactic and grammatical discontinuities, from metaphysics to physics, or from epistemology to rhetoric, they all expose any transcendence or presence to be an illusion created between the cracks of a discontinuous "syntax," whether of sentences or "arguments."

Violating consistencies of syntax, semantic levels, and diction, these poets generate an illicit excess of meaning, which is the "erotic double"—to borrow Ashbery's term— of a spiritual excess of meaning. Such a proliferation of meanings offers an escape from the "law and order" of grammar, rationality, and the reality principle. Dickinson dissects the word, Crane the sentence, and Ashbery the syntax of meditation; but all lay bare the generative gap between the "nature" and the "rhetoric," the "psychology" and the "theology," of their mannered language. The literalist text works on a "carnal" level, for it identifies the literal level as the basis of all other levels of sense, of all other rhetorics, in a postmetaphysical rewriting of a pre-metaphysical, "debased" or "base" literalism. By circling back to literal meanings, Dickinson not only subverts the Christian theory of symbolism but deconstructs all metaphysical systems. Her "sentimental" use of Christian vocabulary and the hymnal form ("naive" in more than one sense), Crane's "sentimental" rewriting of the Christian and the Whitmanic Logos to the tune of the metric beat, Ashbery's "sentimental" meditations on the philosophical issues of representation or the theological issues of prayer—all are deconstructions in the ironic phase. Poetic forms and conventions are also used ironically or paradoxically, as authorities set up to be deconstructed or subverted. I will use "anomalous" rather than "ironic" to refer to this phase in order to distinguish such discontinuous structures from the stylistic "letterism" and the ironic tone that may be present in other phases.[30]

The poets I discuss in each group illustrate the same poetic theory and practice as they unfold through the romantic, modern, and postmodern periods, assimilating changes in historical and cultural experience, as well as diverse stylistic influences, in a given poetic. I do not intend to substitute four traditions for a single Emersonian tradition or to trace influences so much as to propose a generic typing of American poetics. In certain groupings, we might well talk about a tradition: the Whitmanic poets, for example, consciously align themselves with Whitman, whom they regard as a predecessor. In other lines, such as Poe-Eliot-Plath and Dickinson-Crane-Ashbery, the generic groupings do not coincide with any conscious, or at least acknowledged, sense of a tradition or historical continuity. Yet a generic typing is useful in dissociating stylistic influences from structural affinities. For example, Crane is stylistically influenced by Eliot, and Ashbery by Stevens; yet the underlying poetic strategies of both Crane and Ashbery differ from those of their stylistic predecessors, who are not particularly helpful in understanding them.

Approached exclusively in terms of a historical tradition or historical lines of influence, certain features of major poets' work have been covered up and structural relationships have been submerged. Grouping poets by rhetorical strategies would provide a synchronic typing, against which a diachronic history may be more usefully plotted. Often, historical links obscure profound differences: the relationships of Emerson and Whitman, Eliot and Pound, and Ashbery and O'Hara would be examples.

A typology offers some guidelines for evaluation as well. For instance, poets who can assimilate stylistic influences from predecessors with different rhetorical strategies are often best able to sound new inflections or offer new angles of vision. Pound advised poets to go to those most distant from them for their education, and this seems sound advice. For if the lines of influence and affinity coincide, and a poet's style and vision are *both* traceable to one predecessor, he or she will be more "derivative," with less "anxiety" about the predecessor and, in turn, less influence on those who follow. Among the Whitmanic poets, for example, Carl Sandburg, Robinson Jeffers, and Allen Ginsberg are not as significant to our poetic history as Pound, H.D., or W. C. Williams—poets who look beyond Whitman for their stylistic influences and thus can devise different varieties of "free" forms, adapting a given rhetorical strategy to an evolving history and exploring its possibilities for their own time. Stevens's assimilation of Whitman and Ashbery's of Stevens provide other examples of successful crossings of stylistic influence and generic cast to fashion new idioms that have proved fertile.

Mine is not a historical study, and it does not claim to be comprehensive. The poets I have chosen to represent the different historical manifestations of the same generic types also represent my value judgments. The choice of Stevens over Robert Frost or Marianne Moore reflects both personal prefer- ence and the fact that Stevens explored the philosophical implications of analogical thinking more exhaustively than the others. My choosing Pound instead of Williams or H.D. was also guided by this double consideration: in his anagogic project, Pound extends the formal and philosophical possibilities of synecdochic thinking farther than his contemporaries do.

The field is more crowded in the contemporary period, and the choices here have been more a matter of personal preference. To follow the example of the Whitmanic paradigm,Charles Olson, Louis Zukofsky, Robert Duncan, Gary Snyder, and Denise Levertov were among possible representatives. Since most of these poets have often been linked to each other and to Whitman, Pound, Williams, and/or H.D., I chose to write instead on Frank O'Hara, who has not received the same kind of critical attention, whose place in the Whitmanic tradition has not been sorted out, and who, it seems to me, resuscitates the Whitmanic breath with greater success than any of his contemporaries. Similarly, my choice of Sylvia Plath was guided by a consid- eration of her position among the poets to whom she is linked—Robert Lowell, John Berryman, W. D. Snodgrass, and Anne Sexton. While Plath *has* received a great deal of critical attention, it has not been the kind that could serve to place her in American poetic history.

Such a study as this cannot be inclusive, but my hope is that readers will be able to place poets not dealt with here somewhere within this schema and that such placement will help clarify the configuration of American poetry. The synchronic typing I propose is meant not to deny but to help define the precise nature of historical development. Romanticism, modernism, and postmodernism remain functional distinctions between poets and poetics. For example, Pound's distance from Whitman, on the one hand, and from O'Hara, on the other, or Crane's difference from Dickinson and Ashbery measures the extent and significance of historical variation. But historical qualities that make for literary classification by period meet resistance from, play off against, and help reshape shared generic tendencies that survive through historical modulations.

TROPES, TIME, AND TRADITION

Even before American poets developed their distinctive poetic idioms of the English language, they wrote with a consciousness of their historical, American difference. Just as American poetry is never simply naive, it is never simply subject to the prior authority of the English tradition. The idea of a dynastic literary tradition has always been anachronistic for American literary history, because it can account for neither the original deviance nor the resultant variousness of American poetry. According to what idea of tradition can contemporaries like Whitman and Dickinson, Stevens and Pound, Plath and Ashbery, be placed in a continuity? A monolithic tradition cannot allow for such great substantive differences as between these poets, unless one reduces their differences to value judgments like "good" and "bad" or "strong" and "weak." I would maintain, for example, that Stevens and Pound are equally strong poets, on any scale of value but that of a single tradition. Not only is each poet's relationship to the past substantially different; each poet would define what he considers to be his tradition differently. For instance, Homer is part of Pound's "live" tradition but is not as "live" for Stevens as Wordsworth is, who in turn is not very "live" for Pound. If we approach Pound and Stevens with the idea that the relevant predecessors for American poets are the English romantics, we would have to agree with Harold Bloom that Stevens is a "stronger" poet at mastering the tradition—or the "prior plenitude of meaning"—than Pound.[31] Yet, while Stevens confronts the romantic tradition head-on and Pound evades it, such a basis of judgment is not adequate to evaluate a poet of Pound's achievement and influence, for, unlike Stevens, he responds to a global tradition and fully engages the implications of modernism; and the question remains, as Marjorie Perloff has put it, "Pound/Stevens: Whose Era?"[32] Perhaps a typology such as I propose, which substitutes a systematic network of relationships for a dynastic tradition, can help us understand and evaluate differences that can reduce to mere value judgments within a one-directional, patristic understanding of tradition and literary history.

If we see that different rhetorical models imply different temporal configurations, we can map their relation to English literary tradition with greater discrimination. As I have suggested, tropes are not limited to synchronic figuration, because they posit temporal relationships, both between the intratextual axes of a poem and between its language and extratextual experience. The different internal time-structures of the four rhetorical models not only clarify the conception and function of poetic form that distinguish one poet's practice from another's, but explain a given poet's or poem's relationship to the tradition that would prefigure it. Within the retrospective framework of allegory, for example, the signifier is invariably subsequent to the referent, and authority resides in priority, whether of nature or tradition. In analogy, however, process and form, soul and body, the present and tradition are defined in interaction. Now the poetic imagination actively discovers the prior reality of both nature and tradition. Whereas in allegory the referent is always prior to and independent of its representation, metaphor in part creates the model or reality. Such representation is not simply belated; it prefigures its model as prior and timeless. In metaphoric thinking, then, even if nature and the tradition have ontological priority, they do not have logical priority.

American poetry in the nineteenth and twentieth centuries belongs in the larger context of the revolution that romanticism represents. This is a shift from a conception of the sign as an allegorical marker to sign as symbol—a representation that partakes of the thing represented. Or, in Tzvetan Todorov's account, the period from 1750 to 1800 marks the critical shift from the classical idea of art as imitating nature in allegories of reality to the romantic conception of the artist as imitating the Creator by using symbols to produce works of art on a par with nature.[33] Todorov's historical account of European romanticism works with a metonymic-metaphoric axis. This framework would accommodate the poetics of Poe and Emerson and help distinguish their relation to tradition. Historically, allegory links to formal or "associative" analogy, more prevalent in pre-romantic poetry, and metaphor relates to the romantic "symbol," based on organic analogies, vital affinities, or correspondences. However, the dichotomy of allegory vs. symbol—or metonymy vs. metaphor—cannot prefigure a Whitmanic poetic of apocalyptic identities or a Dickinsonian poetic of structural irony. Thus Poe and Emerson may be more profitably discussed within the context of English romanticism; Whitman and Dickinson far less so, for they stand outside the romanticist debate over allegory vs. symbol.

   To a certain extent, even the four types have a historical sequence among themselves: Poe is most closely aligned with the English tradition, and Emerson's work represents a mediating, tropological, or "moral" relationship to English forms. Whitman, however, breaks with that tradition in order to return to more "original" traditions. Synecdoche is a synchronic and synchronizing trope, proposing two-way, duplex equivalences. Its particular fiction identifies synchronic and diachronic time, so that before and after, tenor and vehicle, coincide. The "tradition" of anagogic poetry, which is ecological and nonhierarchical, is not delimited by historical or national bounds and aspires to be primal, global, and "projective." Likewise, the temporal framework of irony is ahistorical; irony is belated to rhetoric itself and is thus forever removed from a prior authority. As in Dickinson's variations on her American predecessors, irony plays off against other rhetorical models; it parodies and deconstructs metonymic, metaphoric, and synecdochic claims to truth; and it is regarded as originating later than the other tropes. "Irony certainly could not have begun until the period of reflection," Vico writes in his classification of historical ages according to the dominant trope, "because it is fashioned of falsehood by dint of a reflection which wears the mask of truth."[34] While irony's consciousness of the discontinuity between language and experience ties it to allegory, it does not share allegory's generically diachronic structure.[35] Irony dissociates historical or temporal priority from authority: here, time is not the "originary constitutive category," as it is in allegory.[36] Thus the internal temporal structures of the four rhetorical models prefigure the relation of their discourse not only to nature but to tradition and suggest just what would constitute a relevant past or tradition. Making use of such distinctions may enable us more fairly to discriminate and assess the varieties of American poetic experience.

Part One

Chapter One

Edgar Allan Poe, the Poet to a T

> The undying voice of that dead time,
> With its interminable chime,
> Rings, in the spirit of a spell,
> Upon thy emptiness—a knell.
> > "Tamerlane"

Edgar Allan Poe's failure as a poet appears to be a matter of consensus among his English and American readers, who find it difficult to account for his exalted status in France. Yet he is best placed in a transatlantic context, for his failure—and his success—directly stem from his American displacement. Poe not only inaugurates a species of estheticism that modulates into Symbolism, but sounds an abiding inflection of American poetic language, which is heard in the modernism of T. S. Eliot and the expressionism of poets like John Berryman, Robert Lowell, and Sylvia Plath. The reverberations set off by Poe's poems follow not so much from their esthetic achievement as from the peculiar note they strike for the first time.

Poe begins with the problem of literary authority: "You are aware of the great barrier in the path of an American writer. He is read, if at all, in preference to the combined and established wit of the world. I say established; for it is with literature as with law or empire—an established name is an estate in tenure, or a throne in possession."[1] Lacking a dynastic authorization or an inherited legal status, the American writer faced an impossible choice between a provincial colonialism ("a most servile deference to British critical dicta") and a provincial nationalism—a "misapplied patriotism" with its "puerile inflation of vanity" (*CW,* 8:276–77). Poe urges us not to forget that "*the world* is the true theatre of the biblical histrio"; his world, however, is curiously suspended between England and America, in a midatlantic

Atlantis outside history. It is this estrangement from both his English and American backgrounds that shapes his work.

Poe's distance from a dynastic tradition enabled him to question its metaphysical assumptions of central authority and to recognize the textuality of writing. This recognition initiates a species of modernism and accounts for his high esteem in France. Modernism may be defined as a transition from representational to reflexive fictions, from closed or "readerly" works to open or "writerly" texts, from dynastic to "fraternal" texts with plural rather than singular, prescribed meanings.[2] Poe is a practitioner of the "writerly" text, and the irony of his all but dynastic position in France points up his problem: he is the foreign author of the "unauthorized" text. The poet of pure writing, he commands not the Logos but only the written word, which lacks authority, access to truth, and the status of knowledge—all privileges, according to Jacques Derrida, only a metaphysical "father" can grant the word.[3] Poe does without transcendentalisms and myths of fathers: his "truth" is only a self-authorized or textual truth—that is, a mere duplication and multiplication of the word's original "untruth," the spatial-temporal gap between the signifier and the signified. Deconstructionist readings of Poe's fiction properly locate him in a textual universe, where there is no origin, authority, or Word but only a library of texts and signifiers circulating multiple images of the absence of nature or God.[4] Such recent readings have helped expose Poe's linguistic assumptions about the root alienation of writing—the abyss between words and things—and are useful guides to the configurations of his fictions.

Yet this approach is not particularly helpful when it comes to Poe's poetry, for it fails to register his historical problem with the library of texts he finds himself in. His metaphysical liberation from dynastic fictions of a central truth and authority forces him to acknowledge the thoroughly conventional nature of verse. Thus his delivery from spiritual fathers only delivers him over to historical fathers and requires him to recognize the authorizing line of a living tradition. For the only exit from metaphysics is into history, and even Derrida's library of thefts, texts, and palimpsests records a history of patricidal, fraternal deconstructions of metaphysical presence. A history of writing—indeed, a history purged of temporality itself—comes to constitute a reconstructed "ground." Poe's nostalgic yet disdainful references to the tradition he lacks reflect his American difference. For example, he remarks that the "supremacy" of the products of the "elder and riper climes of Europe" is "rarely questioned but by prejudice or ignorance"; their "innumerable men of leisure, and of consequent learning, drink daily from those august fountains of inspiration which burst around them everywhere from out the tombs of their immortal dead" (*CW,* 8:276). Such double-edged irony defines Poe's impossible position of being neither in nor out of a litearry tradition.

As a nineteenth-century American poet, Poe found himself exiled not only from a metaphysical absolute but from the textual history that would have given his exile a constructive continuity. No doubt his life reinforced this problem. His six years at the Stoke Newington School in England are described in "William Wilson": "My earliest recollections of a school-life, are connected with a large, rambling, Elizabethan house, in a misty-looking village of England, where were a vast number of gigantic and gnarled trees, and where all the houses were excessively ancient" (*CW,* 3:300–01). It is here that Wilson acquires his double, and the story can be read as an allegory of the education of the American poet: speaking and schooled in a language and literature he is historically alienated from, the American poet is double at the source. He is not just Will's son, William; he has a double, *another* William Wilson—a coeval fake hounding him and questioning his very legitimacy by doubling or mimicking the line of succession. William Wilson detests his double all the more because he underscores the protagonist's "uncourtly patronymic, and its very common, if not plebeian praenomen," until the name to which he "had always felt aversion" grows to be "venom" to his ears (*CW,* 3:308). The commonness of the name is itself a mockery: "For, notwithstanding a noble descent, mine was one of those everyday appellations which seem, by prescriptive right, to have been, time out of mind, the common property of the mob" (*CW,* 3:305). It aptly represents the comparative position of "the noblest and most liberal commoner at Oxford" (*CW,* 3:316), that bastion of tradition and learning, circulating among the "haughtiest heirs of the wealthiest earldoms in Great Britain" (*CW,* 3:315). And the name, of which so much is made and with which the story is titled, is a pseudonym; thus its internal doubling and external repetition may be read as a literary mechanism as well. The lack of a legitimate, dynastic inheritance opens up the poet to pure textuality—to the fraternal, free play of doublings and duplications. Yet Poe is less than comfortable with such a liberation. The double—a masterly "copyist, who, disdaining the letter, (which in a painting is all the obtuse can see,) gave but the full spirit of his original for my individual contemplation and chagrin" (*CW,* 3:310)—starts out as a barely audible echo: "My rival had a weakness in the faucial or guttural organs, which precluded him from raising his voice at any time *above a very low whisper*" (*CW,* 3:307–08). But this "*singular whisper,*" which "*grew the very echo of my own*" (*CW,* 3:309), becomes identical with the protagonist's voice at the end of the story, thus robbing him of life itself in the final scene of self-murder. The American writer's anxiety about his voice—his ironic claims to legitimacy, on the one hand, and to uniqueness, on the other—is what "William Wilson" chronicles.

A number of Poe's concerns, as well as the peculiarities of his poetic practice, are corollaries of his ambiguous relationship to the authority of tradition. His paranoia about plagiarism, for example, is a symptom of the William Wilson complex, and the lengths to which he carries his tireless attacks on "Mr. Longfellow and Other Plagiarists" may be seen as half-parodic, half-hysterical expressions of the nineteenth-century concern for an original, national American literature. Yet Poe ends his attack on plagiarists by reversing himself in his final paragraph and admitting that poetry *is* plagiarism. His closing argument suggests that the greater the "poetic senti-ment"—which does not necessarily entail "poetic power"—a poet is blessed with, the greater his need to "assimilate" past beauty and, therefore, the greater his liability to plagiarism (*CW,* 12:105–06). Accordingly, Poe's pronouncements on originality prepare the way for Eliot's "Tradition and the Individual Talent": "[Poesy's] first element is the thirst for supernal BEAU-TY—a beauty which is not afforded the soul by any existing collocation of earth's forms—a beauty which, perhaps, *no possible* combination of these forms would fully produce. Its second element is the attempt to satisfy his thirst by *novel* combinations, *of those combinations which our predecessors, toiling in chase of the same phantom, have already set in order*" (*CW,* 11:73). Through a complex juggling of terms, Poe defines literary originality as the novelty of *effect.* This is achieved by "novel arrangements of old forms which present themselves" to the imagination, and he uses the analogy of a "*chemical combination*" to describe the creation of a new "compound" (*CW,* 15:13–14). Literary originality, then, consists of variations on established patterns and thus returns poet and reader alike to the tradition. Unlike Longfellow, who is Poe's alter ego and quite earnestly adopts the tradition, Poe can only use and abuse it at once. His allusiveness, for example, becomes exaggerated into a fake erudition complete with footnotes for the more arcane references, a parodic precedent Eliot more than lives up to in *The Waste Land.* Similarly, Poe's dependence on English meters becomes exaggerated in his insistence on more and more artificial meters, again in parodic fulfillment of his require-ment for originality—the most novel and, therefore, outré combinations possible of the known, given, age-old components of English meters.

Poe's formal and stylistic excesses appear to take over in his poems, undercutting his substantive aims. His English and American readers have defined his failure in just these terms. Aldous Huxley articulates the English version of this critique, and his view has become a cliché of Poe criticism:

"The substance of Poe is refined," he argues; "it is his form that is vulgar." Poe's vulgarity, Huxley specifies, is that of a "parvenu" and is comparable to wearing a diamond ring on every finger. In objecting to Poe's rhymes, however, Huxley tips his hand. In "Ulalume," he argues, "newly" and "Thule" do not rhyme or rhyme only "on condition that you pronounce the adverb as though you were a Bengali, or the name as though you came from Whitechapel."[5] Huxley's argument turns on a nationally and socially restrictive definition of who are the proper trustees of the purity of the English tongue, and thus reveals, if inadvertently, the difficulty of Poe's relation to the poetic language at his disposal. As an American poet, Poe is both "disadvantaged" and a "parvenu"—and too self-conscious to pretend otherwise. Other readers have tried to account for Poe's excesses—his transgressions against both English proprieties and decorum and American literary values—precisely in terms of his American situation, and Edwin Fussell presents the American version of Poe's difficulty. He observes that Poe repeatedly "complained about all those iambic pentameters, but his usual answer to the problem was to complicate it with the introduction of meters even more artificial." Poe's awkwardness in diction and meter, his offensive rhymes and alliteration, are deliberate verbal outrages designed "to parody and attack a presumably agreed-upon tradition of poetic language in which such things are simply 'not done.'" Such a reading is sensitive to the parodic distance inscribed in Poe's formalism, which his English and French readers miss. Yet Fussell tips *his* hand when he invokes Walt Whitman's "barbaric yawp" solution: "[Poe] was never to realize that only through a violent break with English tradition might he relieve his discomfort."[6]

Fussell's implication that Poe was in bad faith or unequal to his task as an American poet says less about Poe than about Whitman and, to some extent, Emerson. Both Whitman and Emerson were able to break with the authority of tradition by claiming the living word for poetry—by appealing to the authority of the Logos. According to Emerson, a divine natural law authorizes the poetic word and is incarnate in poetic forms, which are absolute and not historically contingent; thus Emerson bypasses the tradition but retains its metaphysical assumption. According to Whitman, law and history coincide, and he bypasses the tradition by replacing it with a secular history as the ground of the continuous revelation of the Logos; Whitman projects the Heideggerian concept of poetry as the ground where truth becomes historical, where "something permanent" is revealed and preserved in "ravenous time."[7] Poe's double displacement distinguishes him from Emerson and Whitman. Poe is exiled not only from the absolute into history but from history itself—whether the textual, synchronic history of the "library" or the diachronic history of Whitman. The explicit rhetoric of Poe's poems and criticism suggests that his relentless emphasis on temporality in his poetry expresses his primal alienation, as a mortal user of language, from eternal beauty, harmony, and unity. But the parodic exaggeration of such techniques as purposely artificial meters and rhymes adds another dimension to his predicament of temporality. Finding himself at the mercy of time, he registers the temporal machinery of poetic forms as an absolute, external power, because he stands outside any history that could sanction it. Without a history of preservation and continuity, poetic conventions and forms only aid and abet "ravenous time" instead of counterpointing and countering it.

Poe's "exile" in America can so easily become the paradigm of his "exile" on earth because it provides historical reinforcement of the split between form and force. The absolute division that Poe perceives between form and force is upheld by his cosmology, his esthetic theory, and his psychology. His work tells and retells one story of dispossession, a tale of a fall and an exile into time, which he knows to be the generic story of all stories. A prelapsarian and postapocalyptic unity brackets our present, which is an "abnormal" state of temporal and historical diffusion, and the poet—the person of double vision—is the proper author-hero of this story. He can envision "glories beyond the grave" and recall glories immemorial; yet he is also a mortal, whose very heartbeats cut him off from this imagined-remembered paradise: "for Heaven to them no hope imparts / Who hear not for the beating of their hearts" (*CW,* 7:39).

In a sense, poetry aims to displace such worldly passion and "discourse": it demands "no mere appreciation of the Beauty before us—but a wild effort to reach the Beauty above. Inspired by an ecstatic prescience of the glories beyond the grave, we struggle, by multiform combinations among the things and thoughts of Time, to attain a portion of that Loveliness whose very elements, perhaps, appertain to eternity alone" (*CW,* 14:273–74). Yet the rhetorical discrepancy between the "prescience of the glories beyond the grave" and the "combinations among the things and thoughts of Time" suggests that the project is doomed from the start. Moreover, the "things" of time include language itself, and the entire drama of temporal and rhetorical disjunction is reenacted in the relationship between word and thought, signifier and signified. Poetry only displaces passion by substituting a time measured by formalizing the physical properties of the linguistic signifier for the time measured by biological processes. "The Raven," for instance, employs this strategy: "So that now, to still the beating of my heart, I stood repeating" (*CW,* 7:95). As the poem illustrates, however, the rhythm of poetry—achieved by combining "things and thoughts of Time"—blocks access to "Heaven" no less than the passion it displaces.

Similarly, while the poet can hear the music of the spheres—a harmony that precludes sounds or, as Poe puts it in "Al Aaraaf," "A sound of silence on the startled ear / Which dreamy poets name 'the music of the sphere'" (*CW*, 7:28)—he cannot "name" this "silence" without the means of the music of verse—the music, so painfully measured, of "The Bells." In other terms, Poe insists that poetry *cannot* be defined: "Words cannot hem it in. Its intangible and purely spiritual nature refuses to be bound down within the widest horizon of mere sounds. . . . If, indeed, there be any one circle of thought distinctly and palpably marked out from amid the jarring and tumultuous chaos of human intelligence, it is that evergreen and radiant Paradise which the true poet knows, and knows alone, as the limited realm of his authority—as the circumscribed Eden of his dreams. But a definition is a thing of words—a conception of ideas" (*CW*, 8:281). The disjunction between ends and means, the substance and the medium of the poet, is clear. The poet has authority over "the circumscribed Eden" of dreams; the circumscribing or defining words subscribe to another authority and are subject to time and history, thus rendering the dreamed-of paradise unspeakable and unrecoverable. This paradise is both a radiant center before time and a nature before history, for it bears a certain resemblance to

> —a land new found—
> Miraculously found by one of Genoa—
> A thousand leagues within the golden West . . .
> A fairy land of flowers, and fruit, and sunshine,
> And crystal lakes, and over-arching forests,
> And mountains, around whose towering summits the winds
> Of Heaven untrammelled flow . . .   [*CW*, 7:73–74]

The "Art-scarred surface" (*CW*, 4:205) we now have in the "dotage" of the earth shows that the "widest ruin" is "the price of highest civilization" (*CW*, 4:204), and the loss of the American paradise to history offers a correlative of the descent of the poet's dream into time and words.

Thus Poe's poet can only confirm the absolute separation of the eternal and temporal worlds, which seems to be the message of his angelic poet "Israfel":

> If I could dwell
> Where Israfel
>   Hath dwelt, and he where I,

He might not sing so wildly well
   A mortal melody,
While a bolder note than this might swell
   From my lyre within the sky.   [*CW,* 7:48]

Israfel contrasts with Emerson's Transcendentalist angelic poet, Uriel, whose message sounds *through* the natural processes. Such integration of the angelic imagination with natural law, which Harold Bloom terms the "American Sublime," remains beyond Poe. Emerson's sublime is the American version of the romantic nostalgia for a union of the subject and the object. Poe's irony distances him from Israfel and the nostalgias he signifies. In Paul de Man's terms, Poe would be an allegorical poet:[8] his imagination is the antithesis of the symbolic imagination, just as his forms are the opposite of the organic form that fulfills the rhetoric of symbols. Far from effecting the union of the subject and object, poetic form reinforces the separation of the mental and physical realms: "POETRY, in its most confined sense, is *the result of versification,* but may be more properly defined as *the rhythmical personification of existing or real beauty.* One defines it as the 'rhythmical *creation* of beauty;' but though it certainly is a 'creation of beauty' in itself, it is more properly a personification, for the poet only personifies the image previously created by his mind" (*CW,* 11:225–26). Thus Poe's conception of poetic beauty as the objective correlative of a "real," prior beauty renders his form an allegorical representation of a prior content and complicates his temporal problem. Not only are poetic forms temporal mechanisms that are historically determined; they are intrinsically belated as well, for they come after an original vision that they merely personify and represent.

    Poe's recognition of the absolute separation of the imagination or vision from natural or poetic forms shapes his peculiarly self-defeating formalism. According to Poe, our yearning for "supernal Beauty" is the force that initiates a poem: "This thirst belongs to the immortality of Man. It is at once a consequence and an indication of his perennial existence. It is the desire of the moth for the star" (*CW,* 14:273). Yet the means of poetry—the "multiform combinations among the things and thoughts of Time"—belong to our fallen estate and are at odds with the transcendent aims of poetry. Poe's statement that beauty is not a "quality" but an "effect" (*CW,* 14:197) can be understood in this context. "Beauty" is an effect created precisely by our failure to reach "supernal Beauty"; it is an effect of our recognition of our limits:

    And thus when by Poetry—or when by Music, the most entrancing of the Poetic moods—we find ourselves melted into tears—we weep then—not . . . through excess of pleasure, but through a certain, petulant, impatient sorrow at our inability to grasp *now,* wholly, here on earth, at once and for ever, those divine and rapturous joys, of which *through* the poem, or *through* the music, we attain to but brief and indeterminate glimpses. [*CW,* 14:274]

Poe's poetic is no less self-reliant than Emerson's: the more the temporality of poetic form is emphasized, the more final the failure will be and, therefore, the more intense the effect of beauty—the sense of the absence or lack of "supernal Beauty." Thus, although Poe's style is distinguished by his purely technical manipulations of the physicality of the signifier, he cannot be read—without distorting him—as the symbolist-formalist he has been generally taken for. Symbolist readings of Poe accept the mind-nature opposition in his work but align poetic language and forms with the intellect, opposing "artistic" form and order to "natural"—including psychic—entropy and formlessness.[9] I would suggest that the absolute division between mind and nature, soul and body, carries over into art and poetry and renders Poe's poet incapable of such transcendence as the Symbolists aim to achieve through formal art. Regarding Poe as a formalist does not do justice to the violence his form perpetrates, the psychic disorder and entropy it precipitates. His emphasis on technique does not argue the powers of art for art's or sanity's sake but lays bare the intrinsic and maddening limitations of art, which can point to paradisal harmonies only by a grotesque distortion—in time—of such timeless orders.

Poe's double alienation suggests that Mnemosyne is not the mother of the American muse. Time and loss occasion poetry, bringing into play the temporality of language; the play of temporal resonance in language, however, is subject to conventions that govern the purely physical sequentiality of syllables, phonemes, and letters. The poet is the repository of this kind of memory also, the purpose of which is to make us "forget" personal and cosmic loss by repeating, sustaining, and resuscitating a common memory inscribed and embodied in poetic language. Thus Mnemosyne is traditionally the mother of the Muses, whose music brings "forgetfulness of sorrows."[10] Poe's alienation from a historical authority rendered impossible such a productive dialectic of memory and forgetfulness. The props of public memory, the conventional building blocks of poetry, became for Poe—as they would become for Eliot[11]—the stumbling blocks to repossessing personal and cosmic memory and dwelling in time. Public memory and history, encoded in artistic conventions and recorded in the voices of one's predecessors, bring only "forgetfulness" and anesthesia, robbing the Poe poet of life and breath. In "Loss of Breath," Poe studies the loss at once of life and inspiration and the resultant croaking sound that is the fake double of inspired, bona fide language. This "guttural" sound, "depending . . . not upon the current of the breath, but upon a certain spasmodic action of the muscles of the throat" (*CW,* 2:153), is the desperate speech of one buried alive in a dead body—"alive, with the qualifications of the dead—dead, with the propensities of the living" (*CW,* 2:152). The person robbed of his voice lives a death-in-life, where one faculty predominates: "Memory, which, of all other faculties, should have first taken its departure, seemed on the contrary to have been endowed with quadrupled power. . . . I could repeat to myself entire lines, passages, chapters, books, from the studies of my earliest days" (*CW,* 2:358–59).

The paradigm of the American poet inadvertently placed in the English tradition, Poe begins with an absolute separation between form and force and ends up with a Gothic landscape and a Freudian inscape.[12] Forms, and the past that determines present forms, are experienced as alien enclosures that incarcerate the soul, force, or life. This basic pattern is not only literary but modulates into other plots. In philosophical terms, we have a Cartesian dualism—an "angel inhabiting a machine";[13] in psychological terms, we have a psyche inhabiting a dividing and decaying body. And Poe avenges himself on his medium in poems like "The Raven" and "Ulalume," where the tyrannical memory of forms and plots becomes a hypnotic, soporific aid to the forgetfulness of bona fide life and language. Forms are allowed to invade and usurp personal, existential experience, so that the poet can only say: "I was neither / Living nor dead."

Thus Poe's formalism is curiously self-negating and ranges in tone from reckless parody to intense hostility. The Poe poet knows himself to be a scholar; his settings are unnatural, characteristically indoors in a chamber that is a library and a museum for "in-graving" and sustaining the relics of a dead past. Poe and the allegorical poets who follow him consistently represent the past as stone-dead forms—as architecture, as archaeological sites of stony rubble, ruined cities, decaying towers, crumbling pillars, falling bridges, and moss-encrused colossi, as engravings, writings, legends, and cryptic messages. Premature burial is a recurrent theme in Poe's work, and chambers, tombs, and cemeteries or places of "sculpture" (*CW,* 2:363) are his locales. The chamber/museum/tomb is the crypt where the letter of the law—the law of time and the formalities or "legalities" of writing—buries the poet-scholar alive. Thus neither Whitman's "natural" mockingbirds and thrushes nor Keats's traditional nightingale could be Poe's poetic emblem. His emblems are birds that rob the poet's language of transcendent significance or of the possibility of such significance, just as they deprive it of a significant history. His birds are on the order of parrots—"painted" parakeets that teach him the alphabet and ravens that structure the burdens or refrains of his poems. For Poe's nature only repeats human language, echoing it mechanically and draining it of meaning. Yet Poe's raven is no golden bird of artifice, either; his croaking song parodies as much a transcendent artifice as the transcendent meanings we are impelled to attach to certain combinations of certain phonemes.

II

Search narrowly the lines!—they hold a treasure
Divine—a talisman—an amulet
That must be worn *at heart*. Search well the
    measure—
The words—the syllables! Do not forget
The trivialest point, or you may lose your labor!
.   .   .   .

Its letters, although naturally lying
.   .   .   .

Still form a synonym for Truth.
                    "A Valentine"

"The Raven" best illustrates the operations of Poe's nonorganic form and helps us see in practice the complex of his cosmology, psychology, and esthetics. The poem is "about" the process of its own development, for its narrative content reduces to the operations of its form. In a narrative poem, the fictional time of the story transpires against the backdrop of a systematic, formal time, giving us two superimposed temporal orders. Poetic features such as repetition, metrical and stanzaic regularity, and line breaks set up an objectively measurable time system—a kind of clock-time—and this formal, nonfictional time measures and plays up the fictional status of narrative time. In "The Raven," however, such formal devices are themselves played up in their relentless regularity, until the poem becomes a formal mechanism that controls the possibilities of its content. The most prominent formal features of the poem are its refrain and its *abcbbb* rhyme scheme. The *b* rhymes consist of the long "o" and "r" sounds and rhyme with "nevermore," echoing this "melancholy burden" throughout the poem. The refrain makes certain that the final answer to all of the speaker's questions will be "nevermore," or one of its semantic and aural equivalents. Tracing the antecedents of "nevermore," however, we get a different story than that which the poem's narrative—or Poe's critical essay—tells. "Nevermore" has an antecedent in "Lenore," which explains the speaker's psychological compulsion to torment himself by asking questions and demanding signification of a dumb creature whose use of language is limited to an automatic response. The speaker himself suffers from a letter fetishism, a species of necrophilia. If we see him as a bereaved lover, his desire to repeat the letters of his beloved's name and the pleasure—if illusory and substitutive—such repetition offers become the forces that drive him, perversely, to despair finally of ever uniting with his beloved. What would resurrect his beloved by a substitutive process ends up finalizing her loss and establishing as the supreme force the spirit-killing letters.

Yet the condition of the speaker does not appear to be peculiar to him. We learn that "Lenore" is not necessarily the proper name of his beloved, "the rare and radiant maiden whom the *angels name* Lenore— / Nameless *here* for evermore" (*CW,* 7:94; initial emphasis mine). Instead, "Lenore" appears to be Poe's magic word, a talisman. Its echoic and etymological connections to other Poe names—"Eleonora," "Ulalume," and "Helen"—suggest that it may be a generic name for a psychic source, the male speaker's anima-muse. Yet this source is also rooted in history, as its connection to "Helen" implies. Furthermore, the long "o" and "r" of "Lenore" occur first in line two, in the "many a quaint and curious volume of forgotten lore" the narrator pores over, seeking "to borrow / From my books surcease of sorrow—sorrow for the lost Lenore." The student's chamber is a bedroom and a library or museum, for "Lenore" represents both a maternal, "natural" source language and a "lore."

Indeed, the word "Lenore"—the angels' name for the beloved—names the poetic possibilities of language, the emotional resonances and properties inherent in or attached to particular letters. In such use of language, letters are not mere signifiers, absenting themselves in order to present an absent "meaning"; rather, the letters are emotional presences, offering oral pleasures. The oral, infantile satisfactions that letters offer—the pleasures of vowels and consonants—define the "maternal" axis of poetic language,[14] and the exclusive hold that long, sonorous sounds—such as combinations of long *o, r,* and *l*—have over the poet points up his necessary attachment to the phonic, maternal axis of language. Linguistic studies of the senses or semantic resonances of vowels would enlarge the implications of the maternal function of language, linking it to sorrow and loss. The **long** vowels *u* and *o* are perceived, in a variety of languages, as "deeper" and "darker," and such perception is encoded semantically in many languages.[15] Universally, we appear predisposed, without having loved and lost Lenore, to perceive the long *o* and *r* as mournful sounds—perhaps because they are the generic vowels of the past, being produced farther back in the mouth.

If we thus amplify the resonances of "Lenore," the speaker's story becomes an allegory of the poet's psychic and formal progress. He begins in "gladness," prompted to repeat a certain sequence of letters and phonemes. What promises pleasure is soon formalized into patterns of alliteration, rhyme, and stanzas, complete with a refrain; and when the maternal source of the poem becomes encoded in an established pattern, pleasure turns to pain, ending in "despondency" and "madness." "Nevermore" both echoes and drowns out "Lenore," and the physical delight in letters turns into a limitation in and by the letter, as the word "nevermore" blocks the spirit at every turn, prevents union with the poetic source, and thwarts the very life of poetry—the pleasures of literal substitutions. In the terminology of Poe's critical recapitulation, the poet's necessary progress is from beauty to death: the "sole legitimate province of the poem" is beauty, whose "highest manifestation" is melancholy, "the most legitimate of all the poetical tones" (*CW,* 14:197–98). It follows that death—specifically, the death of a beautiful woman—is the most legitimate of poetic subjects. The sequence is a logical representation of "the fact . . . that in efforts to soar above our nature, we invariably fall below it" (*CW,* 16:161). The legitimating and legalizing of the impulse to reach a transcendent, supernal beauty only anchors us more firmly in the "things" of time. The poetic process enacts the reduction of the transcendent impulse to death, just as it embodies the reduction of the anima-muse to poetic forms and script. Poe's theory replays the progression of "The Raven," from the initial attempt to recover maternal language and its pleasures to the defeat by paternal language and its codified formal and semantic patterns.

The maiden and the raven represent the two extremes of the poet's language. Just as the angels name the maiden "Lenore," the raven carries the "lordly name" of "Nevermore" on "Night's Plutonian shore." He is as much demonic language as Lenore is angelic, and the two are coeval opposites. Poe takes great pains to develop these figures as mirror images: the "rare and radiant maiden" is linked to the "stately Raven of the saintly days of yore" by the literal patterns of insistent alliteration and rhyme. The two figures are also linked by the imagery, which presents the "flirting" and "fluttering" raven as a parody of the "radiant maiden." The pleasures "Lenore" offers are those of an oral mother tongue, of memory and repetition, and the raven offers a mechanical, pornographic reproduction of such language. "Lenore" and "Nevermore," angel and demon, heaven and hell, hope and despair mark the beginning and the end of the poet's progress, as the attractions of oral, maternal language modulate into the compulsion of letter fetishism. And Poe's poet is trapped within these limits, for the letters of the alphabet rule his persona's consciousness: the letters the "grave" if not "craven" raven speaks are graven or engraved in the mind of the raving persona. Descent into the psyche does not liberate but enchains the poet in certain key patterns of letters. The psyche is not a counterforce against form; the psyche itself is form, and "Lenore" necessarily leads to "Nevermore." The psychic need to repeat certain letters upholds the materiality of the signifier, which has been culturally and historically codified in and as poetic conventions and forms. Thus the deeper the Poe poet delves into the psyche, the more he finds himself at the mercy of alien and alienating forms. For the psyche is ancient and communal, and "Lenore" is not a personal beloved. The sonorous letters of her name, its etymological connection to "Helen" and its echoic connections to *lore* and *yore,* make her the archetypal beloved, a representative of maternal language as it is inscribed in poetic conventions and history. And it is Poe's ambiguous relationship to literary history that renders him incapable of achieving the unity his lost beloved represents. "Lenore" represents precisely the lost unity of force and form—the blissful, prelapsarian unity of maternal language, which roots the poet in nature and grants him an intimate knowledge of death, and the paternal language of the tradition, conventions, and "lore."

In mythology, the raven signifies death and sometimes appears as the bird of Hermes.[16] Hermes is the god of writing as well as the guardian of the passage to the underworld. As Hermes' bird, the raven embodies the link between writing and loss of life. These associations account for his presence at the scene of Poe's poem, the scene of the traffic with the underworld that Poe's would-be Orphic poet initiates. He conjures up the raven, who promises to echo the letters of Lenore's name. But when the formal mechanism takes control of the poem, the means abort the end, and the Orphic drive turns into necrophilia—a letter fetishism practiced by the failed poet or, in Emerson's terms, a "jingle man." The chamber/poem is cut off from a productive intercourse with the underworld and the world of nature, and the speaker remains arrested in a mediation that fails to mediate. In the end, then, the poem becomes a "legended tomb." We move forward and backward at the same time, as pleasure turns to pain, future hope reverts to past despair, and "*raven*" and "*never*" forever mirror each other.[17] Neither the questions nor the answers can do any more than play with the possibilities delineated by the physical shape of words and poetic conventions. Such a pervasive determinism marks the poem as a premature burial, with the refraining raven naming the poem, guarding the door, and preventing access to "Lenore." The door offers only an illusion of escape from the "legended tomb"[18] of the chamber/poem, for "door" itself fits into and reinforces the closure of the "Lenore"-"Nevermore" rhyme.

Above the door sits the third presence in the chamber/poem, the "pallid bust of Pallas." In mythology, Pallas is associated with reason and craft. She embodies utilitarian language—the use of words as tools of thought and knowledge—and thus is properly posed above the door, offering an exit from solipsism and tautology. A figure of tradition, consensus, and culture, she relates the psychic needs and oral pleasures engraved in letters to meaning, sense, and communication. A goddess who is her father's brain-child, she represents the tradition of craft, which encourages the mediation between father and mother the poet must effect. In making Pallas Athena an arbiter figure, Poe may be thinking of a story in Ovid[19] that also concerns the question of artistic legitimacy and authority. The story is told by one of the Muses to Athena: nine sisters, the daughters of a "landowner Pierus," are impressed with their "numbers," their quantitative resemblance to the daughters of Mnemosyne, and challenge the Muses to a contest of poetry and song. Calliope represents the Muses and sings the story of Death and Proserpina. The story ends with Proserpina's eating forbidden food—a pomegranate—in "Death's formal gardens," witnessed by one Ascalaphus, whose gossip ultimately prevents Proserpina's return to earth. Enraged, Proserpina changes Ascalaphus into "an obscene bird"—"that hated creature, / Scritch-owl of fatal omen to all men"—and settles down to her divided life. This story within a story proves apt, for Calliope wins all the honors for the Muses with her song. The defeated challengers are changed into nine crows: "They were / Gossips in trees yet all had human voices— / A fearful noise, they talk, talk, talk forever." In Ovid as in Poe, the black birds, "which imitate whatever noise they choose," represent failed poets, uninspired chatterers. In Ovid's story, the presence of Athena legitimates the Muses' victory, for she legitimates the very distinction between the authentic and the fake. Indeed, such a distinction *is* a matter of legitimacy and authority, which are conferred on the Muses by the superstructure of myth. In Poe, of course, the arbiter is not the living Minerva or Pallas but the *bust* of Pallas, which itself begs the question of legitimacy.

And this piece of sculpture, this stone representation, witnesses the victory in reverse of the failed poet—the "raven," the "jingle man"—over the lover, the would-be Orpheus, who is first moved to speak by the promptings of his true muse, the memory of "Lenore":

Deep into that darkness peering, long I stood there wondering, fearing,
Doubting, dreaming dreams no mortal ever dared to dream before;
But the silence was unbroken, and the stillness gave no token,
And the only word there spoken was the whispered word, "Lenore!"
This I whispered, and an echo murmured back the word "Lenore!"
    Merely this and nothing more.   [*CW,* 7:95]

When the word the raven repeats by rote echoes and replaces the word the poet repeats by heart, and the mechanism of form takes over for the inspiration of memory, the poet's defeat is complete:

And my soul from out that shadow that lies floating on the floor
           Shall be lifted—nevermore!   [*CW,* 7:100]

The false rise of "lifted"—a purely metrical rise—makes all the more precipitous the poet's fall with his assumption and parroting of the raven's name-word. Far from repossessing and remembering his Lenore, the poet succumbs to the oblivion of the raven's repetitions. The raven, "emblematical of *Mournful and Never-ending Remembrance*" (*CW,* 14:208), represents the fake double of authentic memory. To borrow Derrida's terms for this Platonic distinction, the raven's language is the "rememoration" of writing, which is non-knowledge, forgetfulness, or oblivion, as opposed to true memory, which is knowledge or a repetition of truth.[20] The only force capable, in postmythological times, of distinguishing between the true poet's "angelic," Orphic music and the failed or fake poet's hellish chatter is the standard, established by history, of craft. Athena, a representative of this history and herself a relic of it, watches the contest unmoved and holds her peace. Given Poe's alienation from a tradition—that is, his illegitimacy—he has no way of connecting the letters inscribed in the psyche, both personal and collective, to the letters encoded in poetic conventions. Since, for Poe, psychic memory does not connect to literary history, his formalism becomes arbitrary—a mere fetish and a perversion of the "sanctities" it is supposed to uphold.[21] Without cultural and historical authorization, he works in an echo chamber of forms empty of significance and is condemned to self-parody—to exposing himself his manipulation of the physical and temporal properties of the language he would sound celestial notes with.

    Tautology appears to be the logical end or fulfillment of Poe's forms and rhetoric. "*Verse* originates in the human enjoyment of equality, fitness," he writes; "to this enjoyment, also, all the moods of verse—rhythm, metre, stanza, rhyme, alliteration, the *refrain,* and other analogous effects—are to be referred" (*CW,* 14:218). In practice, such equality is "merely a proximate equality," since "absolute equality" in rhyme, for example, would involve "the use of identical words"—a "duplicate sameness or monotony—that of sense as well as that of sound" (*CW,* 14:227). The threshold of the "pleasures of repetition" is "absolute equality" or "tautology"—the perfect self-identity of death, the perfection of an unconscious object. Poe's "Nevermore" comes close enough to this threshold to render semantic differences illusory. Semantic difference is the freedom temporality gives for all that it takes, and his refrain in effect reduces this freedom to an illusion. The rhetoric of his form, then, follows the model of tautology and thus reaffirms his placement in a world where "flowers are merely—flowers" and things are only what they seem. Tautology is the limit or threshold of a formalist dependence on fixed equivalencies; it also marks the perfection of allegorical rhetoric, since it presents an equivalence purged of temporal sequentiality and difference.

Poe's rhetoric reinforces the closure of his formalism, for he does not invoke expansive metaphorical dissonances or symbolistic fusions but pairs off sets of allegorical equivalencies, and his use of emblems functions like his "letterism." Limited in meaning and limiting interpretation, emblems and their allegorical meanings—predetermined by cultural usage or by authorial design—serve to rule out transcendent meanings.[22] For example, as an emblem the raven questions the very project of using natural objects as symbols or metaphors. The raven is either an emblem with given associations or merely a natural object. Either way, he is securely ensconced in the closet/mind of the student, which is both a library/museum furnished with volumes, busts, and emblems enthroning the past, and a bedroom—a carpeted, cushioned, secluded scene of literal or natural pleasures and pains. Poe's method implies that metaphysical discoveries and expanding meanings are illusory, and collective human wisdom, nature, and poetic form all collaborate in closing off the poem and making a mockery of the human desire for transcendence of mortal limits—whether of the library/museum of history, the mortal body, or the rhyme scheme. All poetic techniques— not simply meter, rhyme, and other such formal features but also representation and figuration—are limited, conventional, and strictly determined by the past. What can be said is limited; what cannot be limited is chimerical. Once again, the only way out of illusion is into history and time.

Poe's reduction of signs to signifiers, tropes to objective correlatives, and symbols to allegorical markers reaffirms the triumph of the deadly letter over the life-giving spirit. Psychoanalytic criticism would judge such poetic strategies to be necrophiliac.[23] In different terms, such strategies may be seen as the self-reliant response of an American romantic poet to his ambiguous historical situation. The possibilities of poetic form and figuration are established by history and precedent. Poe, who stands outside this tradition and authority, willfully imposes upon himself the most stringent limits possible within that tradition and authority. He wills himself to be victimized by the past, and the pattern of his obsession with the life-denying past unfolds along the lines of the speaker's progress in "The Raven." The very thing he must acknowledge in order to begin to be a poet—temporality and the past, both personal and cultural—he proceeds to let annihilate him.

III

"I would fain have them believe that I have been, in some measure, the slave of circumstances beyond human control. I would wish them to seek out for me, in the details I am about to give, some little oasis of *fatality* amid a wilderness of error."

CW, 3:300

Poe's historical and metaphysical deracination or "erring" leads him to seek an "oasis of *fatality*" in the closed chamber of "The Raven," and the psychological compulsion and technical determinism that shape the poem are mirrored in the esthetic theory proposed in "The Philosophy of Composition." In the essay, temporal development is replaced by logical sequence, and compulsion and determinism give way to choice or the intentional creation of effects. Much as Eliot's prose—his essays in general and his notes to *The Waste Land* in particular—functions in relation to his poems, Poe's essay downplays any psychological motivation and provides a sane, "scientific" account of his creative process. It is useless to debate whether his creative procedure was, in fact, the way he describes it in the essay. While the essay most likely does not accurately narrate an actual sequence of events, it remains, in another sense, a valid piece of criticism. Kenneth Burke phrases this distinction when he proposes that "The Philosophy of Composition" is not only serious but a generic piece of criticism: it provides the conceptual framework that enables the poet's intuitions to be translated into their corresponding critical principles. Criticism prophesies after the event to demonstrate how the poem should be logically deducible from the given appropriate critical principles—in this case, those having to do with the creation of certain effects. In other words, although poetry is temporally prior to criticism, criticism is *logically* prior to poetry. According to Burke, Poe confused the issue and misled his readers by presenting the generic critical account of the poem as a *genetic* account—as a narrative of how the poem was historically composed, which is highly unlikely.[24]

Thus we can see why Poe—given his poetic—had also to write criticism in order to resurrect himself from his premature burial. When logical sequence replaces temporal sequence, what is for Poe the unmistakable message of language is invalidated. Compare, for example, the lines

"No more—no more—no more—"
(Such language holds the solemn sea
To the sands upon the shore)   [*CW,* 7:86]

or the mounting effect of the repeated line "Quoth the Raven 'Nevermore'"
with: "Having made up my mind to a *refrain,* the division of the poem into

stanzas was, of course, a corollary: the *refrain* forming the close of each stanza. That such a close, to have force, must be sonorous and susceptible of protracted emphasis, admitted no doubt: and these considerations inevitably led me to the long *o* as the most sonorous vowel, in connection with *r* as the most producible consonant" (*CW,* 14:199–200), and so on. Poe clearly states his purpose in the essay: "It is my design to render it manifest that no one point in its composition is referrible [*sic*] either to accident or intuition—that the work proceeded, step by step, to its completion with the precision and rigid consequence of a mathematical problem" (*CW,* 14:195). The essay merely proposes to substitute another kind of determinism for the compulsion the poem's narrative and form act out. Causality and choice, aimed at producing a certain effect, replace psychic and linguistic compulsion. The temporal closure of narrative—all stories that begin with "Once upon" must end with "nevermore" in order to complete the time span they initiate—the closure of allegory, and the closure of form are all opened up or reversed in criticism, which writes the story backwards. In making good the temporal loss that words inflict in their physical, sequential, and historical nature, criticism enjoys the compensatory power of logic over language.

Poe's criticism has been seen as a precursor of New Criticism,[25] and his insistence on technique, which may have made his poetry a failure, has been thought to account for his success as a critic. His criticism focuses on the work of art as an autonomous structure and avoids such nonliterary considerations as biography, history, sociology, and psychology. His problematic relation to the tradition—very much like Eliot's—accounts for his interest in generic and structural principles. Such practical criticism, based on the analysis of the functions and effects of forms, provided grounds for using and manipulating inherited poetic rules and conventions. Thus Poe's criticism itself is a response to the American situation and initiates what has become identified as an American criticism. A pragmatic criticism that operates without metaphysical authority, it regards rhetoric and irony as strictly intratextual matters and aims to substitute the mechanisms of craft, which are viewed as self-justifying, for the authority of tradition. Liberated from history, it proposes to replace historical synthesis (the assimilability of a work) with formal analysis (the work's analyzability) as the basis for evaluation. In this practice, the poet becomes the best-qualified critic—a twist that is the final, characteristic inversion of Poe's career—to report on "the wheels and pinions—the tackle for scene-shifting—the step-ladders and demon-traps—the cock's feathers, the red paint and the black patches, which, in ninety-nine cases out of the hundred, constitute the properties of the literary *histrio*" (*CW,* 14:195).

Chapter Two

T. S. Eliot and the Archaeology of Poetry

> And other withered stumps of time
> Were told upon the walls; staring forms
> Leaned out, leaning, hushing the room
>   enclosed.
>
> *The Waste Land*

In a lecture presented at the Library of Congress in 1948, T. S. Eliot acknowledges so early an acquaintance with Poe that he cannot be sure whether his own work has been influenced by him. He then distances himself from his predecessor by focusing on Poe's relation to the French Symbolists Baudelaire, Mallarmé, and Valéry.[1] This detour through another country and another language is the standard reading of the Eliot-Poe connection: Poe's insistence on the poem as a formal artifact, as well as his critical self-consciousness, influenced the French Symbolists, who in turn influenced Eliot. Clearly, Eliot shares the Symbolists' interest in the poem-as-object and their preoccupation with the critical process. Yet Eliot also hints at a direct connection to Poe, which may account for the indirection of his approaching Poe via the French. According to Eliot, Poe "certainly" does not belong in the English tradition; but neither does his position seem to be "wholly" explained by his being an American—especially, as Eliot notes, "when we consider the other American writers of his own and an earlier generation." Poe does not fit in either tradition: "There is a certain flavour of provinciality about his work, in a sense in which Whitman is not in the least provincial; it is the provinciality of the person who is not at home where he belongs, but cannot get to anywhere else. Poe is a kind of displaced European . . . he seems a wanderer with no fixed abode. There can be few authors of such eminence who have drawn so little from their own roots, who have been so isolated from any surroundings."[2] This description of Poe parallels Eliot's account, in a letter to Herbert Read in 1928, of his own sense of displacement and disorientation:

Some day I want to write an essay about the point of view of an American who wasn't an American, because he was born in the South and went to school in New England as a small boy with a nigger drawl, but who wasn't a southerner in the South because his people were northerners in a border state and looked down on all southerners and Virginians, and who so was never anything anywhere and who therefore felt himself to be more a Frenchman than an American and more an Englishman than a Frenchman and yet felt that the U.S.A. up to a hundred years ago was a family extension.[3]

Eliot's sense of dispossession is compounded by a historical belatedness. The nineteenth-century archetype of the alienated poet or *poète maudit,* which Eliot invokes to "place" Poe's displacement in the transatlantic context of Byron and Baudelaire, will not help locate Eliot. His early work attests to a profound national, historical, and literary displacement, which would be "corrected" only by his becoming the archetype of belonging—his somewhat anachronistic conversion to become a royalist, Anglo-Catholic, and classicist. Ezra Pound could well find Eliot's remedy an "irrelevance,"[4] for Pound's difference is that he is at home *everywhere.* The poet of empire, who "translates" and assimilates any tradition that interests him into the capital of an international epic, Pound can gather "from the air a live tradition."[5] But Eliot's "fit" is always a "misfit," whether in American, English, or European traditions. A poem like *The Waste Land,* however un-American William Carlos Williams and others may have considered it, could not have been written by a legitimate heir to the English poetic tradition: it is the work of a poet overwhelmed by a past to which he has a less than direct connection.

The physical and psychological enervation of Eliot's early personae may be read in part as correlatives of his literary situation; this is the way Prufrock, for example, states his problem:

And I have known the eyes already, known them all—
The eyes that fix you in a formulated phrase,
And when I am formulated, sprawling on a pin,
When I am pinned and wriggling on the wall,
Then how should I begin
To spit out all the butt-ends of my days and ways?
    And how should I presume?[6]

Prufrock does not know how to presume to begin to speak, both because he knows "all already"—this is the burden of his lament—and because he is already known, formulated. His consciousness of the other's eye-I haunts his language at its source: "Let us go then, you and I." An "I" who addresses a "you" becomes subject to the laws of communication, and his voice is subsumed by expression. In his critical replay of the poetic process, Eliot remarks that the poet expresses not a personality but a particular medium.[7] The particular medium expressed in "Prufrock" is a confession or a dramatic monologue. The you-I split being the formal ground of his medium, Prufrock's problem is in fact the problem the expressive medium introduces, and this identification of the formal and rhetorical dimensions of the medium with the emotion or psychic burden of the speaker makes for the airless closure of the poem. As in Poe's "Raven," the speaker's relationship to the form within which his adventure transpires constitutes the nature of his adventure: his form determines the content of his story.

And if Prufrock's problem coincides with the dynamics of Eliot's particular medium of dramatic monologue, Eliot's problem coincides with the dynamics of the poetic medium itself; just as Prufrock is paralyzed by his consciousness of the other, his author is paralyzed by his consciousness of the tradition. In the line "It is impossible to say just what I mean!" the dramatic character and his author meet, "uttering the words in unison, though perhaps with somewhat different meaning,"[8] and displaying the rhetorical advantage a dramatic poet holds. And Eliot's imprisoning his speaker in the very medium of expressive or even confessional speech may register his own intertextual interment in a medium inscribed with prototypes of original or central speech—whether prophetic, like John the Baptist's, or epic, like Dante's, or dramatic, like Shakespeare's—which are codified in and reinforced by conventions precluding the possibility of saying "just what I mean." Eliot's ironic use of rhyme and meter in "Prufrock" acknowledges the complicity of the poet's conventions with his persona's "de-meaning" language. On the one hand, the "comic" meter of lines like "In the room the women come and go / Talking of Michelangelo" equates poetic forms that channel force and the social forms of keeping conversation light. On the other hand, dreams of escape from the pre-formulating formulae are themselves recounted in formulaic lines, for the solution to Prufrock's problem would be a "solution" for Eliot as well—forgetting the present and the separate self, surrendering to the oblivion of an unconscious nature and the "natural" meter of English poetry:

I should have been a pair of ragged claws
Scuttling across the floors of silent seas.

The epigraph to "Prufrock" formally subsumes its hero's problem with expressive language to the poet's problem with textuality. The poem is a dramatic monologue, a mimesis of speech, yet it opens with an epigraph that identifies it as writing and diminishes its urgency by absorbing it within the prototype of another confession, so that the beginning "let us go" is already the "end of something." At the same time that the epigraph consigns the persona to the company of his "semblables"—all those confined in the deadly circle of their solipsistic-confessional speech-likenesses—it seals the poet in the prison of literary "truth," which cancels out his life and tells someone else's "lie." Supernatural vision and natural blindness—issuing in prophetic or lyric utterances—would alike deliver Prufrock from himself; but such ascents and descents are not possible within writing, a historically coded and prescribed medium where vision drowns in revision and human voices drown out natural and supernatural music. And if Prufrock—too decorous and conventional to be a prophet or to dally with mermaids—is incarcerated in the echo chamber of his and others' chatter, Eliot finds himself locked in the "room" of literary "talk," too late to "tell all" *or* to "sing." The poem's epigraph at once opens and closes this discourse of a poet-hero generically old before his time. Eliot's early work is unusual in its dependence on epigraphs that mediate between the poet and the poem, preformulating the poem before it can begin, and his epigraphs often ex-plicitly concern belatedness, exhaustion, and endings. Indeed, the epigraph to *Prufrock and Other Observations* locates Eliot's beginning as a poet by placing him in the company of Jean Verdenal and other "shadows"—Statius, Virgil, and Dante. In "Prufrock," the literary epigraph, bespeaking "not only . . . the pastness of the past, but . . . its presence" (*SW,* 49), casts such a shadow over the poem that nature itself disappears, for a "sky" that recalls "ether" is, in fact, "etherized" for the present speaker. Thus, social paralysis resulting from knowing all and being known or seen through parallels a literary anesthe-sia—knowing all predecessors and being preformulated and "epi-graphed" by them. Both kinds of anesthesia subject the individual voice to anterior formulas, forms, and styles.

Prufrock's acute consciousness of his age is thus the classic symptom of Eliot's philosophical and literary problem. Prufrock's body is presented as a text, for he literally carries the burden of the past on his body—in the lines, the thinning hair and arms and legs, and other signs of age that record time's passage. In the same way, his monologue is a "polylogue," superscribed with quotations, allusions, and echoes that document the presence of the past. Since existential experience is subsumed by textual experience in early Eliot, bodily and natural forms correlate with literary forms. The labyrinthine cities and "corridors" of history, the sepulchral drawing rooms with their "at-mosphere of Juliet's tomb" (*CP,* 8), the body aging "on its own," and the formulas of discourse are all experienced as suffocating incarcerations. They are all modeled as texts, as stages set and scripts written before the speaker enters to recite his lines. And attempts to free the individual voice by breaking out of forms register, as in "Prufrock," only as impulses to dismemberment and suicide.

Eliot's objective correlative provides the rhetorical model of his philosophic and poetic reduction of force to form: "The only way of expressing emotion in the form of art is by finding an 'objective correlative'; in other words, a set of objects, a situation, a chain of events which shall be the formula of the *particular* emotion; such that when the external facts, which must terminate in sensory experience, are given, the emotion is immediately evoked." And Eliot adds, "The artistic 'inevitability' lies in this complete adequacy of the external to the emotion" (*SW,* 100–01). A poem like "Rhapsody on a Windy Night" illustrates the complete correlation of the subjective and the objective, where the descent into the psyche and the past mirrors the descent into nature, and memory and imagination supply automatic responses to physical stimuli, throwing up correlatives of the "twisted" phenomena the speaker observes. Although "a crowd of twisted things" (*CP,* 16) holds the poem together, the productive turns of "versus" and "trope"— which generate and regenerate, infusing form with vital force and meaning—survive only in the title as ideas evoked by the etymology of "rhapsody" and the resonances of "wind." Eliot's expressive technique renders the subjective a repetition of the objective, and vice versa, so that memory-time and lamp-time, past and present, psyche and city, response and stimulus only mirror each other, and technique—formal and rhetorical control—reigns supreme, manipulating subject and object alike.

A precedent for such a tyrannical "mediation" that shapes both the mind and nature can be found in Poe, whose "Raven" and "Haunted House" exemplify the absolute closure of objective correlation. Like Poe's preference for emblems—which are "pre-scribed" and therefore prescribe rather than generate meanings—over symbols, Eliot's preference for fixed, "objective" equivalencies over negotiable, metaphoric relationships checks the influx of meanings and emotion. Such an esthetic, which "corrects" the Symbolists' "deviation," directly links Eliot to Poe. An objective correlative is not a symbol but a dramatic, expressive, and manipulative device; it aims not to expand and discover meanings but to convey already-known equivalencies. In such allegorical representation, the subjective emotion and its objective correlative are never joined; like mirror images, the content and the medium merely reflect each other.

A conception of language as an expressive medium, as the externalization and alienation of the soul in time and nature, also characterizes so-called confessional poetry. Although such poetry has been considered a reaction to Eliotic impersonalism, it is in fact a variation on the pattern of Poe's and Eliot's expressive, dramatic lyric. A confessional poet like Sylvia Plath emphasizes the conventional features of poetry and exaggerates metrical regularity and phonemic repetition in order to stage the abysmal distance between the formal, expressionist language and the psyche, memory, or imagination. Such a poetic subscribes to a species of naturalism, but now the alien, hostile forces are internalized. They constitute the "nature" of one's medium; they inscribe the medium in which the "I" would express itself and be heard. In more technical terms, this poetic internalizes a dramatic awareness of others and the otherness of language within a lyric poem. Such poetry is staged in the very aporia—in Eliot's words, "the difference, the abyss"— between the dramatic voice and the lyric or meditative voice.[9]

An understanding of expression as repression also accompanies a consciousness of the anteriority of a "pre-scribed" poetic language. In "Tradition and the Individual Talent," Eliot begins his discussion of tradition by distinguishing it from "some pleasing archaeological reconstruction." The "science of archaeology" is "reassuring" (*SW,* 47), he points out, presumably because it busies itself with relics and assumes an objective distinction between the living and the dead. As Eliot would have it, however, tradition is a dynamic whole, which includes both "existing monuments" and the "really new" work (*SW,* 50). It includes both the living and the dead: "The whole of the literature of Europe from Homer and within it the whole of the literature of his own country" must be seen by the poet as having "a simultaneous existence" and constituting "a simultaneous order" (*SW,* 49). Thus tradition is a matter less of "reassurance" than of "anxiety"; it is an *internalization* of an archaeology. And for a poet for whom "the whole of the literature of his own country" does not go back very far, this anxiety is exacerbated, for the tradition is largely someone else's past. Tradition, Eliot must therefore insist, "cannot be inherited, and if you want it you must obtain it by great labour" (*SW,* 49). According to this Protestant ethic, great labor will compensate for the lack of an inheritance. Yet this great labor cannot be exactly labor, either. Eliot rejects "erudition (pedantry)" as a sign of the poet who has labored for his tradition; an "appeal to the lives of poets in any pantheon," Eliot argues, will show the irrelevancy of erudition (*SW,* 52). Indeed, this labor works by not laboring: "Some can absorb knowledge, the more tardy must sweat for it." As such rigorous qualifications would suggest, in practice the issue remains unsettled. Does *The Waste Land,* for example, represent the great labor of a poet who would "develop or procure the consciousness of the past" (*SW*, 52), and, if so, how is his work to be distinguished from erudition or the "sweating" of the "more tardy"?

"Tradition and the Individual Talent" shows Eliot's concern with the originality of the traditional poet. Like Poe, Eliot would define originality as "novel combinations,"[10] although Eliot's ingredients would include feelings and emotions as well as poetic conventions. *The Waste Land* best exemplifies such an originality; it is the work of a daring poet who rises above petty worries about his predecessors, belatedness, and plagiarism by elevating stealing to originality (*SW*, 125)—by making a compositional method of stealing. The use of allusion as a structural method makes the issue of authorship and authority the poem's explicit and central concern. Eliot's original title, "He Do the Police in Different Voices," registers the poetic problem with the repressive authority of literary tradition that the poem sublimates to larger cultural issues.[11] His manuscript version of "These fragments I have shored against my ruins" (*CP*, 69) explicitly invokes the writer's problem: "These fragments I have *spelt* into my ruins."[12] From the distance criticism grants him, Eliot writes that "not only the best, but the most individual parts of [a poet's] work may be those in which the dead poets, his ancestors, assert their immortality most vigorously" (*SW*, 48), and argues that the poet's work must "inevitably be judged by the standards of the past" (*SW*, 50). And he adds, in a telling choice of words, "I say judged, not amputated, by them." Yet this is how he uses the past in *The Waste Land*— to splinter, fragment, and "amputate" his text. The body of Eliot's poem is an objective correlative of a synchronic, living tradition: a field of scattered fragments to be studied and annotated, artifacts to be numbered, filed, and typed.

Eliot's archaeological imagery presents the past as a collection of dead and deadening memorials that anesthetize memory itself. The crumbling structures of tradition, the "heap of broken images" (*CP*, 53) and "falling towers" (*CP*, 67), signal both historical destruction—"cracks and reforms and bursts in the violet air" (*CP*, 67)—and a loss of poetic power:

And upside down in air were towers
Tolling reminiscent bells, that kept the hours
And voices singing out of empty cisterns and exhausted wells.   [*CP*, 68]

Thus the impetus and nature of Eliot's experimentalism, his modernism, does not consist of a "pro-jective" destruction of a dead past as preliminary to "dis-covering" a phenomenological present; rather, it is an expression of dejection and a way of striking back at a past that holds the poet in bondage and blocks any return to a primordial, ontological source.[13] Unlike Ezra Pound, whose authorizing *Polis* enables him to assume a composite tradition and to let it speak through his "co-hering" voice, Eliot answers to a "Police" divorced from the very idea of a *Polis*. And for any voice that inhabits an alien form or forms, the only liberation is through destruction—of the body, the body of the text, or the body of literature. Thus Eliot's experimentalism shares something of the suicidal impulse, the overwhelming death-wish, of all the poets in Poe's line.

The "withered stumps of time" that decorate the room in "A Game of Chess" attest to the suffocating weight and castrating, amputating violence of the past, which is more graphic in the original manuscript:

And other tales, from the old stumps and bloody ends of
    time
Were told upon the walls, where staring forms
Leaned out, and hushed the room and closed it in.[14]

In this museum/bedroom, overfurnished in the style of Poe, "the change of Philomel" is indeed a framed "sylvan scene":

Above the antique mantel was displayed
As though a window gave upon the sylvan scene
The change of Philomel, by the barbarous king
So rudely forced; yet there the nightingale
Filled all the desert with inviolable voice
And still she cried, and still the world pursues,
'Jug Jug' to dirty ears.
And other withered stumps of time
Were told upon the walls.   [*CP, 56*]

To the woman buried alive, Philomel offers the possibility of transformation; to the poet likewise entombed, Philomel's natural, liquid music offers another way out. Yet such hopes remain illusory, for her "inviolable voice" is no longer heard but only pictorially represented, visible "*as though* a window gave upon the sylvan scene." Philomel remains a figure of the tradition and, much like Poe's raven, oversees another scene of solipsistic enclosure: a woman asking urgent questions that meet with silence. Thus Philomel only mirrors the woman "savagely still" in her "coffered" chamber, for her original metamorphosis is superseded by the metamorphosis of representation and its second silencing:

And *still* she cried, and *still* the world pursues,
'Jug Jug' to dirty ears. (Emphasis mine.)

Her second amputation and change issue in the conventional representation of the nightingale's song, "Jug Jug." In her second loss, Philomel also mirrors the poet, who is cut off from nature and shut up with "fragments" of "synthetic" facsimiles—including Ovid's story of Philomela and Keats's "Ode to a Nightingale."

The same associations are at work in "The Fire Sermon," where the mating of the typist and the clerk and the subsequent gramophone music contrast with the rape of Philomel and her subsequent command of natural music. Eliot again links sexual potency and poetic power: the scene is "seen" by Tiresias, who has already seen all there is to see, and is "told" in a Shakespearean sonnet, which is as encoded and inscribed as a gramophone record. The poet's paraphernalia of myths, forms, and meters likewise cuts him off from the original experience myths codify—a violent change or break with the past, issuing in "natural" language or music. All else is secondhand and already recorded, counted, typed, used, and used up. Thus Tiresias is an ironic "seer": he has *foresuffered* all, and what he sees is only a past endlessly repeated. What he sees now are the clerk and the typist, who are his mirror images. A clerk counts, records, and files; a typist types letters and words; a prophet "types" myths and stories; and a poet counts syllables and types rhymes, stanzas, and sonnets. The coding governs at all levels. And if the clerk gropes blindly and the typist feels no passion, Tiresias can see nothing that is not there, and the poet can tell nothing that has not been told before—by Tiresias, Shakespeare, or Goldsmith—for all the characters, the poet among them, share in the general enervation.

"What the Thunder Said" entertains the possibility of a poetic source in nature:

If there were the sound of water only
Not the cicada
And dry grass singing
But sound of water over a rock
Where the hermit-thrush sings in the pine trees
Drip drop drip drop drop drop drop
But there is no water   [CP, 67]

Such a natural music as the "water-dripping song" (CP, 74) of the thrush is not audible to Eliot as it was to Whitman, who could hear and tally the songs of birds and more:

I hear you whispering there O stars of heaven,
O suns—O grass of graves—O perpetual transfers and
    promotions,
If you do not say any thing how can I say any thing?[15]

Eliot's other predecessor here is Keats, whose sonnet on the thrush also appeals to nature—if with an implicit acknowledgment that "all this is a mere sophistication." Eliot may well have been thinking of this sonnet, for the renewal "Thunder" promises the "dead land," Keats's "Thrush" would offer its archaeologist:

O thou whose only book has been the light
Of supreme darkness which thou feddest on
Night after night, when Phoebus was away,
To thee the spring shall be a tripple morn.
O fret not after knowledge—I have none,
And yet my song comes native with the warmth;
O fret not after knowledge—I have none,
And yet the evening listens . . .[16]

But even ironic appeals to nature are beyond the poet of *The Waste Land*, whose sole authority is the past—"the whole of the literature of Europe from Homer" that is "in his bones" (*SW,* 49).

Since "Tradition and the Individual Talent" limits the tradition to the literature of Europe from Homer,[17] it is significant that the only positive "message" of *The Waste Land* is conveyed through "DA DA DA," which originates outside the Western tradition. Moreover, it originates in nature, as the thunder "speaks" in an onomatopoeic sequence. Yet such a coincidence of force and form is merely a poetic device or a foreign tongue or even nonsense, for surely "Dada" lurks behind "DA DA DA." Thus efficacious language is divorced from meaning, and for the poet to speak with Whitman's "original energy," he would have to move beyond sense. Eliot may take Poe to task for poeticizing at the expense of sense,[18] but it is Eliot himself who takes Poe to his logical conclusion. Like Poe's, Eliot's language alternates between a parodic super-sense or God's-eye view and a parodic sub-sense or nature's echolalia. In "DA DA DA," these two extremes of the language of *The Waste Land*—ranging from "Son of Man" to "Twit twit twit"—meet, as God speaks "nonsense" through the medium of nature. While this language is more than currency, it is also parodic and less than currency—the wisdom-nonsense of another country, another time, and another language, even if it is the original language, Sanskrit. For the beginning merely echoes the end, "DA DA DA" echoes "Dada," and the origin repeats ruin and disintegration. By descending below articulate signification, Eliot hints at a music-language above articulation. Thus nature's echolalia mimics, but necessarily parodies, the "music of the spheres."[19]

The "Shantih shantih shantih" that ends the poem points to a future direction. The last line is properly a deus ex machina: it delivers the poet not only from the tradition that informs and encloses the poem but from history itself. For it is the language of a theological center, even if in a foreign tongue—as indeed the language of faith, for the characters of *The Waste Land,* is a foreign tongue. "The Peace which passeth understanding" is what follows the historical ruin of the poem, the collapse of textual authority and the dismemberment of texts of centrality. Ruins in general impart such peace because they celebrate oblivion. In Jean Starobinski's words, "The ruin *par excellence* indicates an abandoned cult, a forsaken god. It expresses neglect, desertion. The ancient monument had originally been a memorial, a 'monition,' perpetuating a memory. But the initial memory has now been lost, to be replaced by a second significance, which resides in the disappearance of the memory that the constructor had claimed he was perpetuating in this stone. Its melancholy resides in the fact that it has become a monument of lost significance."[20] This species of the sublime, which is also found in Poe, may account for the final peace or sense of relief at the end of *The Waste Land.*

Allen Tate's description of Poe as a "religious man whose Christianity, for reasons that nobody knows anything about, had got short-circuited" would characterize Eliot as well.[21] Christianity is the theological correlative of what would have solved Poe's and Eliot's poetic problem. In the poetic worlds of Poe and early Eliot, divinity and nature, the immortal soul and mortal form, are forever separate, without a unifying sign or Logos. Instead, language signifies the poet's distance from both nature and divinity and renders him incapable of either natural blindness or divine vision. Force and form merely reflect each other in a collapse of difference that parodies a primal unity "above" or "below" the severing language. In such poetry without faith in the word's incarnational power, language is at best an expressive tool to be manipulated by the poet to create desired effects. The more the formal means are played up, however, the more the spirit suffocates; conversely, the more the spirit is animated, the more forms become dead and deadening enclosures, the more the body becomes a decaying husk. Poe and Eliot share a horror of such decay, as even the details of their subject show. For example, Eliot observes that "the ladies in [Poe's] poems and tales are always ladies lost, or ladies vanishing before they can be embraced."[22] "Ladies," of course, are rushed offstage because they force the crisis between the "angel" and the "machine" he inhabits. In Eliot as well, ladies are problematic. They tend to be embodiments of the "machine": objects of horror as in Poe, they are usually reduced to natural forms (they are "downed" with hair) and empty chatter (they "talk, talk, talk"). Or, less characteristically, they can be projections of the "angel," as the "hyacinth girl" clearly is. Yet the speaker's encounter with this girl is ambiguous, suspended as it is between life and death. For just as empty chatter has its poetic analogue, so does this paralysis.

While the "hyacinth girl" is surrounded by a redeeming silence, her allusion to Poe's "Helen" of "hyacinth hair"[23] suggests a silence less than transcendent. Thus a spiritual-sexual experience that "passes" telling correlates with a literary experience in search of its proper expression.

The "text" of "Mr. Eliot's Sunday Morning Service" offers a clinical diagnosis of the poet's problem. Eliot begins by distinguishing the "poly-philoprogenitive" "sapient sutlers of the Lord" from the "Word" that was "in the beginning." The monosyllabic "Word" contrasts with the polysyllabic impurity of "polyphiloprogenitive" and, appropriately, rhymes with "Lord." But the rhyme is also a symptom of the problem the poem studies, and it indicates that the priests/poets of the Lord/Word—those who do the Lord's dirty work—have indeed more than one origin:

In the beginning was the Word.
Superfetation of τό ἔν,
And at the mensual turn of time
Produced enervate Origen.   [*CP, 47*]

The name "Origen" conflates *origin* and *genesis* and suggests that the proper name is propagated (by polyphiloprogenesis) out of "Origin." Such propagation is an enervation of "Origin" by the pollution or "de-generation" of nature, for *mensual* seems to conflate *mensural* ("of measure") and *mensis* ("month") or *menses* and even *sensual*. Thus *measure* has links to natural periodization and reproduction, and the poet, like the "enervate" priest, has mixed parentage, half Lord/Word and half "mensual" "polymath." The "painter" of the Lord/Word provides another model for the poet:

A painter of the Umbrian school
Designed upon a gesso ground
The nimbus of the Baptized God.
The wilderness is cracked and browned

But through the water pale and thin
Still shine the unoffending feet
And there above the painter set
The Father and the Paraclete.   [*CP, 47*]

The "Paraclete," rhyming with "feet," intercedes between the Father and the Son, and this intercession authorizes the painter's "designing" "upon a gesso ground / The nimbus of the Baptized God." And the "Paraclete"—the Holy Spirit—would authorize the poet as well: the baptized God's "feet" mark the natural base and basis of the Word, both the Christian Word and the poetic. But the poet cannot connect to that authorizing translation, that "tallying" authority, and the God's "unoffending feet" degenerate into the offensive "Sweeney shifts from ham to ham / Stirring the water in his bath" (*CP,* 48), just as the poet's word degenerates to Latinate diction (the dialect of "enervate Origen"), a "polymath" stutter of *ps* above which is perched τό ἕν—"The One," characteristically existing outside the poet's "native tongue" but already marked by "superfetation," of Greek over Aramaic.

In Eliot's early work, the Word that is "superfetated" to produce bodies and "super-scribed" to produce words, the Word that disseminates into polysyllabic "polymath," is lost beyond recovery, and the poet wanders through a waste land of enervated products—bodies, words, sites, and forms—as a veritable ghost of himself. And tradition is no help, for it only erects history as the authority and institutionalizes a secular descent or progeneration of words from the original Word. Eliot's necessary alienation from a tradition not his own plays up the deracination of all history and all language from the Word.[24] Joining the Anglican Church and becoming a British citizen allow Eliot to align spiritual and historical authorities and to correct his dislocation as a mortal and an American. And the two authorities are interdependent for the American poet; a legitimate tradition that will be more than an alien imposition can be justified only by an appeal to an authority outside history altogether. Submission to a non-secular authority allows the poet to inhabit a temporal or natural language that is inscribed with a secular history or tradition without being *of* it. Thus the poet of *Four Quartets* can confront the complicity of his medium in the devastation of the spirit and the fragmentation of the Word into nature, history, and words. By centering himself outside history, Eliot can regard history as "a pattern / Of timeless moments" (*CP,* 208) and see "movement" as a "detail of the pattern" (*CP,* 181), which gathers the "mensual" time of the poet's medium:

Words move, music moves
Only in time; but that which is only living
Can only die. Words, after speech, reach
Into the silence. Only by the form, the pattern,
Can words or music reach
The stillness.   [*CP,* 180]

In *Four Quartets,* the "Peace which passeth understanding" enables Eliot not only to accept that time is conquered "only through time" (*CP,* 178), but to understand the nature of his own struggle with history and tradition:

And what there is to conquer
By strength and submission, has already been discovered
Once or twice, or several times, by men whom one cannot
  hope

To emulate—but there is no competition—
There is only the fight to recover what has been lost
And found and lost again and again: and now, under
    conditions
That seem unpropitious. But perhaps neither gain nor
    loss.
For us, there is only the trying. The rest is not our
    business.   [*CP*, 189]

Chapter Three

Sylvia Plath's Black Car of Lethe

Years later I
Encounter them on the road—
Words dry and riderless,
The indefatigable hoof-taps.
While
From the bottom of the pool, fixed stars
Govern a life.

"Words"

The constellation of personal, historical, and esthetic forces that shape Sylvia Plath's poetic and plot her life traces the same pattern that Poe's ill-starred poet originally marked. With Plath, we once more begin "in a kingdom by the sea," before all separations and departures. In such a prelapsarian mythic matrix, human breath, the breath of the sea, and the breath of poetry pulse in unison. Plath recalls this origin in "OCEAN 1212-W": "Breath, that is the first thing. Something is breathing. My own breath? The breath of my mother? No, something else, something larger, farther, more serious, more weary." This larger breath is the measure of all other sounds: "There might be a hiss of rain on the pane, there might be wind sighing and trying the creaks of the house like keys. I was not deceived by these. The motherly pulse of the sea made a mock of such counterfeits." Eventually, the "pulse" of poetry comes to hold something of the "motherly pulse of the sea": "And I recall my mother, a sea-girl herself, reading to me and my brother—who came later—from Matthew Arnold's 'Forsaken Merman.'" In this final inflection of the maternal breath, the child is marked: "I had fallen into a new way of being happy."[1]

The birth into poetry is a "fall" into "substitutive satisfactions." As such, it enfolds the knowledge of otherness, of separation, of difference. Thus the brother—"who came later"—is a necessary actor in the drama of the poet's birth. Plath's account of her brother's birth records the elision of her *breath* into an *other:* "I who for two and a half years had been the centre of a tender universe felt the axis wrench and a polar chill immobilize my bones. I would be a bystander, a museum mammoth." This de-centering marks the "awful birthday of otherness": "As from a star I saw, coldly and soberly, the *separateness* of everything. I felt the wall of my skin: I am I. That stone is a stone. My beautiful fusion with the things of this world was over."[2] And with this "dif-fusion" comes the otherness of language: the tautological "I am I" is as much a "wall" as the skin is.

Plath rehearses the "script" of the birth of otherness over and over. In "Morning Song," the mother mourns another birth:

Love set you going like a fat gold watch.
The midwife slapped your footsoles, and your bald cry
Took its place among the elements.

Our voices echo, magnifying your arrival. New statue.
In a drafty museum, your nakedness
Shadows our safety. We stand round blankly as walls.

I'm no more your mother
Than the cloud that distills a mirror to reflect its own slow
Effacement at the wind's hand.[3]

Plath consistently presents the "fall" into otherness in images of stiffening, freezing into forms, or turning into stones or statues or even into the museums housing the statues. Images of water and archaeology hold the same antithetical values in Plath as they do in Eliot. The text of her Gothic drama is the generic text of otherness, because it spells out the generic otherness of texts. Plath's childhood reminiscence ends abruptly by sealing her prehistory, her origin, into a text: "And this is how it stiffens, my vision of that seaside childhood. My father died, we moved inland. Whereon those nine first years of my life sealed themselves off like a ship in a bottle— beautiful, inaccessible, obsolete, a fine, white flying myth."[4] Diffusing from this center, "Memories growing, ring on ring, / A series of weddings" (*CP*, 257), repeat this divorce and record its history.

The texts that bottle and seal the myths are forms of otherness. Plath also presents them as enclosures, stony forms that rob of breath, or plaster casts that imprison the soul. Her tautological "I am I" is one inflection of texts of otherness, of texts of closure, and it modulates into other voices—the "I am I am I am," for example, of the body-machine. This line is used twice in *The Bell Jar*. The first scene reads:

I thought I would swim out until I was too tired to swim back. As I paddled on, my heartbeat boomed like a dull motor in my ears.

I am I am I am.[5]

Here, the line marks the refrain of the body, and it keeps time to the suicidal wish to silence the "machine" and set the "angel" free. Later, the line denotes the "old brag of my heart,"[6] the brag of the survivor body. The tautological language of separation, which becomes a suicidal equation of life and death, also modulates into the "iambs" of poetic meter. The association is clearest in "Suicide off Egg Rock":

Sun struck the water like a damnation.
No pit of shadow to crawl into,
And his blood beating the old tattoo
I am, I am, I am . . .   [*CP*, 115]

The rhythm of the body—"A machine to breathe and beat forever"—and poetic rhythm conspire in the man's suicide, so that

The words in his book wormed off the pages.
Everything glittered like blank paper

and "he walked into the water." As Pamela Smith has argued, this "suicidal 'I am'/iamb holds the key to Plath's use of iambics. The lub-dubb of the heartbeat becomes the 'I am' of a man realizing his own death."[7]

Somewhat in the manner of Poe's "The Bells," the coded, formal way of registering the life force comes to defeat the life. The "blood jet" (*CP*, 270), the biological birthright to poetry, is a "tattoo"—both a drum beat and a writing, a text engraved on the very skin and flesh. The military and primitive associations of the two senses of "tattoo" are telling: the aggression of the physical, time-bound body is absorbed in a self-inflicted wound. The meanings of the word fit the pattern of other suicidal internalizations of victimizer and victim in Plath's poetry. Thus her melodrama derives from the same source as Poe's: a sensational, histrionic language, which aims at the nerves and is directed at "effects," dramatizes its self-defeating strategy. Plath's theatrics are not failed drama but generic melodrama,[8] which demonstrates how technique negates structure, surfaces bury depths, the "plaster casts" of bodies entomb souls, the "machine" overrides the "angel," the public memory encoded in literary forms erases all traces of the private memory in expressing it. The prototype of Plath's work is "The Raven": in Poe's anatomy of the mechanism of poetry, the machinery of repetition, meter, and rhyme denies all freedom, and a psychology of stimulus and response usurps the psyche and yields a pure style (the word has the same root as *stimulus*) without responsibility. Poe's poem is the first to show the inadvertent and necessary reversal of pure estheticism (the word means "sensation") or sensationalism into an *an*esthetic.

"Daddy" is Plath's most theatrical example of this operation. The "you" of otherness strikes the keynote of the poem and raises the rhyming to a pitch of compulsive repetition that effectively drowns out the "I." Even the "do" of action or choice is only an echo of *du,* the father's *ich.* The poem's regressive form is less a "manic defence" against a painful subject⁹ than a confirmation of the defeat of the poet's language, its total surrender to the "you" of otherness:

I never could talk to you.
The tongue stuck in my jaw.

It stuck in a barb wire snare.
Ich, ich, ich, ich,
I could hardly speak.   [*CP,* 223]

"Ich, ich, ich, ich" is the poem's skeleton, the pure reductive form that supports its four-stress rhythm. Thus "ich" is also the "barb wire" of a language that checks the poet's tongue and cuts off her speech by being not hers but Daddy's "I"—already there, already encoded. This "ich" is a foreign language to the self; its consonants set "a barricade of barb and check" (*CP,* 50) against the open vowel "I," which yearns to be free.¹⁰ Yet "ich" rhymes with "speak" and thus makes a mockery of the "I"'s very drive for self-expression.

If this encoded, anterior, foreign "ich" is Daddy's sign, the daughter's repetition of it can only inflict pain on her and magnify her separation, and the drama of the father's language silencing the daughter easily translates into a variety of internal or civil wars. The Nazi-Jew struggle becomes a recurrent emblem of destructive, preempting, silencing language. "Cut" provides other models: the poet branches out from her personal pain to Pilgrims, Indians, "Redcoats," "Homunculus," "Saboteur," "Kamikaze," "Ku Klux Klan," and "Babushka," for all the "foreign" languages say the same thing—a Babel of tongues amplifying her inner war with her own "foreign" language. In the end, she can only circle back to "Dirty girl, / Thumb stump" (*CP,* 235–36), with its suggestion of amputation or even castration. And "the thin / Papery feeling" of the cut suggests that the violent excision of the signifier's force amounts to a reduction of life to writing. Thus Plath's "foot fetishism" is a perfectly ironic symptom of her "sickness." While a Freudian analysis would point to the father's sexual hold over the daughter, Plath suggests that even the father-daughter sexual drama is not properly her own, for the psychic drama reduces to a poet's problem. The father is a "black shoe / In which I have lived like a foot" (*CP,* 222); he is the container-form that reduces the poet's "I" to a foot, the existential "I am" to an iamb. Elsewhere we read:

This black boot has no mercy for anybody.
Why should it, it is the hearse of a dead foot,

The high, dead, toeless foot of this priest
Who plumbs the well of his book.   [*CP,* 197]

The tongue held in the barbed wire of a metrical beat is an analogue of the foot in the shoe, and the well is plumbed—fathomed and sealed up with lead (pencil)—by this fetishized signifier. The process whereby desire is metonymically transferred to a fetishized signifier, container, or equivalent of the original object provides a model for this kind of poetic mechanism. The literal signifier, the form, becomes Jacques Derrida's "dangerous supplement"[11] that usurps the signified or the content and erases the metaphoric difference or distance. In poetic terms, the fetish that kills the erotic is the letter that kills the metaphor, the form that kills the force, the public memory or history that usurps and kills personal remembrance.

The desire to achieve presence via poetic language leaves the poet at the mercy of formal contraptions and a spectator to the pathetic discrepancy between ends and means. In the stiffened language of exile, we get formally ordained or compulsively chosen repetitions rather than the magic "spells" that just might give back, "like a conch, the susurrous of the sea." Here, Plath is recalling the "incantation, a fine rhyme," of her grandmother's phone number, "OCEAN 1212-W,"[12] which is also the title of her reminiscence and carries her back to the voices of the past. The phonic connection between words and what they promise to give back, the susurrous of that larger breath, is broken by the exile into consciousness and history. And, as Plath reveals in the later poems, the formal and compulsive repetitions of words conspire in the exiling: rather than "ferrying" her home (*CP,* 95), poetic language becomes "obscene // An engine, an engine / Chuffing me off like a Jew" (*CP,* 223), taking her farther away from the oceanic rhythm and deeper inland into an alien history. Trains are a recurrent emblem of the paternal language:

The train is dragging itself, it is screaming—
An animal
Insane for the destination.   [*CP,* 249]

When the speaker gives herself over to the engine and its momentum, she regresses to a mechanical repetition, as in "Daddy." Now rhyme and repetition ("Ocean one-two, one-two, double-*u*") parody the larger breath that swaddles and cradles the child—the infantile rhythm they would recover—and the poet is "finally through"; the "phone" is "off at the root" (*CP,* 224). As the line "Love set you going like a fat gold watch" (*CP,* 156) warns us, "Between the essence / And the descent / Falls the Shadow."[13] And the "black car of Lethe" (*CP,* 249) will not ferry one anywhere; the estranging and "dif-fusing" language is the engine that will "kill" the track (*CP,* 264), obliterating both past and future.

As in Poe, the psychic impulse to recover a lost paradise where breath, nature, and language were in step sets in motion a machine, a cacophony of mechanical repetitions that can only exile the poet deeper into an anesthetic "Lethe." Thus the poet who internalizes the exiling mechanism becomes both victim and victimizer, whose "barbs" engrave her own skin. She is both the ant and the spider of "The Spider":

The ants—a file of comers, a file of goers—
Persevered on a set course
No scruple could disrupt,
Obeying orders of instinct till swept
Off-stage and infamously wrapped
Up by a spry black deus
Ex machina . . .   [*CP,* 49]

The spider's web, the "deus / Ex machina" of poetic form, takes over, finishes the procedures initiated by instinct, and concludes the drama; but it is already someone else's drama. Unlike the Greek concept of character as destiny, which internalizes fate, Plath's melodramatic understanding casts form as destiny, which externalizes character and subjects the psyche to the forms of its objectification. Thus poetic forms loom as external, alien powers, for the "deus," in descending to the "machina," is externalized, objectified, and *x*ed or crossed out, and the unconvincing device comes to convince.

Plath's problematic relation to her medium accounts for the distinctive marks of her poetry. The combination of a cool distance from and a helpless surrender to the emotional states she portrays[14] is a function of the jux-taposition of rigid formal control and the increasingly uncontrolled states of mind that the formal control stimulates. Thus tight nets of sound underlie wild imagistic jumps; rhymes and meter anchor an excessive, "pathological" diction. As in Poe, the inner wildness, incoherence, and psychic disintegra-tion increase in direct proportion to the rigidity of control and formal decorum. This disparity is the source of Plath's brand of "comedy"[15] and explains her tonal impurities and mixtures,[16] as serious "confession" turns into "light verse" with the increase in formal archaism and control. After *The Colossus,* Plath's forms are not inherited or conventional orders but self-imposed rules, and for this reason certain critics have devalued her later poems. According to Hugh Kenner, for example, the poems in *Ariel* show "more of compulsion neurosis than mathematics"; their control is only the "*look* of control," a "cunning" rhetoric designed to manipulate readers and to turn their attention "from perversity to craft."[17] What gives the impression of "perversity," however, is the very disjunction between form and content, craft and passion. We never know whether passion is acting out a confession on the stage of craft, or whether craft is plotting a poem on the stage of passion. This disjunction is a "madness" like the one Eliot diagnosed in *Hamlet*—"less than madness and more than feigned."[18] For Plath's "madness" is internal to the structure of her poems, a function of the process of expression. The internal division between means and ends, between craft and passion, is the explicit subject of a number of poems and appears to inform her consistent treatment of the poet as double—in, for example, "Rhyme," "In Plaster," and "Two Sisters of Persephone." Here, the first sister

. . . works problems on
A mathematical machine.
Dry ticks mark time
As she calculates each sum

at her "barren enterprise," while the other is the "sun's bride":

Bronzed as earth, the second lies,
Hearing ticks blown gold
Like pollen on bright air.   [*CP,* 32]

Similarly, it is not the family drama that explains Plath's poetics, but her problem with her medium that conjures up and installs the family drama as the central, allegorical text of her life. The facts of her biography reinforce this drama and enable her to conflate problems of poetic authority and Oedipal themes, thereby bringing a psychological urgency to poetic anxieties. This conflation accounts for the range of imagery and plots that Plath musters to flesh out her esthetic argument with her medium that does not mediate. For example, the father who freezes the maternal matrix into a text appears, in one of his masks, as the allegorical "Man in Black," the

Fixed vortex on the far
Tip, riveting stones, air,
All of it, together.   [*CP,* 120]

The father who becomes an emblem of death's absolute otherness is an end that has replaced the beginning. He represents the foreclosure of all flux, whether of nature or of poetry:

It stands at my window, big as the sky.
It breathes from my sheets, the cold dead center
Where split lives congeal and stiffen to history. [*CP*, 207–08]

Since he marks the passage out of a "mythic" childhood and the "stiffening" into history and consciousness, he blocks access to the past and memory or imagination itself:

Miles long
Extend the radial sheaves
Of your spread hair, in which wrinkling skeins
Knotted, caught, survives
The old myth of origins
Unimaginable. [*CP*, 92]

The "myth of origins" is the myth both of childhood and of a language that sounds the larger breath, and both are caught in the father's net. The poet who would regress to the maternal language—who would regress to infancy and crawl "straight for the coming wave," trusting its "infant gills" to take over and ferry it through the "looking-glass" to a primal regression-home[19]—finds that the father guards the shore:

You defy other godhood.
I walk dry on your kingdom's border
Exiled to no good.
Your shelled bed I remember.
Father, this thick air is murderous.
I would breathe water. [*CP*, 93]

But the net of the father's text traps her: one can remember the maternal "bed" or "cradle" of the sea only in the voices of other "fathers." The lines echo the ending of "Prufrock," and the poem's title, "Full Fathom Five," takes Plath *and* Eliot back to Shakespeare, where we find the poet-father Prospero pulling the strings of even the airiest spirit, his servant Ariel. Yet Prospero himself is not free but held in bondage by the play. Thus the father who exiles the poet into history is also an ancient, archaic "father" of writing, who encodes the sea-psyche itself:

For the archaic trenched lines
Of your grained face shed time in runnels:
Ages beat like rains

On the unbeaten channels
Of the ocean.   [*CP,* 93]

   It is the patriarchal tradition of "stony" predecessors, as well as the
paternal language of articulations and the poetic "adhering to rules, to rules,
to rules" (*CP,* 206), that stands between the poet and the origin. Plath
addresses "The Colossus" to this literary father-figure rather than to her own
father; her choice of a statue—of Apollo, the god of music and oracles, who
commands both the lyre and the earth's omphalos—makes this fact clear.
For Plath, as for Eliot, the powers of prophecy and song alike are denied the
poet who is exiled into history and writing. Yet this self-proclaimed oracle of
a colossal father has "silt" blocking his throat, and despite the poet's efforts to
"dredge the silt" and clear his throat, he mouths neither articulate speech nor
song; instead,

Mule-bray, pig-grunt and bawdy cackles
Proceed from your great lips.
It's worse than a barnyard.   [*CP,* 129]

Plath's colossus makes a mockery of both oracular speech and natural music.
Her colossus is Poe's "pallid bust of Pallas" and croaking raven[20] in one. The
gods are silent, and nature croaks away. Since the fallen poet is lost to deity
and nature at once, prophecies are hard to tell from mule-brays. "On the
Decline of Oracles" again presents a father who rules the voice:

My father kept a vaulted conch
By two bronze bookends of ships in sail,
And as I listened its cold teeth seethed
With voices of that ambiguous sea

. . . .

My father died, and when he died
He willed his books and shell away.
The books burned up, sea took the shell,
But I, I keep the voices he
Set in my ear . . .   [*CP,* 78]

The father is the keeper of the books *and* the conch; the poet holds only their
echoes in her ear. And her voice is threatened by both the literary past and
nature.

"Hardcastle Crags" concerns this double threat.[21] Just as the "Colossus" of Apollo sounds "mule-bray" and "pig-grunt," the "babel" here is both nature's echolalia and the "racket of echoes" the poet's feet strike "from the steely street." Both threaten to choke off her breath, and she becomes a blank slate, a sounding board that echoes both:

Nor did any word body with a name
The blank mood she walked in. Once past
The dream-peopled village, her eyes entertained no dream,
And the sandman's dust

Lost lustre under her footsoles.   [CP, 63]

The echoes of her feet stamp out her dream—ironically, cast by the "sand-man's dust"—of being distinct from dust:

The long wind, paring her person down
To a pinch of flame, blew its burdened whistle
In the whorl of her ear, and like a scooped-out pumpkin crown
Her head cupped the babel.

Conversely, the mute landscape frozen into stone threatens to silence her. And as the echoes of her feet modulate into nature's echolalia, nature's silence freezes into the stone weight of a dead past:

The whole landscape
Loomed absolute as the antique world was
Once, in its earliest sway of lymph and sap,
Unaltered by eyes,

Enough to snuff the quick
Of her small heat out . . .   [CP, 63]

Her anxiety is both a poetic anxiety and a natural anxiety, a fear of being overcome by a babel of voices and by silence, for nature and the tradition mirror each other in her allegorical universe.

This double threat is felt in a variety of poems and seems to inform Plath's division of women into barren women and mothers, with a good deal of ambiguity about both. Reproduction serves Plath well as a metaphor for poetic production because it reveals the discrepancy between the initiating force and what necessarily follows: bodies turn to statues and museums on the occasion of birth; love winds a "fat gold watch" (CP, 156); children are "right like a well-done sum" (CP, 141). Childbirth puts one at the mercy of nature's processes and threatens to "efface" one and to steal one's "voice."

Yet "barrenness" is no answer, either, as "Spinster" suggests: "intolerably struck / By the birds' irregular babel / And the leaves' litter," the spinster withdraws and erects an impenetrable "barricade of barb and check / Against mutinous weather" and against all "lover's gestures" that might "unbalance the air" (*CP*, 49–50). But the spinster (the root of the word, "spinner," renders her a poet figure), the upholder of formal perfection, only becomes a mirror image of the otherness of nature's "litter," the wind's "babel." The "leaves' litter" (the waste of natural reproduction) and the lettered leaves (the waste or reduction of poetic production to nature) are mirror images. And if nature's babel is threatening, so is formal perfection, for it is equally alien to the desired unity of form and force, words and breath; in fact, it is equally at the mercy of others' voices. The poet's medium is both a temporal, entropy-bound "machine" that measures out the speaker's time, and a historically determined and encoded vehicle. Poetry marks and is marked by two kinds of time, both of which remain alien forces for Plath. Thus, if the "Heavy Women" listening "for the millennium, / The knock of the small, new heart," are attended by "the axle of winter" grinding "round" and "bearing down" on them (*CP*, 158), the "Barren Woman" is subject to a different otherness:

Empty, I echo to the least footfall,
Museum without statues, grand with pillars, porticoes, rotundas.

. . . .

I imagine myself with a great public,
Mother of a white Nike and several bald-eyed Apollos.
Instead, the dead injure me with attentions, and nothing can happen.   [*CP*, 157]

Thus, if it isn't the "leaves' bicker and whisk in babel tongues" (*CP*, 67) threatening the poet's voice, it is Daddy's thesaurus,[22] the old god's "talking whirlwind" (*CP*, 77), the ghosts the poet is "riddled with" (*CP*, 71), the ghost of the "old god" the poet conjures up on her ouija board:

The glass mouth sucks blood-heat from my forefinger.
The old god dribbles, in return, his words.

The old god, too, writes aureate poetry
In tarnished modes, maundering among the wastes,
Fair chronicler of every foul declension.   [*CP*, 77]

A number of readers have noted the early Plath's easy assumption of other poets' voices as lyric masks. Marjorie Perloff, for example, suggests that Plath does not exhibit what Harold Bloom terms the "anxiety of influence"—the sense of a struggle with a powerful predecessor for one's own voice, for the right to work the same ground; rather, Plath seems to write in other poets' voices in order to escape her own voice.[23] The concept of her own voice is problematic for Plath. In one sense, she sounds from the beginning a distinctive voice and articulates a distinctive set of preoccupations; in another sense, however, her voice is always already distanced, and her changes are changes only in the masks she assumes in exile. In her earlier work, these masks tend to be the voices of other poets; in the later work, they tend to be the voices of the poetic mechanism itself. Indeed, Plath appears to think of her own voice in rather literal terms—as literally a voice that internalizes and speaks the masking process. She sees her development as a change from "written" poems to "spoken" poems. She says about her later work: "I have found myself having to read them aloud to myself . . . I speak them to myself. Whatever lucidity they may have comes from the fact that I say them aloud."[24]

Yet the shift to a voice-bound poetry only binds her more closely to a medium that "shortchanges" her "continuously" (*CP,* 106). If "the word, defining, muzzles,"[25] so does the voice. The dramatic monologue, which is dependent on an audience of a "you" to "let" the "I" speak, becomes theatrical—as in "Lady Lazarus"[26]—and the mask of openness, of an effect-bound or "confessional" performance, muzzles the "I." For in drama, the very transparency of the expressive medium prohibits expression; Plath's figures for such transparent prisons include not only her ubiquitous mirrors but a bell jar, the cellophane tent of the "Paralytic" (who appears to be another poet figure), and even the blurred vision of an eye in which a splinter seems permanently lodged, "needling it dark" (*CP,* 109). Moreover, drama has its own cast of "fathers," and her assumption of given dramatic roles, such as Electra ("Electra on Azalea Path"), Clytemnestra ("Purdah"), and Medea ("Edge"), amounts merely to borrowing "the stilts of an old tragedy," which casts the speaker as another one of the "stony actors" who "poise and pause for breath" (*CP,* 117). Thus the graveyard becomes the proper stage for the father-daughter drama, a stage where the poet may approach the father but not on *her* feet.

Drama muzzles the voice the more decisively by sounding it; it stages the transcription of one's breath as a plot or text. "The Eye-mote" addresses this process directly:

I dream that I am Oedipus.

What I want back is what I was
Before the bed, before the knife,
Before the brooch-pin and the salve

Fixed me in this parenthesis;
Horses fluent in the wind,
A place, a time gone out of mind.   [*CP,* 109]

The parenthesis is a punctuation mark, a writing *before* the poet, a plot that
codes her dreams and puts her feet on "stilts." This writing splinters the eye-
I, blurs and darkens the vision of one who started out "blameless as daylight,"
and cuts her off from nature and herself, already memorializing her memory
and speaking her lines. Unable to ascend or descend to a fluency "above" or
"below" the scripts that assign her her words, the poet is arrested on the
impossible ground of literary language, a middle ground of exile where she
wanders on the stilts of iambs.

Plath's ambivalence toward her expressionist medium often registers in
images of the skin as a writing surface. Not only are people devoid of the life
force reduced to "paper" people,[27] but the poet's skin is reduced to cloth or
paper that records her victimization by her medium. "Lady Lazarus"
provides a sensational example:

A sort of walking miracle, my skin
Bright as a Nazi lampshade,
My right foot

A paperweight,
My face a featureless, fine
Jew linen.   [*CP,* 244]

Plath's presentation of the self-destructive process of expression—"the big
strip tease"—recalls other expressionists. John Berryman, whose "Henry's
pelt was put on sundry walls" to delight "them persons," cites Gottfried
Benn as a predecessor: "We are using our own skins for wallpaper and we
cannot win."[28] But such imagery is also found in Eliot, whose Prufrock is
pinned on a wall for exhibit. The expressionist poet is characteristically
reduced to a public surface, a wall with the generic handwriting on it. For
expression is a destructive process, and these poets often present it as a
process of fragmentation—a reduction of the person to depersonalized body
parts, mere signifiers. Eliot's Prufrock, Berryman's Henry, and Plath's Lady
Lazarus share this unhealthy condition: an expressionist prying open of the
self disarticulates the person and exposes the absence or erosion of an
inhering and informing spirit: "Ash, ash— / You poke and stir. / Flesh, bone,
there is nothing there—"(*CP,* 246). The verdict of Berryman's analysts—
"'Underneath,' / (they called in iron voices) 'understand, / is nothing. So
there'"[29]—only repeats the findings of all such "prying."

Plath's expressionist conception of language traps her in a divided world, reducing the subject to the language of its expression and the outside world to characters and props on the stage of the subject's expressionist drama. The two separate worlds of the mind and nature relate only through culturally over-determined emblems, through psychologically over-determined objective correlatives, through automatic "releaser" mechanisms[30] of stimulus and response. Natural objects in Plath tend to have given values: whether moons or skulls, oceans or stones, poppies or tulips, they are characteristically used as allegorical pointers that "talk" or "correspond" to her "wound" (*CP*, 161). For Plath's poet is "fallen" from "grace": "Tongues are strange, / Signs say nothing. The falcon who spoke clear / To Canacee cries gibberish to coarsened ears" (*CP*, 100) and only recalls the nightingale who cries "'Jug Jug' to dirty ears." "Incommunicado," the poet can only "spin mirrors, / Loyal to [her] image" (*CP*, 259). Thus Plath's figuration reaffirms the closure of her formalism. One of her last poems, "Words" spells the defeat of her doubly alien language. The formal mechanism of poetry, "the indefatigable hoof-taps" (*CP*, 270) marching onward and outward from the center, perfectly reflects the mechanisms of nature—rings freezing around the sap, echoes radiating from sound, horses running out riderless. And the "ringing"—the temporal dispersal of hoof-taps and the spatial divagation of similes—leaves behind the ax that cuts, the axis that centers, the felt loss. Thus the "sly nerve" that "knits to each original its coarse copy" (*CP*, 69) is severed, the "simulacrum" "leers" (*CP*, 69), and the "fixed stars / Govern" (*CP*, 270).

Part Two

Chapter Four

Ralph Waldo Emerson: Essaying the Poet

> Philosophers are lined with eyes within,
> And, being so, the sage unmakes the man.
> > "The Philosopher"
>
> Bring us . . . men-making poets.
> > "Poetry and Imagination"

In being set up as the spiritual and literary father figure of American poetry, Emerson has become a tangle of contradictions. His work has been splintered into numerous "oppositions" and "dialectics," and his insistence on the necessity of poetic forms has been largely ignored so that he can sustain his role as the father of all his unlikely brood. If obviously antithetical poets come out of Emerson, there must be a basic contradiction between his early or Orphic and late phases, between his essays and poems, between "Bacchus" and "Merlin," and so on. By restoring the unity of Emerson's career and regarding his poetic theory and practice as of a piece, we can assess more accurately his place in American poetry.

Emerson's theory of language, which reflects an idealist's world-view, reveals the conceptual limits of his poetic theory. In brief, Emerson conceives of language as a system of symbolic, metaphoric, or analogical relationships representing the correspondences between nature and the mind. "Man is an analogist," Emerson claims,[1] and language represents, analogically, our perceptions of analogies. He argues that these analogies are not merely "lucky or capricious" (*CW,* 1:19)—unless, of course, "man" himself is. The laws of the human mind validate analogizing language, and analogizing language validates the mind; as the source or maker of all analogies, connections, and relationships, the human mind in effect replaces the Creator. Emerson insists that the "relation between the mind and matter is not fancied by some poet, but stands in the will of God" (*CW*, 1:22). But this only means that "God" is a species of poet, a trope for the analogizing principle. Likewise, Emerson contends that "every correspondence we observe in mind and matter suggests a substance older and deeper than either of these old nobilities. We see the law gleaming through."[2] But this law is only the law of correspondences, which constitutes the "grammar" of nature, language, and the mind.

Language is the middle term of this trinity, which language itself posits *as* a trinity. Emerson is not simply "assuming" correspondences and having "the whole system of language . . . reflect the order of reality";[3] instead, his medium *is* the "radical correspondence" of nature and thought. As he analyzes it in "Nature," language is double—a system of signs of facts *and* symbols of Spirit. Since a word as a sign is also a natural fact on the order of trees and stones, language is part fact and part Spirit. Emerson calls language, which is "material only on one side," a "demi-god" (*W*, 7:43): it is our "finest tool," "nearest to the mind" (*W*, 7:163), but it is also divine law, the law of the mind, which "*thinks* for us as Coleridge said."[4] Thus language "unites" the mind and nature by taking upon itself the duality of mind and nature.

The law of the mind becomes incarnate in language as the law of nature: the Word becomes flesh. As a result, temporality is the essence of language, which enacts the metamorphosis whereby Spirit flows into objects, "Being passes into Appearance, and Unity into Variety" (*CW*, 3:9). The unity of the mind and nature—symbolized by language—can be apprehended only in language, where it ceases to be a unity. Expression in language, then, recapitulates the genesis of the world: "The Germans believe in the necessary Trinity of God,—the Infinite; the finite; & the passage from Inf. into Fin.; or the Creation. It is typified in the act of thinking. Whilst we contemplate we are infinite; the thought we express is partial and finite; the expression is the third part & is equivalent to the act of Creation" (*JMN*, 5:30). Expression represents the metamorphosis of spirit into nature, of soul into natural law: "That soul which within us is a sentiment," Emerson writes, "outside of us is a law. We feel its inspiration; out there in history we can see its fatal strength" (*CW*, 2:60). The eternal law enacts itself in time and space. Since it is in language that thought enters history and becomes outer law, Emerson regards the "Representative Man" or the poet as a god who condescends to be born, for "it is indeed a perilous adventure, this serious act of venturing into mortality, swimming in a sea strewn with wrecks, where none indeed go undamaged[.] It is as bad as going to Congress; none comes back innocent" (*JMN*, 11:417). Thus language not only embodies correspondences between the mind and nature by virtue of the symbolic status of its sign-words and its metaphorical rhetoric; it also creates such correspondences by doubling sentiment into history and thought into expression, which is then part of nature.

The price paid for language's transformation of nature into thought—into "pictures" of the mind—is the countertransformation of soul into fatal law. Emerson's thought centers on this metamorphosis: language is alternately thought and law, power and fate. Language as a correspondence-making tool controls, tames, and uses the world; it is power. Language as the law of correspondence puts limits even on thought (W, 6:21), for it thinks us; it is fate. The duality of language enables Emerson to say both that "Intellect annuls Fate" (W, 6:23) and that fate limits even thought (W, 6:20–21). Language as power and fate renders one self-reliant, since "self-reliance is precisely that secret,—to make your supposed deficiency redundancy," so that one's "very impotency . . . shall become a greater excellency than all skill and toil."[5]

Emerson's self-reliant career reveals in practice the two faces of language. As essayist, Emerson uses language as power—as the human tool by which thought subsumes nature. Yet language can have such power *only* if it is also perceived as law, and Emerson's essays exercise and validate their human power by continually positing and yearning for a use of language as divine and natural law. Emerson calls the spokesman for language-as-law the Poet, and this idea of poetry is required to validate not only Emerson's prose but language itself. For poetry demonstrates that "this correspondence of things to thoughts is far deeper than they [great poets] can penetrate,—defying adequate expression; that it is elemental, or in the core of things" (W, 8:29). In other words, this correspondence is of the nature of nature or fate, which Emerson describes in similar terms as a "cropping-out in our planted gardens of the core of the world" (W, 6:19). Poetry discloses the "core of the world," for in the temporal laws of poetic forms the spirit discovers language as fatal law.

THE ESSAYS: WAITING FOR THE POET

In the preface to his discourse on the creation of the cosmos, Plato's Timaeus includes this disclaimer: "Concerning a likeness, then, and its model we must make this distinction: an account is of the same order as the things which it sets forth—an account of that which is abiding and stable and discoverable by the aid of reason will itself be abiding and unchangeable (so far as it is possible and it lies in the nature of an account to be incontrovertible and irrefutable . . .); while an account of what is made in the image of that other, but is only a likeness [the world of phenomena], will itself be but likely. . . . If then, Socrates, in many respects concerning many things . . . we prove unable to render an account at all points entirely consistent with itself and exact, you must not be surprised. If we can furnish accounts no less likely than any other, we must be content, remembering that I who speak and you my judges are only human, and consequently it is fitting that we should, in these matters, accept the likely story and look for nothing further."[6] This is the Platonist speaking: if the world of phenomena is seen as a likeness—if it was created by a mimetic act—all accounts of its creation are at best but likely. The Platonist-critic who is the speaker of Emerson's essays holds the same position: all accounts of the phenomenal world—including interpretations of poetry—are likely stories and no more.

Following the Neoplatonists, Emerson exempts poets from the burden of such relativity. As M. H. Abrams has shown, Neoplatonists conceived of poems as imitating not the phenomenal world but the world of forms.[7] In the terms of Timaeus's distinction, then, poets give an account of what is "abiding and stable and discoverable by the aid of reason." To that extent, their discourse is "abiding and unchangeable"—insofar as any account can be. For Emerson, the poet's discourse is far more than a likely story: the poet stands at the center, which he "composes" by his presence. Thus the figure of the poet replaces God, and the critic becomes the priest of this central man. And yet the poet represents not so much a center as the critic's *desire* for a center. Emerson's "Representative Man" embodies the Platonist's lack; he is an abstraction, as Emerson knows: "Of course, when we describe man as poet, and credit him with the triumphs of the art, we speak of the potential or ideal man,—not found now in any one person. You must go through a city or a nation, and find one faculty here, one there, to build the true poet withal. Yet all men know the portrait when it is drawn, and it is part of religion to believe its possible incarnation" (W, 8:26). "Poetry is faith," Emerson writes (W, 8:31), anticipating Wallace Stevens: it is the faith that posits a center by believing in it. The poet is an abstraction that proves a reality, or, in Stevens's words, an "impossible possible philosophers' man"[8]—a center that holds and redeems the eccentric discourse of the Platonist and critic.

Emerson's stance in the essays, then, is one of waiting and desiring. Emerson the essayist is "not a poet but a lover of poetry, and poets, and merely serving as writer, &c. in this empty America, before the arrival of the poets."[9] In 1844 Emerson writes, "I look in vain for the poet whom I describe" (CW, 3:21), and in 1850 he judges Shakespeare "a half-man" for being too playful and reiterates, "The world still wants its poet-priest, a reconciler" (W, 4:219). Twenty-two years later, in 1872, the dream remains as distant: "Poems!—we have no poem. Whenever that angel shall be organized and appear on earth, the Iliad will be reckoned a poor ballad-grinding" (*W,* 8:74). The terms escalate from poet to priest to angel (at which stage the poet is identical with the poem), and the dream recedes.

Emerson's obsession with the figure of the poet goes beyond a nationalistic desire for an American poet and the democratic enterprise of revelation for the common man.[10] If Emerson's poet were to appear, it would amount to a second coming, for the distinctions between the poet and the people would disappear along with all other oppositions, including the ideal versus the real. Emerson's poet, then, is not someone who can exist. The shape and nature of Emerson's poet, this idea-man, are delineated in answer to the needs created by living in a fallen, divided world. He is an imaginary figure who ministers to the hunger of our being in the world, for "divine Providence" does seem to observe "a certain parsimony": "It has shown the heaven and earth to every child and filled him with a desire for the whole; a desire raging, infinite; a hunger, as of space to be filled with planets; a cry of famine, as of devils for souls. Then for the satisfaction,—to each man is administered a single drop, a bead of dew of vital power, *per day,*—a cup as large as space, and one drop of the water of life in it" (*W,* 4:184). In such a fix, "man helps himself by larger generalizations" (*W,* 4:185); the remedy of a larger vision helps us to live in a world of separation, to carry on the "feud of Want and Have" (*W,* 9:270). But "poetic peace" (*W,* 9:122) it brings not. For the peace that Emerson's conception of the poet offers is a state beyond the last generalization, the final circle. In a way, "Circles" is the ideal Emerson essay. In constantly enlarging his point of view, the "endless seeker" (*W,* 2:188) acts out the rhetorical progression of an essay, which is the medium of desire. The poet represents a fulfillment of, or an end to, this desire; in contrast to the ever-expanding consciousness of the "circular" essays, the poet is perfected, self-contained, and "spherical":

And he the bard, a crystal soul
Sphered and concentric with the whole.   [*W,* 9:322]

Stevens echoes this in his redefinition of the poet:

The central man, the human globe, responsive
As a mirror with a voice, the man of glass,
Who in a million diamonds sums us up.[11]

In both Emerson and Stevens, the idea of the poet represents a union that is impossible, given the analogical model of language. "The universe is the bride of the soul" (*CW,* 3:44), Emerson writes, again anticipating Stevens's nuptial imagery. The marriage is never consummated, however, for language—part "universe" and part "soul"—can only yearn after a union it itself renders impossible. If the mind and world are related as and by analogy, they are condemned to eternal separation. Thus the poet—the bridegroom who *can* consummate his marriage, whose intellect *can* be "ravished" by "the fact" (*CW,* 3:16)—actually stands for a deliverance from language itself. Hence the abundance in Emerson and Stevens of images of glass and transparency, which indicate the perfect alignment of the mind, word, and world. The figure of the poet is a personification, a metaphor for the destruction of metaphor, language, separation. The poet represents an end to representation, an apocalyptic union not just of fact with Spirit but of fact and Spirit with language. Thus poets are "liberating gods" (*CW,* 3:18) *only* if we remember that gods do not normally "liberate"—that their liberation is impossible to tell from necessity or fate. The liberating message of Emerson's Uriel, for example, resounds in the inexorable processes of nature. Similarly, the poet's marriage to nature can only be a death—a return to the "Rock," which, after a "skeleton's life" lived in the mind, is truly a consummation devoutly to be wished.

Yet the essays are ambivalent. Emerson does not really want his poet to appear; he only wants to propose him in order to desire him. In part, this desiring is the very nature of Emerson's genre, which Georg Lukács analyzes so well: "The essayist is a Schopenhauer who writes his *Parerga* while waiting for the arrival of his own (or another's) *The World as Will and Idea,* he is a John the Baptist who goes out to preach in the wilderness about another who is still to come, whose shoelace he is not worthy to untie. And if that other does not come—is not the essayist then without justification? And if the other does come, is he not made superfluous thereby? . . . He is the pure type of the precursor, and it seems highly questionable whether, left entirely to himself—i.e., independent from the fate of that other of whom he is the herald—he could lay claim to any value or validity."[12] Emerson's poet, not only yearned for philosophically but desired critically in order to validate Emerson the essayist, was and had to remain an impossibility.

Lukács continues: "For in the system of values yet to be found, the longing we spoke of would be satisfied and therefore abolished; but this longing is more than just something waiting for fulfillment, it is a fact of the soul with a value and existence of its own: an original and deep-rooted attitude towards the whole of life, a final, irreducible category of possibilities of experience."[13] If we see the "longing" of Emerson's essays as itself a variety of spiritual experience—indeed, as a way of sustaining the possibility of experience itself—it would seem that he found his true form after all, despite the judgment of Henry James and others to the contrary. Emerson's true form lay in not finding, for essayists are not simply failed poets; they are Plato-nists—poets who want to fail. Lukács goes on to distinguish the realms of the poet and the essayist: "The poet writes in verse, the Platonist in prose. The one lives within the strict security of a structure of laws, the other in the thousand hazards and vagaries of freedom—the one in a radiant and en-chanting perfection-within-itself, the other in the infinite waves of relativity. . . . Perhaps both are equally homeless, both stand equally outside life, but the poet's world (although he never reaches the world of real life) is an absolute one in which it is possible to live, whereas the Platonist's world has no substantiality. The poet says either 'Yes' or 'No,' the Platonist believes and doubts all at once, at the same moment."[14]

The poet and the Platonist mark the two poles of the bipolar unity that Emerson is. The Platonist's discourse is free, abstract, and unlimited: "There is no outside, no enclosing wall, no circumference to us" (*CW,* 2:181). But without a circumference there is no center, either, and the idealist is caught in cycles of relativity: "All is riddle, and the key to a riddle is another rid-dle. . . . We wake from one dream into another dream" (*W,* 6:313). Without an outside wall, there is no inside, either: "We fancy that we are strangers, and not so intimately domesticated in the planet as the wild man, and the wild beast and bird. But the exclusion reaches them also. . . . Fox and woodchuck, hawk and snipe, and bittern, when nearly seen, have no more root in the deep world than man, and are just such superficial tenants of the globe. Then the new molecular philosophy shows astronomical interspaces betwixt atom and atom, shows that the world is all outside: it has no inside" (*CW,* 3:37). The figure of the poet enables the Platonist to get out of this continuous discourse, this endless rhetoric of appearances, and to posit the center, the "vast affirmative, excluding negation, self-balanced, and swallow-ing up all relations, parts and times, within itself" (*CW,* 2:70). At this point, of course, there is not much difference between affirmation and negation, and poetry itself is ultimately impossible. For the only exit from illusion is into fate. Thus the debate goes on, as the Platonist or language as freedom, relativity, and flux longs for the poet or language as law, which in turn nullifies the very being of the Platonist.

Emerson was aware of the distinction between the two kinds of writing. For him, prose was always human: "Eloquence shows the power and pos-sibility of man" (*W,* 8:112). And the orator, the public essayist, instills in his audience yearning and desire: "The orator is the physician. Whether he speaks in the Capitol or on a cart, he is the benefactor that lifts men above themselves, and creates a higher appetite than he satisfies" (*W,* 8:113). Like money, "the prose of life" (*CW,* 3:136), prose is the medium of desire. It functions through self-negation: it gets by spending, attaining to truth by absenting itself. "No sentence will hold the whole truth," Emerson writes, "and the only way in which we can be just, is by giving ourselves the lie" (*CW*, 3:143–44). In other words, prose must deconstruct its own rhetoric and erase itself as it unfolds. For after all, the essay is not really even a genre; it is language in search of a genre, a form, a home. As Emerson knows, "all writings must be in a degree exoteric, written to a human *should* or *would*, instead of to the fatal *is*" (*W*, 8:30–31). Prose, at least, is always exoteric, and by remaining forever separate from the whole it at once yearns for and undoes, it maintains its freedom.

THE POETRY: THE "FATAL *IS*" OF FORM

"Poetry is the *gai science*. The trait and test of the poet is that he builds, adds and affirms. The critic destroys," Emerson writes in "Poetry and Imagination" (*W*, 8:37). Poetry satisfies the desire or lack of prose, for the construction of poetic form represents a fulness, as opposed to the self-destructive rhetorical progression of prose. "For poetry is science," Emerson continues, "and the poet a truer logician. Men in the courts or in the street think themselves logical and the poet whimsical. Do they think there is chance or wilfulness in what he sees and tells? . . . He is the lawgiver, as being an exact reporter of the essential law. He knows that he did not make his thought" (*W*, 8:39). By keeping in mind Emerson's abiding idea of the poet as lawgiver and of poetry as *gai science,* we see that for Emerson there is no difference between the Dionysian poet and the Apollonian lawgiver. When Emerson's poet "suffers" the "ethereal tides to roll and circulate through him" (*CW*, 3:16), he discovers law—the order of nature—so that he and Bacchus can

> write my old adventures with the pen
> Which on the first day drew,
> Upon the tablets blue,
> The dancing Pleiads and eternal men.   [*W*, 9:127]

The adventures are the "old" adventures; the Bacchic poet creates the world anew but according to the same old law. He asks to be liberated from forgetfulness or illusion into law.

It is this kind of "liberation" that is the function of poetry, "where every word is free, every word is necessary" (*W*, 7:50). Indeed, "every work of art, in proportion to its excellence, partakes of the precision of fate" (*W*, 7:50), and we delight in such art because we recognize in it "the mind that formed Nature, again in active operation" (*W*, 7:51). Harold Bloom's idea of a dialectic in Emerson between the Bacchic poet of inspiration and Merlin, the poet of fate, needs to be qualified.[15] In Emerson, *all* poetry is formal, and *all* form is identified with fate, Nemesis, or death. When the poet is possessed, he is possessed by fate: he becomes an instrument of the necessity of nature. For the poet, inspired by "some random word" of the gods, becomes "the fated man of men / Whom the ages must obey" (*W*, 9:312). These lines from Emerson's poem "The Poet," which declare, in effect, that the poet is fated and makes fated, revise the statement "They are free, and they make free" from the essay "The Poet" (*CW*, 3:18). Of course, the figure of the poet exists in order to make such distinctions between freedom and fate disappear, for he liberates us into the law which "rules throughout existence; a Law which is not intelligent but intelligence" (*W*, 6:49).

Emerson's conception of poetry provides his escape from solipsism. For Emerson, poetry is not "exoteric" discourse: it is in poetic form alone that language attains to the "fatal *is*." But the "is," if it is to center or ground language in nature, is fatal—it is death itself. Consequently, Emerson both yearns for and recoils from poetry and its strict, "liberating" form. Poems mean by becoming instruments of fate: their language connects to truth—the human truth, death—and becomes something more than the chirping of birds; it becomes part of human destiny. The Platonist critic must take just this view of poetry if his *own* discourse is to be more than the chirping of birds—if his discourse is to partake of human truth. In the "fatal *is*" of the poem, death validates language; nature confers reality on Spirit. Therefore, whether ascending to Spirit or descending to nature, the Apollonian-Dionysian poet discovers the same law—"this cropping-out in our planted gardens of the core of the world" (*W*, 6:19). Since "the laws below are sisters of the laws above" (*W*, 4:83), however, the law of nature "rhymes" with spiritual law—"that Law, the joy of the whole earth, which alone can *make thought dear and rich;* that Law whose fatal sureness the astronomical orbits poorly emulate" (*CW*, 1:88; emphasis mine). For Emerson, building "your own world" only means self-reliance or making "liabilities redundant," which means building "altars" to "Beautiful Necessity" (*W*, 6:49).

Thus the spiritual law of form and the natural law of death are identified in poetic form. Yet poets do not take up traditional poetic forms automatically; they rediscover them in their freedom. Although the resulting poem may use conventional devices, it does not originate from them, for "the thought and the form are equal in the order of time, but in the order of genesis the thought is prior to the form" (*CW*, 3:6–7). Indeed, this view affirms the universality and efficacy of conventional poetic forms. Poets begin not with meters but with the argument, yet meters are what they end with. Emerson's phrase "metre-making argument" (*CW,* 3:6) means just what it says, and should not be read as advocating free verse. This free rediscovery of conventional forms explains Emerson's ambiguous relation to English forms. Edwin Fussell suggests that Emerson tried to sound like an American poet, "without having any adequate idea, or auditory sense, [of] what an American poet might sound like."[16] For Emerson, however, sounding like an American poet never meant sounding a "barbaric yawp"; it simply meant recutting "the aged prints" (*W,* 9:127), or rediscovering English forms in their original vitality. Thus Hyatt Waggoner's observation that Emerson's is a curious, "unconventional handling of conventional forms" is all that can be said.[17] While Emerson calls for the poetic use of native material, he does not ask for indigenous poetic forms; to him, poetic forms are absolute, not relative to time, place, or circumstance: "The poet affirms the laws, prose busies itself with exceptions,—with the local and individual" (*W,* 8:32).

Although Emerson sees forms as limiting and as belonging to the domain of the senses and thus imprisoning the intellect (*W,* 8:23), he also knows that they *are* the intellect: "And thou shalt serve the God Terminus," Emerson writes, "the bounding Intellect, & love Boundary or Form: believing that form is an oracle which never lies" (*JMN,* 8:405). When we recall the poem "Terminus" and its "God of bounds" with his message of death, we come full circle. Forms must be rejected in order to be discovered beyond forgetfulness. As in "Bacchus," the ecstasy of this discovery ascribes to poetry an ecstasy "beyond the pleasure principle," for one rejects meters so as to rediscover the argument that *must make* meters. In other words, Emerson's American poetry rediscovers forms as humanly necessary; it says "no" to say "yes."

Emerson's association of poetry with fate or death is most striking in "Merlin" and its theory of rhyme. Rhyme, the heart of Emerson's *gai science,* performs three simultaneous functions. To begin with, rhymes are productive:

Solitary fancies go
Short-lived wandering to and fro,
Most like to bachelors,
Or an ungiven maid . . .   [*W,* 9:124]

Rhymes are a species of metaphor, generating new meanings by coupling unlike senses. Hence they lead to discovery: the poet must reject formal schemes, leave "rule and pale forethought," in order to "climb / For his rhyme" and "mount to paradise / By the stairway of surprise" (*W,* 9:121). Or, as Emerson puts it elsewhere, "Rhyme which builds out into Chaos & Old night a splendid architecture to bridge the impassable, & call aloud on all the children of morning that the Creation is recommencing. I wish to write such rhymes as shall not suggest a restraint, but contrariwise the wildest freedom" (*JMN*, 7:219). Rhyme as metaphor means freedom: it reveals the metamorphosis that is "the nature of things," and thus touches off that "shudder of joy with which in each clear moment we recognize the metamorphosis, because it is always a conquest, a surprise from the heart of things" (*W*, 8:71). But the imagery is already ambiguous: the "heart of things" is the "core of the world," the dread law Emerson calls fate. Thus freedom turns into fate at the point that it discloses the heart of nature, for "there is a crack in every thing God has made. It would seem, there is always this vindictive circumstance stealing in at unawares, even into the wild poesy in which the human fancy attempted to make bold holiday, and to shake itself free of the old laws,— this back-stroke, this kick of the gun, certifying that the law is fatal" (*CW*, 2:63).

As a result, the second function of rhyme is to embody fate—as music and as Nemesis. The music of rhyme gives pleasure, but now the "stairway" leads rather to a Dickinsonian "awe"; we see in "Merlin II" that the paradise to which the rhyming stiches "climb" is the realm of law. In less transcendent terms, rhyme embodies fate simply as a stairway of time. The argument is stated again in "Art":

'T is the privilege of Art
Thus to play its cheerful part,
Man on earth to acclimate
And bend the exile to his fate,
And, moulded of one element
With the days and firmament,
Teach him on these as stairs to climb,
And live on even terms with Time . . .   [*W*, 9:278]

That is, the artist or poet is the cheerful Angel of Death, the "gai" scientist. Prose, for Emerson, remains free because it proceeds by deconstructing itself; again, "no sentence will hold the whole truth, and the only way in which we can be just, is by giving ourselves the lie" (*CW*, 3:143–44). The principle of justice works in prose by un-building discourse (hence the critic's freedom); by contrast, the same principle is carried out in poetry by building, by sealing a statement with its rhyme—the "posterity" that makes "the lie afraid." For

Perfect-paired as eagle's wings,
Justice is the rhyme of things;

Trade and counting use
The self-same tuneful muse;
And Nemesis,
Who with even matches odd,
Who athwart space redresses
The partial wrong,
Fills the just period,
And finishes the song.   [*W,* 9:124]

Poetic form is incontrovertible discourse: "Rhyme, being a kind of music, shares this advantage with music, that it has a privilege of speaking truth which all Philistia is unable to challenge" (*W,* 8:51), and "you shall not speak ideal truth in prose uncontradicted: you may in verse" (*W,* 8:52). Accordingly, the more formal the poetic discourse is in Emerson, the more incontrovertible the truth expressed. In "Hamatreya," for example, the unspiritual "facts" defy all meter (ll. 1 and 3), while the poet's blank verse marks the realm of exoteric and conventional poetic discourse. Only the truncated line 16 ominously breaks the pattern:

Who steer the plough, but cannot steer their feet
Clear of the grave.

The final line of the poet's speech, "Hear what the Earth says," echoes line 16, to which it is connected by initial and end rhymes, and leads into the highly stylized "Earth-song," which rhymes and uses a dominant two-stress line. In this form, the earth speaks the truth none can challenge, the truth that withers even earthly poets, the truth of the law that "disdains words" (*W,* 6:49). Thus, when Emerson wants to go beyond iambic pentameter, he replaces it with a line more fundamental, even archaic: a two-stress or two-part, four-stress line that alludes to Anglo-Saxon verse. The regression to this primal pattern coincides with the use of an oracular, truth-sounding voice. For Emerson bypasses the historical authorities governing exoteric discourse only because he appeals to a more fundamental divine/natural authority underwriting poetic forms.

Emerson's theory of rhyme reflects his view of the correspondences between mind and nature: "This methodizing mind meets no resistance in its attempts. The scattered blocks, with which it strives to form a symmetrical structure, fit. This design following after finds with joy that like design went before. Not only man puts things in a row, but things belong in a row" (*W,* 12:20). Yet "things belong in a row" because the mind requires that they do, for "without identity at base, chaos must be forever" (*W,* 12:20). Thus rhymes can set the "material universe" dancing by revealing that it is "mated" at the source.

This brings us to the third function of rhyme: rhyme is a species of metaphor that is able to descend below rhetoric. For example, "Hamatreya" ends:

When I heard the Earth-song
I was no longer brave;
My avarice cooled
Like lust in the chill of the grave.   [*W*, 9:37]

Since the first three lines of the quatrain do not set up an expectation of rhymes, rhyming "brave" and "grave" has a rhetorical function similar to that of metaphor. The coupling changes our perceptions of "brave"; we perceive the word and all its meanings differently when it is rhymed with "grave." Paul Ricoeur makes the point that in metaphor the perception of new meaning arises from "the collapse of the literal meaning."[18] If we accept this definition, we can see how rhyme functions like metaphor in generating new meanings yet is grounded in a way metaphor cannot be. Metaphor has no center; it is a passage back and forth between sets of meanings; it is eccentric; it is evasive; it is pure rhetoric; and it is free. As seen in the example above, however, the metaphoric transformation in rhyme is grounded in the letters of the words. The new meanings arise precisely from the reinstitution of the literal shapes of the words. Thus the rhetoric, the implied commentary, and the free flow of meanings between the two words appear as surface flux only, for the rhyme reveals the basic otherness that exists within each word, exterior to signification and untouched by meaning. The revelation of this unrelenting object-ness, this factuality of the symbol, this stasis underlying the metamorphoses, provides a backdrop of irony that implicitly qualifies any free play with these words in the way of interpretation. Such objective equality is death itself; rhyme is always a grave business.

Thus rhymes are central to Emerson's idea of poetry because they sound the dread truth, which kills us but can save our discourse. The final lines of "Merlin" capture wonderfully the external and internal forces of fate that rhyme both expresses and embodies:

Subtle rhymes, with ruin rife,
Murmur in the house of life,
Sung by the Sisters as they spin;
In perfect time and measure they
Build and unbuild our echoing clay.

As the two twilights of the day
Fold us music-drunken *in*.   [*W,* 9:124; emphasis mine]

At the end of "Merlin" it is as much the terminal rhyme of "spin" and "in"
that folds us in as the "two twilights," as much the internal rhymes that
"measure" us as the subtler "murmurs" that "build and unbuild our echoing
clay." Our "clay" or physiology only echoes the perfect rhymes sung by the
Fates and their poet. Moreover, since "subtle" and "folded" suggest texts,
paper, and books, they reinforce the implication that we are fated in rhymes
and "folded" in poems. In other words, poetry is gay, but it is a science; as
such, it offers us self-reliance—the secret that makes our "supposed deficiency redundancy." In the poetic use of rhyme, then, meaning is generated
in the same act in which a time period is completed, fate is chosen, the
world's time is internalized, and form is taken upon us and celebrated. By
contrast, in the unrhymed and unrhyming universe of "Blight," time remains
an alien force, and life *seems* too short:

And nothing thrives to reach its natural term;
And life, shorn of its venerable length,
Even at its greatest space is a defeat,
And dies in anger that it was a dupe.   [*W,* 9:141]

   The "formality" of poetry separates it from mortals and their language yet
enables it to be "the consolation of mortal men" (*W,* 8:37); as Stevens informs
"the One of Fictive Music," poetry—"our likest issuance"—must not be
"too like . . . / Too near, too clear."[19] This view of poetic language precludes
experimental or open forms that mimic the rhythms of experience and
speech. As the closing lines of "Merlin" make clear, what remains outside the
"folding in" of poetic form is nothingness itself. Such is the truth that poetic
form conveys: its being "artifice" only argues its necessity.[20] The revolutionary truth of Uriel's message, for example, is apprehended not in "free" forms
but in the "fated" processes of nature, for "the book of Nature is the book of
Fate" (*W,* 6:15). Thus poets are necessarily "in-human": we would not need
them if they were otherwise. According to Stephen E. Whicher, while Uriel's
utterance "shakes society," it "transforms him also into something fey and
inhuman. In this poem, as elsewhere in his writings, we touch the chilling
core of Emerson's idealism and sense the presence there of something with
which no community is possible"[21] But that "chilling core" is the burning
heart of the Emersonian poet; as Uriel knows, "ice will burn." The chill is the
poet's identification with natural law or necessity—his absorption by fate.
Yet the subsuming of the mind to nature is impossible to distinguish from the

consuming of nature by the mind, or the sacrificial assumption of fate upon oneself. As Emerson writes, "Why should we fear to be crushed by savage elements, we who are made up of the same elements?" (*W*, 6:49). Thus poems rhyme and discover for us that nature rhymes, that God created nature by rhyming, and that God is a poet. Either the poet "writes" a rhyming nature and a rhymer God, or God rhymes nature and hence the poet's poems: these are two terms of an equation. The book of nature is the book of fate; but it is a book. If we regard language in general and poetry in particular as earthly discourse, rhyme is a compositional device, just as analogy is a rhetorical device. If poetry and language are sacred, however, rhyme and analogy are revelation. And in Emerson's theory of language, the earthly and sacred faces of language are analogous; they rhyme. The bipartite structure of "Merlin" shows us that causing nature to rhyme and powerlessly chiming with its rhythms constitute one and the same act. This is the message of poetry: we are our fate.

Poetic forms, which align phenomena and concepts, nature and Spirit, stand above both. Form is absolute and cannot be "capricious": the original poet "wrote without levity and without choice. Every word was carved before his eyes into the earth and the sky; and the sun and stars were only letters of the same purport and of no more necessity" (*W*, 4:269).[22] The Emersonian poet must become a sacrificial figure and submit to language as the law of nature in order to liberate us from being bound by fate, even to license us—and Emerson—as critics. Uriel is imprisoned in his knowledge of circularity so that we may be freed in "Circles." The knowledge of circularity condemns gods and poets; the same knowledge saves humans and essayists. The poems projected by the essays in turn make possible the vision of the liberated and liberating essays. And the essays with their human time redeem the poems with their inexorable balances and fated forms, just as the "central" poetry licenses the "eccentric" essays. In this way, the bipartite whole of Emerson's work can constitute a "supreme fiction"—both the supreme law and, thankfully, still a fiction, that is, still abstract instead of concrete, still changing instead of finally formed, and still giving pleasure instead of *the* pleasure "beyond the pleasure principle."

Emerson's concept of poetry as the language of law—or even as language *as* law—makes clear that his idea of poetry is much more restrictive than what has been termed the musical or inspired speech of his essays; indeed, visionary insight into the nature of nature necessitates going beyond prose to "create" the whole "apparatus of poetic expression" (*W*, 4:143). For poetry embodies the dread, liberating laws of creation precisely through the poetic apparatus of line divisions, "pairing rhymes," and, yes, "chiming meters."

Prose, however musical, is not music: "I know what you say of mediaeval barbarism and sleighbell rhyme, but we have not done with music, no, nor with rhyme" (*W,* 8:52). And he reiterates: "O no, we have not done with music, nor must console ourselves with prose poets. . . . We wish the undrawn line of tendency to be drawn for us. Where is the Euclid who can sum up these million errors, & compute the beautiful mean?" (*JMN,* 9:379). To regard the essays, for whatever reason, as more "poetic" is to overlook the centrality of order, Nemesis, or fate to poetry. For Emerson, poetry is our way of discovering fate in ourselves and ourselves in fate—which is why we *need* it.

Seeing Emerson's poems and essays in terms of their different yet complementary intentions enables us to reassess his position in American poetry. The poems are formal constructs meant to parallel the correspondence of the orders of nature and Spirit. As such, they offer more than the "likely stories" of prose—but at the expense of becoming identified with death itself. The unity Emerson's "vehicular" essays yearn for is shown, in the "homestead" of the poems, to be only the unity of death. Among the poets who may be regarded as Emersonian are Robert Frost, Wallace Stevens, Marianne Moore, Elizabeth Bishop, and James Merrill, all of whom acknowledge the centrality of poetic forms but are able to incorporate into their poems the Platonic awareness of the eccentricity of our propositions about our fate. These poets are able to internalize within poetry the bipartite structure of Emerson's discourse. For Emerson, the analogical relationship between the mind and nature yields a divided language, which serves him alternately as power (essays) and as fate (poems). The poets who share Emerson's analogical conception of the relationship between nature and the mind are able to go beyond the limits of his poetic by conceiving of poetic language as itself embodying the analogies between the mind and nature—between poetic rhetoric and poetic form. Thus poets like Stevens and Bishop can define a poetic ground where form is less than central—less a "homestead" and more "homemade"—and where rhetoric is more than "eccentric," less "vehicular" and more the necessary mode of our passage through time.

As for Emerson's essays, they may well be more successful as essays than the poems are as poems. Perhaps Emerson was a minor poet and a major essayist; indeed, the logic of his career would have required him to be so.[23] This, however, is the most one can say. Waggoner shows that Emerson's essay style was in no way experimental—that it followed the dicta of the high rhetorical mode in vogue.[24] Not even by analogy, then, can one jump from Emerson's essays to the poetry of experimental forms, and the weakness of all the arguments for his experimental connection to Whitman and beyond is that no one has ever shown what new poetic form Emerson discovered. He only discovers, to his surprise, that his form is Form and his fate, Fate. The irony is that Emerson has become the father—the archetype—of American poets who could, miraculously, *center* American poetry, when his own idea of a center, as the poems sadly demonstrate, was death itself. If we stop reading the essays and the poetry in isolation from each other and begin to see the interplay of the rhetoric of both forms (the "oracles" that never "lie") as they mirror and sustain each other in Emerson's discourse with himself, we can comprehend his work as a whole and save him from the responsibility for American modernism and American poetry from the burden of Emersonianism.

Chapter Five

Wallace Stevens: The Exquisite Errors of Time

> It must change from destiny to slight caprice.
> And thus its jetted tragedy, its stele
>
> And shape and mournful making move to find
> What must unmake it and, at last, what can,
> Say, a flippant communication under the moon.
> "The Auroras of Autumn"

"Poetry and reality are one." Wallace Stevens echoes Emerson, but immediately adds "or should be. This may be less thesis than hypothesis. Yet hypotheses relating to poetry, although they may appear to be very distant illuminations, could be the fires of fate, if rhetoric ever meant anything."[1] If. . . . And, luckily, it does not, the philosopher knows, and he proceeds to expose his rhetoric of a poetry coincident with reality. And, luckily, it does, the poet knows, and he sets out to prove the "truth" of his rhetoric. Stevens retains the Emersonian distinction between the philosopher and the poet: "If the end of the philosopher is despair," he writes, "the end of the poet is fulfillment" (*NA*, 43). Forever deconstructing, "the philosopher fails to discover. Suppose the poet discovered and had the power thereafter at will and by intelligence to reconstruct us by his transformations. He would also have the power to destroy us. If there was, or if we believed that there was, a center, it would be absurd to fear or to avoid its discovery" (*NA*, 45). The function of the philosopher is to make certain that we do not believe in a "center," for we do not want to be fulfilled; he must keep things rhetorical, so that the "fires of fate" stay metaphorical. And he does this by rigorously maintaining the poverty at the center—maintaining

The self as sibyl, whose diamond,
Whose chiefest embracing of all wealth

Is poverty, whose jewel found
At the exactest central of the earth
Is need.[2]

The lack of a metaphysical or physical center that would preempt or negate freedom liberates the philosopher, but only into a discourse of desire:

> The philosopher desires.
And not to have is the beginning of desire.
To have what is not is its ancient cycle.[3]

This is the discourse of Emerson's essayist, and Stevens's philosopher like-wise desires what he lacks—a "central man, the human globe . . . the man of glass, / Who in a million diamonds sums us up" (CP, 250). But Stevens's project diverges from Emerson's at this point: Stevens's poet does not contract to play the part of the central man, satisfy the philosopher's need, and license his freedom. Instead, the poet indulges the philosopher in his fiction, his dream of "a large-sculptured, platonic person, free from time" (CP, 330), for the poet finds his diachronic truth precisely in the eccentric discourse of the philosopher, begotten in need and begetting lack.

Stevens's poet, a connoisseur of the "old chaos of the sun" (CP, 70), centers in eccentricity, the temporal passage in which humans and their discourse are made and unmade. The poet does not discover a central truth, but he discovers the truth all the same: he discovers it to be eccentric. "False flick, false form, but falseness close to kin," Stevens writes of the magnolias in "Notes Toward a Supreme Fiction" (CP, 385). The flicks and forms of all phenomena, including poems, are false. But while "truth" would destroy, falsenesses are fecund and generate their own relations: "false" is close to "close," which in turn is close to "kin." The "falseness" of the exaggerated alliteration and consonance here resolves itself into a kind of kinship. And the interplay of falseness and kinship, both in the semantic content of the line and in its phonetic form, calls into question the distinction between the natural and the artificial. The magnolias are "false" and therefore "kin" to us, hinting at "the extent of artifice within us" (NA, 141); poetic language is "false"—the alliteration and consonance set it off as relatively "unnatural"—and therefore "kin" to a certain "excessiveness" or rhetoricity in nature, as evidenced in the magnolias. The kin might not be "kind"; yet the unnatural-ness of the bond proves to be a kindness after all, so that "our likest issuance"—our "fictive music"—is "not too like,"

> not so like to be
Too near, too clear, saving a little to endow

Our feigning with the strange unlike, whence springs
The difference that heavenly pity brings.   [*CP,* 88]

That "difference," which is a grace, is both our temporal difference from
nature and the language of our difference or metaphor, which names the
kinship of falsenesses, their unlikely likenesses. Thus the "music summoned
by the birth / That separates us from the wind and sea, / Yet leaves us in
them," measures our temporal passage in its metaphoric rhetoric.

Stevens shares Emerson's idealism and his analogical conception of the
relationship between nature, language, and the mind, but locates poetry
within this network. "Poetry," Stevens writes, "is almost incredibly one of
the effects of analogy. This statement involves much more than the analogy of
figures of speech, since otherwise poetry would be little more than a trick"
(*NA,* 117). According to Stevens, a "significant" component of "the structure
of reality" is "the resemblance between things" (*NA,* 71). This "resemblance
between things in nature" is analogous to the "resemblance" in which "the
mind begets" (*NA,* 76). For "there is always an analogy between nature and
the imagination, and possibly poetry is merely the strange rhetoric of that
parallel" (*NA,* 118). Since the rhetoric of poetry is one of resemblances,
analogies, and likenesses, however, it is a rhetoric that bespeaks or is spoken
by the very structure of reality; hence, "the structure of poetry and the
structure of reality are one"—"or should be" (*NA,* 81). Stevens sees the
rhetoric of analogies—the language of resemblance, the figuration of metaphor—as the link between the mind and nature, just as it is the link between
thought and the sounds of words. "We are not dealing with identity," he
admits: "Both in nature and in metaphor identity is the vanishing-point of
resemblance" (*NA,* 72). But "nature is not mechanical," any more than the
imagination is, and "its prodigy is not identity but resemblance" (*NA,* 73).
The "center of resemblance" (*NA,* 89)—a natural identity *and* the "azury
center of time" (*CP,* 425) the philosopher's man would inhabit—is either an
inert and deadly fact or a fanciful fiction, whose realization would be deadening to the vital/evil imagination. For the significant, human drama begins
with a fall, when that "center of resemblance" is defined *as* "the inhuman
making choice of a human self" (*NA,* 89)—the natural identity choosing
metaphorical resemblances and exiling itself into time and space, history and
geography.

Stevens's diachronic understanding of metaphor enables him to perceive a
timeless center—whether a metaphysical "first idea" or a natural "muddy
centre before we breathed" (*CP,* 383)—as peripheral to humans and lan-

guage, and he is always ironic in depicting the desire for such a center. Stevens insists that ours

> is an intellect
> Of windings round and dodges to and fro,
>
> Writhings in wrong obliques and distances,
> Not an intellect in which we are fleet: present
> Everywhere in space at once, cloud-pole
> Of communication.   [*CP*, 429–30]

In rhetorical terms, both a Whitmanic fusion and a Poundian superimposition of subject and object—a modernist *nostos* to the same nostalgia[4]—are foreign to Stevens's idea of poetry, for they proceed "as if / There was a bright *scienza* outside of ourselves, // A gaiety that is being, not merely knowing" (*CP*, 248). For Stevens, the very eccentricity of metaphor is its "truth," since the "world" of the human "beholder" is itself temporal and rhetorical in nature:[5]

> The world? The inhuman as human? That which thinks not,
> Feels not, resembling thought, resembling feeling?
>
> It habituates him to the invisible,
> By its faculty of the exceptional,
>
> The faculty of ellipses and deviations,
> In which he exists but never as himself.   [*CP*, 493]

Given Stevens's universe of analogy with its "endlessly emerging accords" (*CP*, 493), our eccentric language is adequate to nature, which appears to us not in its timeless "truth" but in the temporal "rhetoric" of its changes and seasons,

> *As if* nothingness contained a métier,
> A vital assumption, an impermanence
> In its permanent cold, an illusion so desired
>
> That the green leaves came and covered the high rock,
> That the lilacs came and bloomed, like a blindness cleaned,
> Exclaiming bright sight, as it was satisfied,
>
> In a birth of sight.   [*CP*, 526; emphasis mine]

The deviation of "as if" is a "birth of sight" nonetheless; as Stevens writes elsewhere, "What the eye beholds may be the text of life. It is, nevertheless, a text that we do not write" (*NA*, 76). By avoiding the Emersonian dualities of falseness and truth, artifice and nature, desire and fulfillment, rhetoric and meters, Stevens can go beyond the deadly identification of poetry and truth in which Emerson sought to ground his rhetoric.[6] The fate that was natural law for Emerson becomes for Stevens an internal truth—the truth of human nature—adequately expressed in an admittedly eccentric rhetoric, of which meters constitute a conventional part.

Stevens's search for a rhetoric more than fiction and a nature less than an external fate begins with "Sunday Morning" and its realignment of the Emersonian and romantic dualities. The poem mourns at once the loss of Christian and romantic mythologies, which offer versions of the same fusion of temporal and eternal realities. "Sunday Morning" does not judge religion to be a fiction and Christ to be but a man in order to exhort us to a species of nature worship. For Stevens portrays the world of sense impressions as a fantastic play of surfaces. The painterly interior, the various trees and fruits, "April's green," and the cockatoo, swallows, and pigeons—birds represented, literary, or "observed"—all become equally phantasmal, passing like "things in some procession of the dead." In these terms, the sun-worshippers of stanza 7 reduce to mere "personae of summer" (*CP,* 377), their bookish status reinforced by Biblical imagery, for pantheism would be as foreign as the religion of Palestine when the sky itself is "isolated" and appears as alien as the "icy Élysée" (*CP,* 56) seems to a temporal speaker. The poem proceeds by contrasting the surfaces and the depths of things: the surfaces of nature—its false flicks and forms, its rhetoric—contrast with its depths, which turn out to be internal to the subject. A "wide water" silently flows below the welter of visible and audible phenomena, and, in contrast to the sensory experience of surfaces, this archetypal river of the unconscious carries the truth of "blood." The river of meditation courses to death—the "dominion of the blood and sepulchre"—and to erotic reveries of "supple and turbulent" men; Christian and romantic mythologies only code its natural course.

Thus Stevens dislocates the Emersonian alignment of nature with fate and the mind with freedom. The imagistic contrast of light and dark in the first stanza corresponds to the thematic contrast of freedom and fate, life and death, rhetoric and truth, the claims of the life of the senses and the life of the mind. It is nature and its sensuous attractions that are free, and their extravagant, ornamental "rhetoric" cannot satisfy the mind. For the mind and its course of meditation give us access to the truth of Eros and Thanatos. In Stevens's realignment, the mind alone knows nature: an undomesticated nature that is more than "a widow's bird" (*CP,* 18) is accessible only in the meditation of the "virile" poet. When Stevens announces, "Death is the mother of beauty," he is talking not only about the changes in nature that constitute its rhetorical appeal to the senses—senses equipped to register and take pleasure in change—but about the truth of the mind. For the seasonal repetitions of nature are temporal changes and intimate death *only* to the human consciousness, and these temporal changes open up the mental space of remembrance and anticipation, of memory and desire (stanza 4), of poetry and its measures. Death is the mother of the imagination—of the mind and memory, the "muttering" that engenders "myths" in the "burning bosom" of a destructive mother. The final stanza reaffirms this alignment:

We live in an old chaos of the sun,
Or old dependency of day and night,
Or island solitude, unsponsored, free,
Of that wide water, inescapable.   [*CP*, 70]

Our dependence on the "chaos" of natural processes, our "freedom" from sponsoring deities, and our being constituted "of that wide water" are grammatical appositives and substantive equivalents. The "wide water" is the "wide water" of stanza 1—the inseparable and inescapable concourse of Eros, death, and meditation that constitutes us and our freedom. In linking the mind with death, Stevens is able to displace the terms of the Emersonian debate: freedom and fate are no longer aligned with the subject and object. Stevens's existential project is to show that our freedom is our fate, our discourse is our nature, our imagination is our destruction.[7]

"Sunday Morning" also marks the beginning of Stevens's stylistic development beyond the reductive dichotomy of rhetoric and meters that arrested Emerson's growth as a poet. In Stevens, the discursive and the Orphic modes are not polar opposites but inflections of the same conventional, exoteric, poetic voice. The range and flexibility of Stevens's diction and blank verse enable him to incorporate the course of nature and the discourse of the mind in the same internal monologue. In the first stanza of "Sunday Morning," for example, he signals the shift from observation to meditation with a switch in diction from polysyllabic, Latinate words to one- or two-syllable, Anglo-Saxon words; with vocalic modulations from front or "light" vowels to back or "dark" vowels; with metrical variations like the increased use of trochees and spondees; and with an insistence on alliteration, assonance, and repetition:

Complacencies of the peignoir, and late
Coffee and oranges in a sunny chair,
And the green freedom of a cockatoo
Upon a rug mingle to dissipate
The holy hush of ancient sacrifice.

She dreams a little, and she feels the dark
Encroachment of that old catastrophe,
As a calm darkens among water-lights.
The pungent oranges and bright, green wings
Seem things in some procession of the dead,
Winding across wide water, without sound.
The day is like wide water, without sound,
Stilled for the passing of her dreaming feet
Over the seas, to silent Palestine,
Dominion of the blood and sepulchre.   [*CP,* 66–67]

The fatal truth has been internalized as an inflection of a poetic language that traces the course of an explicitly eccentric and inherently rhetorical meditation.

The language of "Sunday Morning" remains nostalgic, however, and Stevens has difficulty in developing a form that does not rely on the "magnificent measure" (*CP,* 13) of the English romantics[8] yet can register the truth of rhetoric, the centrality of an explicitly eccentric poetic language. His development of a language both exoteric and central leads through an excessively rhetorical style that remains merely exoteric and thus is ironic about its decorative excesses. "Le Monocle de Mon Oncle," for example, engages this issue. Isabel G. MacCaffrey writes that the methodology of the poem, as well as its subject, addresses the "relationship between opaque, visceral depths and dazzling verbal surfaces," and she suggests that the poem rejects its own rhetoric as "inadequate, bombastic, bland, or self-deceiving," so that another, counter "meaning" can be apprehended "behind the words," which is the "wordless world" of Eros and Thanatos.[9] Stevens's rejection of his own rhetoric comes in the lines,

Last night, we sat beside a pool of pink,
Clippered with lilies scudding the bright chromes,
Keen to the point of starlight, while a frog
Boomed from his very belly odious chords.   [*CP,* 17]

which pass judgment, in Harold Bloom's words, on "all amorous diction."[10] Nevertheless, however inadequate it may be to Eros, rhetoric remains the necessary substitution by which love becomes love, for even the chords of the frog's mating call are natural substitutions for the "foremost law":

If sex were all, then every trembling hand
Could make us squeak, like dolls, the wished-for words.
But note the unconscionable treachery of fate,
That makes us weep, laugh, grunt and groan, and shout
Doleful heroics, pinching gestures forth

From madness or delight, *without regard*
To that first, foremost law.   [*CP,* 17; emphasis mine]

The "foremost law" is itself apprehended in and as substitution. If we are fated, we are fated to substitute one thing for another, to remain at the edge, and to play with words—"le monocle de mon oncle"—stringing together metaphoric or phonetic substitutions. For the poem demonstrates that no one language is more natural or less rhetorical than another.

Elsewhere, too, Stevens despairs of sounding the "saltier well" (*CP,* 13) within, and his language remains mere "gay . . . hallucinations in surfaces" (*CP,* 472). "The Comedian as the Letter C," for example, is regressive and limits the poet's options to subjection to the authority of "soil" or "intelligence"—a reductive natural truth or a reductive rhetoric. In linguistic terms, the options are silence—a "clipped" "relation" acknowledging the triumph of nature—or the verbosity of the "profitless / Philosopher" (*CP,* 45–46) that marks the purely academic victory of the mind. The "Comedian" ends in resignation, for Stevens's etymological divagations and stylistic circumlocutions have unmoored the language of the poem beyond the kind of "relation" that was the impetus of its quest. Crispin, the "stiffest realist," is finally defeated in his confrontation with the "insoluble lump" of the world-turnip (*CP,* 45); yet the world-as-turnip—from the root "to turn"—joins the pattern of "turning" words in the poem, which has already put "the world in a verse" (*CP,* 241).[11] Thus it becomes impossible to tell an irreducible reality from an irreducible rhetoric or troping, and solipsism becomes Crispin's real failing. The "sounds of the letter C," which Stevens suggests make for the real comedian of the poem,[12] have a similar function, serving to annul the poem's philosophical quest. For example, *C* yields both the "sea" that "severs selves" and the "see" of the subject's "eye [I] of land," the self that is severed. Not unlike the "turnip," *C* also dissolves into *S* or *K* or even *Z, X,* or *TS,*[13] so that "soil" and "intelligence," "nature" and "mind," the "turnip" and the "C" are equally fictive. This is a reductively eccentric language lacking any "relation" to the "truth" of rhetoric.

Only when Stevens can harmonize the philosopher's exoteric voice with the esoteric voice of the poet can he remain philosophically rigorous yet sound the "watery syllable" of the "saltier well." We hear this language of meditation again in "The Idea of Order at Key West," where he replaces linguistic and metaphysical dichotomies with a triangular arrangement and places the meditating mind at the apex. The poem returns to the discovery of "Sunday Morning" and to its dramatic form but casts the philosopher, the Emersonian essayist, as its central speaker. While it may revert stylistically to the "magnificent measure" that the post-romantic—with his eccentric truth—must learn to relinquish, "Key West" points to Stevens's way out of the impasse of poems like the "Comedian" and "Sea Surface Full of Clouds." It enables us to understand his subsequent insistence that poetry is the proper subject of poetry to be not a solipsistic withdrawal but an adequate response to just that danger.

The sea that "never formed to mind or voice" is, in "Key West," both the "inhuman," "veritable ocean" and an inner "nature" of Eros and death. And Stevens counterpoints the "grinding water and the gasping wind" of nature with the "song" of the "artificer" in such a way that neither subject nor object speaks through the other:

The sea was not a mask. No more was she.
The song and water were not medleyed sound
Even if what she sang was what she heard,
Since what she sang was uttered word by word.   [*CP,* 128]

Both the pathetic fallacy and realism are rejected. The "plungings of water and the wind" are "meaningless" indeed, and we do not hear them, any more than we ever hear nature in poems. And the woman's song does not copy nature; it is "the voice that is great" (*CP,* 138) within her—her human "spirit" (stanza 3) or "breath"—rising in response to the sea's body and the "gasping wind." Yet we never hear the words of her lyric, either. The sea is an external nature with its meaningless, "constant cry"; its image and counterpart is the "she" who sings "word by word." Her measures and meters utter her song's law, just as the sea's cry sounds nature's law.

Stevens distances the lyric voice to the same extent that nature's echolalia is distanced. Instead, he centers on the speaker, the "connoisseur of chaos," and the "idea of order" he entertains. This meditating and mediating speaker is not a singer but a rhetorician, something of a critic even, and in his words, letters, and internal rhymes "relation appears" (*CP,* 215) between the "she" and "sea." Here Stevens goes beyond "Sea Surface" by explicitly affirming a relation between the sea and song—but only as the subject and predicate of a metaphor about the relationship of life and art. The Emersonian precedent for this poem is "The Snow-Storm," which also centers on the metaphor-making imagination, and invites us to "come see" a process "unseen"—a process not visible to the eye. In "Key West" such "seeing" becomes the link between "sea" and "she."

In this deconstruction of a romantic fusion of nature and subject, Stevens constructs a central rhetoric. In the words of the poem's speaker, the alien

depths of a nature at once external and internal meet in the surfaces of a
poetic language that glosses

The maker's rage to order words of the sea,
Words of the fragrant portals, dimly-starred,
And of ourselves and of our origins,
In ghostlier demarcations, keener sounds.   [*CP,* 130]

The song has a transforming significance only for its hearer, who hears a new,
"amassing harmony" as much beyond the song as beyond the sea. For the
critic, the singer's voice makes "the sky acutest at its vanishing" and measures "to the hour its solitude." Her measures open intercourse between
nature and "ourselves," mastering and portioning out the darkness of inner
and outer seas—but only in the "meta-phoric" speech of the critic who
"inter-prets" and outlines the connection between artifice and sea, form and
nature, music and death. *He* occupies the center, which is a portal or
passageway—spatially and temporally "measured" by the singer—from a
dark sea outside us to a darker sea inside, "dimly-starred" either way.

This metaphoric passage is, appropriately, a "fragrant" portal: the syn-
esthesia makes the image a proper vehicle for its tenor, the earthly and earthy
truth of figurative language. Measuring a space and time, the singer opens a
door that delivers us into yet "separates us from the wind and sea" (*CP,* 87).
The metaphoric/temporal passage is guarded by the "fragrant mother" of
"Fictive Music," who belongs to the same "sisterhood of the living dead" (*CP,*
87), and the poet's muse—the mother of memory and imagination, the
"mother of heaven, regina of the clouds" (*CP,* 13)—is also his earthly source,
the "bearded queen" who would "feed" on him (*CP,* 507). All are imaginings
of the same "mother" who opens and closes our earthly discourse, who binds
the "handbook of heartbreak" (*CP,* 507). Thus Stevens understands metaphoric language as the threshold of fiction and truth, where the philosopher's
"human *should* or *would*" and the poet's "fatal *is*" meet.[14] In Stevens's impure
voice, Emerson's "fatal *is*" becomes a copula that marks metaphoric unions.
While "is" is empty as copula and indeterminate in meaning, without it we
would have not just one fewer verb but, in Heidegger's words, "*no language at
all*": "No essent *as such* would disclose itself in words, it would no longer be
possible to invoke it and speak about it in words." In "is," "essents" come to
be; yet coming to be means "to achieve a limit for itself, to limit itself."[15]
Being enters time, limits itself, and thus begins to be in "is"; as temporality,
this "is" is fatal. And when metaphor is understood as not simply the change
of A to B but the injection of time and change into the static, it becomes the

center of experience. Metaphor embodies the center-as-flux or flux-as-center, because it names "the flux // Between the thing as idea and / The idea as thing" (*CP*, 295). A synchronic expansion coincides with a diachronic limitation in metaphor, where the copula turns into the "fatal *is*." Its couplings *are* fecund, but they bear death. For if metaphoric rhetoric attempts to evade the final fact of death, its rhetorical substitutions remain temporal, offering "the exhilarations of changes" (*CP*, 288).

Stevens considers the dual nature of poetic creation in a number of poems. In "The Auroras of Autumn" he asks:

Is there an imagination that sits enthroned
As grim as it is benevolent, the just
And the unjust, which in the midst of summer stops

To imagine winter?   [*CP*, 417]

Just such an imagination characterizes the philosopher-poet: "the white creator of black, jetted / By extinguishings" (*CP*, 417). The imagination is "jetted" or darkened by extinguishings, "even of planets," "even of earth, even of sight." But the line, which recalls Whitman's "jetting" the "stuff" of future "republics,"[16] also concerns poetic creation. The white creates or "jets" the black by "extinguishings," not just of planets but of the "white creator of black." In "Metaphor as Degeneration," Stevens presents a double or black-and-white poet and similarly defines the imagination as the faculty that "broods"—both contemplates and generates—its own absence. The poet's brooding "jets" the "greenest" life with its "dark / Encroachment," so that all turn "things in some procession of the dead." Thus, when Stevens asks,

How, then, is metaphor degeneration,
When Swatara becomes this undulant river
And the river becomes the landless, waterless ocean?   [*CP*, 444]

the answer must be twofold, for the question is both rhetorical and genuine. Metaphor is not degeneration, for it has generated "being" by turning the river Swatara into

The swarthy water
That flows round the earth and through the skies,
Twisting among the universal spaces   [*CP*, 444]

Yet the change is also a degeneration. In Robert Frost's terms, Stevens's river "runs down in sending up" the metaphorical river of "being"; in Stevens's poem, however, Frost's thematic countercurrent runs in the very motion of language.[17] For metaphor images being in the "reverberations" of words,

And these images, these reverberations,
And others, make certain how being
Includes death and the imagination.   [*CP*, 444]

Since being includes imagination and death, generation and degeneration, language at once generates being and traces its degeneration. Poetry, then, is both "tropic" *and* "entropic"; it both resists and yields:

Here the black violets grow down to its banks
And the memorial mosses hang their green
Upon it, as it flows ahead.   [*CP*, 445]

Time is thus not "the eccentric exterior of which the clocks talk" (*CP*, 478) but the nature of the mind and its works:

Time is the hooded enemy,
The inimical music, the enchantered space
In which the enchanted preludes have their place.   [*CP*, 330]

The "inimical music" makes for an "enchantered space," a place chartered by chants or "enchanted preludes." These beginnings for which time makes room, these "*Preludes to Felicity*" (*CP*, 329), include such music as imagines endings or delivery from time—from this "on, on, forever onward" that "wears out adamant," in Emerson's lament.[18] They include "Credences of Summer" and speculations on

. . . how it would feel, released from destruction,
To be a bronze man breathing under archaic lapis,

Without the oscillations of planetary pass-pass,
Breathing his bronzen breath at the azury centre of time   [*CP*, 425]

For the "enchantered space" that the "inimical music" measures is the space of meditation, the natural landscape of the "inhuman" mind,

. . . the rock where tranquil must adduce
Its tranquil self, the main of things, the mind,

The starting point of the human and the end,
That in which space itself is contained, the gate
To the enclosure, day, the things illumined

By day, night and that which night illumines,
Night and its midnight-minting fragrances,
Night's hymn of the rock, as in a vivid sleep.   [*CP*, 528]

It is in the "habitation" of the "central mind" (*CP,* 524) that we live and die saying, "As if life and death were ever physical" (*CP,* 478).

Nature is not an inert fact for Stevens but something intimately bound up with his temporal "erring," and the "rock" is only "the exact rock where his inexactnesses / Would discover, at last, the view toward which they had edged" (*CP,* 512). For "if earth dissolves / Its evil after death, it dissolves it while / We live" (*CP,* 259). And the "genius of misfortune" (*CP,* 316) knows that "evil"—the "fault" of deviation from the "simplicity" and perfection of a timeless nature—defines the "never-resting mind," the "evilly compounded, vital I" (*CP,* 193–94):

> He is
> That evil, that evil in the self, from which
> In desperate hallow, rugged gesture, fault
> Falls out on everything: the genius of
> The mind, which is our being, wrong and wrong.   [*CP,* 316–17]

And the "fault" is inscribed in language, as the anagram of "evil" and "live" and the off-rhyme of "evil" and "vital"—which at other times conjures up its partner, "fatal"—highlight. Thus, "the whole race is a poet that writes down / The eccentric propositions of its fate," Stevens writes in "Men Made Out of Words" (*CP,* 356). "A Primitive Like an Orb" reverses and completes this statement:

> That's it. The lover writes, the believer hears,
> The poet mumbles and the painter sees,
> Each one, his *fated eccentricity,*
> As a part, but part, but tenacious particle,
> Of the skeleton of the ether, the total
> Of letters, prophecies, perceptions, clods
> Of color, the giant of nothingness, each one
> And the giant ever changing, living in change.   [*CP,* 443; emphasis mine]

Since the eccentric appears to be "the base of design" (*CP,* 151), however, we are not barred from "a *vis* or *noeud vital*" (*NA,* 44). It is at the circumference that we live, tracing "the outlines of being and its expressings, the syllables of its law" (*CP,* 424), by the light of meditation "like a blaze of summer straw, in winter's nick" (*CP,* 421).

Stevens's concurrent dislocation of rhetoric and nature enables him to inhabit a thoroughly human, man-made world without losing sight of the foremost law (*CP,* 17). Since his law is no longer Emerson's central fate, it is adequately represented in eccentric poetic forms, conventional measures of our rhetorical error. In Stevens's redefinition, "the false and true are one"

(*CP*, 253), so that the poet can justly suppose "the thing I hum appears to be / The rhythm of this celestial pantomime" (*CP*, 243). "Notes Toward a Supreme Fiction" provides an example of such a fictive/natural passage:

A bench was his catalepsy, Theatre
Of Trope. He sat in the park. The water of
The lake was full of artificial things,

Like a page of music, like an upper air,
Like a momentary color, in which swans
Were seraphs, were saints, were changing essences.

The west wind was the music, the motion, the force
To which the swans curveted, a will to change,
A will to make iris frettings on the blank.   [*CP*, 397]

The "artificial things" of nature "curvet" to a literary wind out of a will to touch up the blank page or lake surface; the literary music to which the tropes turn, however, is the music of natural time, to which the figures of nature "curvet." Nature's "show" of appearances is the "Theatre / Of Trope," the lake surface is like "a page of music," and the music of the "west wind" is also literary. The poet and nature are identified in the "will to change," which idea itself has a literary history going back to Shelley. And the whole of this natural/metaphoric theater is sustained by the temporal music of the lines—a distinctly conventional music. The literary composing of a physical time, as well as the texturizing of nature with a literary history, renders its "artificial" show (as well as the poet's troping) natural. Thus Stevens accepts blank verse unquestioningly because its very conventionality serves his purposes. The conventionality of Stevens's form underlines its "unnaturalness"; nevertheless, the composing and experiencing of the conventional rhythm are temporal processes and have historical resonance, thereby locating the experience of time in poetic form rather than in nature. In other words, time appears as a conventional human construct, and we need poetry to restore time to nature:

The mind renews the world in a verse,
A passage of music, a paragraph
By a right philosopher.   [*OP*, 103]

Or, as Apollinaire remarked, without poetry we would not have seasons.

In Stevens, poetic form functions as the conventional/natural backdrop for the unraveling of the eccentric/central philosophical discourse. The "objective" formal pace of meter, rhyme, alliteration, stanzaic patterns, and so on counterpoint the philosophical content, which develops—with all its qualifications, leaps forward, and reversals—according to its own rhetorical rhythm. In Marie Borroff's words, "The scholar in Stevens's poetry (more narrowly, the philosopher) expounds and excogitates in a language whose forms and patterns suggest the treatise, the textbook, or the classroom lecture." What Helen Vendler calls Stevens's "pensive" style characteristically relies on conditional statements, expanding similes that veer away from direct statement, mounting qualifications that undo the assertions made, and various other evasive rhetorical, semantic, and syntactic tricks.[19] This rhetorical and syntactical rhythm represents a "shrinking" (*CP*, 288) from the objective form in which its evasions are expressed. As the philosopher unfolds his pensive, eccentric "argument" in pursuit of "logical" knowledge (*NA*, 54), the poet juggles *his* eccentric "meters" in a display of his "empirical" knowledge (*NA*, 54), the "fusky alphabet" taught him by "that elemental parent, the green night" (*CP*, 267). And the rhetorical system does not correspond exactly to the formal system, so that formal features like stanzaic patterns seem slightly irrelevant to the argument that flows through and beyond them. Conversely, the unquestioned presence of formal norms renders the philosophical discourse slightly irrelevant, so that the two discourses make and unmake each other.

Stevens's choice of words from different sources creates a corresponding tension. Native words, words without etymology, and sound-symbolic words of imitative origin constantly move against Latinate words with elaborate etymological backgrounds. Borroff interprets this strategy as Stevens's way of undercutting declamatory and "poetic" language, as a "dampening of eloquence." In the switch from one species of words to another, we find "bravura giving way to sobriety and cynicism, exuberance to restraint, exaltation to uncertainty, even fear." And, one might add, philosophical discourse to nonsense. Indeed, Stevens's terms for the poet's language are "mumbling" and "gibberish"—a language of "flawed words and stubborn sounds" (*CP*, 194), not clear, articulate, rhetorical architectonics. According to Borroff, Stevens insists that "poetic language remain partly inarticulate, partly inhuman, that it incorporate within itself something of the 'incommunicable mass' of external reality."[20] Yet that very sense is internal to the poems' dissonant language. Since Stevens emphasizes the opacity or physicality of words as much as their transparency or referentiality, nature and metaphysics constitute the two poles of his poetic language. For example:

We say: At night an Arabian in my room,
With his damned hoobla-hoobla-hoobla-how,
Inscribes a primitive astronomy

Across the unscrawled fores the future casts
And throws his stars around the floor. By day
The wood-dove used to chant his hoobla-hoo

And still the grossest iridescence of ocean
Howls hoo and rises and howls hoo and falls.
Life's nonsense pierces us with strange relation.   [*CP,* 383]

The Arabian's "astronomy," the "wood-dove"'s mating call, and the howls of
"verbose" Triton compose "Life's nonsense," which "pierces us with strange
relation." Emerson notes: "We try to listen to the hymn of gods, and must
needs hear this perpetual *cock-a-doodle-doo,* and *ke-tar-kut* right under the
library windows."[21] While Emerson's poetry filters out nature's echolalia at
the expense of impoverishing his language, Stevens incorporates nature's
"rhetoric" in order to mark its kinship with ours and to expose its eccentricity to the foremost law.

Stevens's eclectic style, which registers the doubleness of language as part
mind and part nature, part sense and part nonsense, is adequate to his
conception of truth as eccentric and rhetoric as central. And his conventional, eccentric blank verse can hold the fluctuating center between desire and
its fulfillment, between rhetoric and truth. So that, while

                    We seek
The poem of pure reality, untouched
By trope or deviation, straight to the word,
Straight to the transfixing object,   [*CP,* 471]

we find

The accent of deviation in the living thing
That is its life preserved, the effort to be born
Surviving being born, *the event of life.*   [*OP,* 96; emphasis mine]

As the internal rhyme of "accent" and "event" and the parallel syntax
suggest, the "accent" of language in search of "pure reality" is the temporal
"deviation" that *is* "the event of life." Thus the rhetorical and linguistic
difference, deviation, and displacement make a difference, marking the moral
presence of the human imagination. Such rhetoric figures us and our world
for each other: it humanizes the world even as we become "less and less
human" (*CP,* 327). "Poetry," Emerson writes, "was all written before time
was, and whenever we are so finely organized that we can penetrate into that
region where the air is music, we hear those primal warblings, and attempt to
write them down, but we lose ever and anon a word, or a verse, and
substitute something of our own, and thus miswrite the poem."[22] This

miswriting, this generic error, opens the way for Stevens's tropological poems and their likely accounts, which are

A little different from reality:
The difference that we make in what we see

And our memorials of that difference.   [*CP,* 344]

Chapter Six

*T*he Re-Verses of Elizabeth Bishop

Love's the boy stood on the burning deck
trying to recite "The boy stood on
the burning deck." Love's the son
   stood stammering elocution
   while the poor ship in flames went down.
                "Casabianca"

Elizabeth Bishop extends Stevens's revision of Emerson and his bipartite career by engaging in a process of "constant re-adjustment" between subject and object, mind and nature, rhetoric and meters. The seemingly contradictory commentary that her work sustains proves her success in "con-fusing" romantic and modernist oppositions: she has been read as an autobiographical poet with an impersonal touch, as a surrealist given to meticulous observations of natural facts, and as a formalist whose poems are open-ended accumulations of detail.[1] Her distinction is to have developed the kind of diction and formal flexibility that enable her to be at home on the shifting ground between "is" and "as if," between our "unlikely" situation and our "likely stories." Bishop's world is precarious yet secure, being "homemade" or made in the mind's image. Her poetry can be less discursive and more descriptive than Stevens's, for realism and idealism are not antithetical in her work: the objective world of facts is never a natural or prior source but always an already represented or mediated world. Stevens may admonish "geographers and philosophers" that

The sea is a form of ridicule.
The iceberg settings satirize

The demon that cannot be himself,
That tours to shift the shifting scene.[2]

But Bishop begins with an "imaginary iceberg" and suggests that geographers and philosophers consider how it "behooves" the soul. Her iceberg, which "dares" its weight "upon a shifting stage and stands and stares," shows "who treads the boards" to be "artlessly rhetorical,"[3] and the antithesis of the artlessly rhetorical play enacted on the solider ground of the theater stage is not a play artlessly natural but an *artfully* rhetorical drama featuring a "wit" that can "spar with the sun."

On the one hand, Bishop can dissolve the opposition of reality and imagination in the "dazzling dialectic" of the play of natural surfaces and light, which becomes so "moving" in the late poem "Santarém":

I liked the place; I liked the idea of the place.
Two rivers. Hadn't two rivers sprung
from the Garden of Eden? No, that was four
and they'd diverged. Here only two
and coming together. Even if one were tempted
to literary interpretations
such as: life/death, right/wrong, male/female
—such notions would have resolved, dissolved, straight off
in that watery, dazzling dialectic.

                                                                        [*CP*, 185]

On the other hand, since dialectics originate within discourse, it is only in discourse, as in the one above, that oppositions are resolved. It is the poem's "dazzling dialectic" that dissolves nature's course and the mind's discourse. And the poem's dazzle is at once a surface brilliance and an effect of its layers of mediation. First, the experience is recollected: "Of course I may be remembering it all wrong / after, after—how many years?" Second, the temptations of "literary interpretations" are rejected on the signifying stage of a comparison to the Garden of Eden. Finally, Emerson's "Two Rivers" and Stevens's rewriting of it in "The River of Rivers in Connecticut"—poetic precedents of the same convergence of natural flow and discourse, dazzle and dialectic, place and the idea of the place—course under Bishop's dazzle. The conflux of the seen and unseen rivers is more than a meeting of nature and the mind; it is a conflux of different dialectics. For nature is not one—there are, in fact, *two* rivers; the mind is not single but the conflux of a personal remembrance and the archetypal memory of the Garden, which locates the personal past and the scene seen; and the verses that tell this conflux remember others' discourses.

Bishop's poetic remains remarkably consistent throughout her career. An early poem like "The Gentleman of Shalott" can serve as the credo for her kind of "realism," which finds nature to be *in fact* shaped on the model of rhetoric. The poem rewrites Tennyson's "The Lady of Shalott" and revises its opposition of reality and imagination. Tennyson's "Lady" represents the psyche as dwelling in an islanded inner space of reflection, and such a figure implies a mutually exclusive relationship between the inner and the outer. Isolated and forbidden to look down on "many-towered Camelot," the "fairy Lady" is granted only its reflection in a mirror:

And moving through a mirror clear
That hangs before her all the year,
Shadows of the world appear.

And "she weaves by night and day / A magic web with colours gay" of the "mirror's magic sights." She cannot look at Camelot directly, because she is herself a projection and a reversal of the outside world, as the rhyme of "Shalott" and "Camelot" and the near-anagram of "water" and "tower" suggest. Her water-bound existence and her weaving rest on her isolation from "towered Camelot"; when she turns her "glassy countenance" toward Camelot, her web unravels, and her mirror cracks "from side to side."[4]

In Bishop's revision of the poem, the dichotomy of inner and outer disappears; the bilateral symmetry of the human body renders her gentleman a mirror image of himself:

Which eye's his eye?
Which limb lies
next the mirror?
For neither is clearer
nor a different color
than the other,
nor meets a stranger
in this arrangement
of leg and leg and
arm and so on.
To his mind
it's the indication
of a mirrored reflection
somewhere along the line
of what we call the spine.   [*CP,* 9]

Bishop internalizes the mirror, replacing the subject-object duality not with a unity but with a duplication at the subject's source. The dividing line lies within, and the "center" is itself a reflection. Bishop's eccentric gentleman is by nature off-center:

He felt in modesty
his person was
half looking-glass,
for why should he
be doubled?
The glass must stretch
down his middle,
or rather down the edge.
But he's in doubt
as to which side's in or out
of the mirror.
There's little margin for error,
but there's no proof, either.
And if half his head's reflected,
thought, he thinks, might be affected.   [*CP,* 9]

Thought, quite likely affected by the reflective structure of his head, is necessarily affected or duplicitous. With the internalization of the duplication, which preempts the inside-outside dichotomy, the spatial and temporal distinction between an original (nature, fact, or experience) and a subsequent reproduction (a copy, reflection, or art) vanishes. It is impossible to tell which side is the original and which the duplicate; since the "modesty" of the postromantic, peripheral man questions the need for two of him, however, only one side *can* be him, and the other must be a mirror image. There must be a duplication, then, but it is an atemporal, ahistorical doubling. The "middle" or the "spine" now becomes an "edge"; the inner becomes a limit. Bishop concludes:

But he's resigned
to such economical design.
If the glass slips
he's in a fix—
only one leg, etc. But
while it stays put
he can walk and run
and his hands can clasp one
another. The uncertainty
he says he
finds exhilarating. He loves
that sense of constant re-adjustment.
He wishes to be quoted as saying at present:
"Half is enough."   [*CP,* 9–10]

His answer echoes the Lady of Shalott's complaint, "I am half sick of shadows." A survivor, Bishop's gentleman prefers being "half sick" to the Lady's consummation-death: "And her eyes were darkened wholly."

"The Gentleman of Shalott" has significant implications for Bishop's poetic, for the confusion between the original and the representation, the uncertainty and alienation, are built into the gentleman. Duplication, the formative principle enabling his existence, constitutes the beginning of discourse; it constitutes also the end or limits of discourse, for the original is itself a reflection. If one starts with two halves without a historical order of priority, one inhabits a metaphor, the two terms of which—the tenor and the vehicle—are simply equal and coeval in a world "littered with old correspondences" (*CP*, 60).

Indeed, the implications of "The Gentleman of Shalott" go beyond the poetic. The bilateral symmetry of the body and binary logic—which also demarcates and duplicates in order to generate distinctions and meanings—are themselves mirror images. In this hall of mirrors, the dialectic between Tennyson's and Bishop's poetics, or even the distinction between ladies and gentlemen, may be reduced to the same central pattern, thereby reducing physiological distinctions themselves to human duplications. The limitation of this arrangement is solipsism, hinted at by the disappointment registered in the enjambment of "his hands can clasp one / another." Yet the precariousness of the gentleman's position exhilarates:

> The uncertainty
> he says he
> finds exhilarating.

The line "he says he" both sets his limits and sets him free. The solipsistic flanking of "says" with "he" on two sides suggests that the saying itself is the center that divides and duplicates; it is the spine of the duplicitous "book" that he inhabits, binding his fiction and his fact and spanning that chasm with a chiasmus.

Bishop's poetry as a whole overturns the hierarchical dualities of subject and object, inside and outside, center and periphery, original and copy. She repeatedly questions the priority and authority of experience over representation. For example, her use of letters as visual images to depict nature suggests that representation may even be prior to the original. On the one hand, her nature harbors "S-shaped birds" (*CP*, 32); on the other, her uncle's "Large Bad Picture" has "scribbled" on it "hundreds of fine black birds / hanging in *n*'s in banks" (*CP*, 11). "Poem," in *Geography III,* is a multi-layered reversal: it represents a painting of a landscape in which

A specklike bird is flying to the left.
Or is it a flyspeck looking like a bird?   [*CP*, 176]

Nature (the flyspeck) is subsequent to and figures in or litters the "half inch of blue sky." Consequently, Bishop's work neither pays elegiac homage to the life art preempts nor elevates art to Art. As "The Monument" reminds us, a work of art is just as incomprehensible as experience; it signifies nothing beyond the emotion invested in it, the fragments of memory it contains, its allusions to past meanings ("a sort of fleur-de-lys of weathered wood, / . . . pierced with odd holes, / four-sided, stiff, ecclesiastical" [*CP*, 23]), its expression of desire—"wanting to be a monument, to cherish something"—the desire merely to commemorate. "Monuments to every moment, / refuse of every moment, used: / cages for infinity" (*CP*, 275), are what Bishop calls the "minimal, incoherent fragments" Joseph Cornell's boxes hold. Or, as she explains in "Poem," neither experience nor art abides, except in the momentary conjunction of "visions." But

>   "visions" is
> too serious a word—our looks, two looks:
> art "copying from life" and life itself,
> life and the memory of it so compressed
> they've turned into each other. Which is which?   [*CP*, 177]

The life, the memory of it, and the painting "about the size of an old-style dollar bill" are all compressed in "Poem," so that the actual dimensions of the work of art and the excess value conferred by shared "looks" are indistinguishable, together making up "our earthly trust."

Bishop's characteristic points of departure are examples of mediated experience: memories ("Sestina," "First Death in Nova Scotia," "In the Waiting Room"); paintings ("Large Bad Picture," "Poem"); tapestries ("Brazil, January 1, 1502"); monuments or wood-rubbings ("The Monument"); toys ("Cirque d'Hiver"); illustrations and concordances ("Over 2,000 Illustrations and a Complete Concordance"); news stories ("The Burgler of Babylon") and bulletins ("12 O'Clock News"); misprints ("The Man-Moth"); dreams ("The Weed," "Sleeping Standing Up"); books ("Crusoe in England," "From Trollope's Journal"); and other poems ("The Gentleman of Shalott," "Casabianca"). "The Map," which begins the *Complete Poems,* shows why she is interested less in landscape than in its representation on a map, of which her poem is yet another representation. The naiveté of the observer in the poem points up the thoroughly conventional nature of cartography. Representational artifacts, which help us navigate in the world, express a consensus and must be conventional. Yet representation liberates as well as limits. The rift between the original and its representation constitutes an exhilarating uncertainty that leads to discovery by prompting questions one could not put to a landscape alone or to a map as a merely conventional artifact. Only when the map is seen as a new landscape equal to its original is there room for questions and answers, thoughts and feelings.

"The Map" opens on uncertain ground:

Land lies in water; it is shadowed green.
Shadows, or are they shallows, at its edges
showing the line of long sea-weeded ledges
where weeds hang to the simple blue from green.
Or does the land lean down to lift the sea from under,
drawing it unperturbed around itself?
Along the fine tan sandy shelf
is the land tugging at the sea from under?   [*CP*, 3]

Bishop depicts a map in terms one might apply to a natural landscape— "shadows," "shallows," and so on. As her mixing of terms suggests, these questions would not arise from observing the fluctuating shoreline of an actual landscape; nor would they be generated by the conventional, clearly demarcated shoreline on a map. But the difference or disjunction—the questionable relationship—between a map and a landscape makes possible such speculations, which are charged with emotion and constitute a meta-physics. The disjunction embodied in any representational artifact— whether a map negotiating between a landscape and colors and lines on paper or a poem negotiating between the sense and sounds of words—opens up the metaphysical realm.

This disjunction or questionable relationship exists within language itself: does Bishop start by questioning the color differences on the map, or do alliteration and rhyme call "shallows" forth from "shadows" to generate the questions? In "Filling Station," Bishop exploits this process whereby words of similar sounds but different meanings trigger metaphysical speculation. The "dirty" family station, run by the father in a "dirty, / oil-soaked monkey suit" and "several quick and saucy / and greasy sons"—"all quite thoroughly dirty"—hums to a repetition of "oily" and "dirty" and insistent rhymes to them. When Bishop proceeds to the metaphysical question—"Why, oh why, the doily?"—the very question seems generated by the literal pattern of the poem: "doily" includes "oily." "Somebody embroidered the d*oily*"; "somebody / arranges the rows of cans / *so* that they *so*ftly say: / ESSO— SO—SO—SO"; somebody set the poem humming to a rhyme of -*y*, as in dirt*y*, oil*y*, and d*oily*; "somebody loves us all" (*CP*, 127–28; emphasis mine).

The questions and answers repeat and revise the dominant pattern of sounds found in the poem. Although they may arise from observation, they may spring also from the partly fortuitous and partly planned literal pattern of the poem; there is no way of telling which came first.

Moreover, as "The Map" shows, emotion likewise springs from the disjunction between two different representational conventions:

The names of seashore towns run out to sea,
the names of cities cross the neighboring mountains
—the printer here experiencing the same excitement
as when emotion too far exceeds its cause.   [*CP,* 3]

What one unschooled in the conventions of map-making might interpret as an expression of feeling is, in fact, mere convention. Representing cities by circles and allowing their names to "cross the neighboring mountains" are shifts in scale that are part of cartographic convention. For maps superimpose writing, a second symbolic system, on the topographic representation, which works by a *spatial* reduction of scale. And this dissonance creates the illusion of emotion on the part of the mapmaker. The poetic structure of "The Map" enacts a similar superimposition of different conventions. The first and third stanzas have eight lines each, consisting of two quatrains rhymed *abba.* The middle stanza consists of eleven unrhymed lines. Since the content of the stanza seems less abstract and more affecting, we are tempted to think that this stanza is more "natural" and freer—more responsive to the observer's emotion. But we would be as naive as the speaker of the poem if we were to think so. At most, the stanza upholds the convention of spontaneity. For emotion can never exceed form. Flanking her freer verse with more formal poetry, Bishop exposes the convention of freedom. When the speaker asks about the map's colors, "Are they assigned, or can the countries pick their colors?" the quaintness of the very idea of choice or self-expression in such a context becomes clear.

"12 O'Clock News," reminiscent of "The Map" in its witty manipulation of scale, refers more specifically to the poet's landscape. Speaking in prose, the observer—"alien" either to our earth or simply to a poet's world—describes a war-torn terrain. After noting the variety of inscrutable yet menacing artifacts on the poet's desk, the speaker discloses that "aerial reconnaissance reports the discovery of a large rectangular 'field,' hitherto unknown to us, obviously man-made. It is dark-speckled. An airstrip? A cemetery?" (*CP,* 174). Calling the typewritten page of the poem a field alludes to William Carlos Williams's and Charles Olson's "force-field" theories of composition.[5] Bishop implicitly rejects such poetics, which attempt to equate art with action. First, her literalizing the field through the eyes of an alien observer exposes the field theory of composition as itself a metaphor. Second, she suggests that the impulse to reduce artistic representation to nature, to physical action—indeed, to physical laws—leads directly to war—to the bombed-out landscape of the poet's desk. She reverses such nuclear poetics: the field itself is "obviously man-made." Because the field is not natural, the poet need not be bound by natural laws, which only spell disaster. Seen as a man-made space, the page is open to negotiation: it becomes the field of human discourse. Thus the poem may be an airstrip for transcendental take-offs or a cemetery—an interment between the lines. The page—"obviously man-made" yet "hitherto unknown to us"—becomes the source, generating questions and the possibility of answers, interpretations, and meanings. The physics of the poem on the page—in Walt Whitman's words, "those upright lines . . . those curves, angles, dots"[6]—grounds the metaphysics of discourse. And whatever the meanings, whether Crusoe's volcano is christened *"Mont d'Espoir* or *Mount Despair,"* they are articulated by one who has "time enough to play with names" (*CP,* 165). The placement of letters, the play of languages, and the reversals of representation all resist nature itself: they make time for metaphysics.

By questioning the priority of nature, Bishop can inhabit a reflected and therefore thoroughly human world. For representations counter nature: they "re-verse" the world, turn it around, and right its wrong. In "Insomnia" the moon—that "daytime sleeper"—provides a model for the poet:

> By the Universe deserted,
> *she*'d tell it to go to hell,
> and she'd find a body of water,
> or a mirror, on which to dwell.

Since "to dwell on" also means "to contemplate," one dwells or lives by reflection and speculation. "So wrap up care in a cobweb," Bishop writes, and "cobweb," with its long association with poet's "webs," relates her own task to the moon's:

> and drop it down the well
>
> into that world inverted
> where left is always right,
> where the shadows are really the body,
> where we stay awake all night,
> where the heavens are shallow as the sea
> is now deep, and you love me.   [*CP,* 70]

Bishop reports that Marianne Moore called this a "cheap love poem"[7]—
which is exactly what it is. The poem does not effect any changes; it affects a
change.

"Anaphora" illustrates the larger uses of such reversals. The rhetorical
device of progression through repetition, considered by classical rhetoricians
to mimic the movement of thought, is the compositional method of the
poem, which describes the natural repetition of the rising and setting of the
sun:

Each day with so much ceremony
begins, with birds, with bells,
with whistles from a factory;
such white-gold skies our eyes
first open on, such brilliant walls
that for a moment we wonder
"Where is the music coming from, the energy?
The day was meant for what ineffable creature
we must have missed?" Oh promptly he
appears and takes his earthly nature
    instantly, instantly falls
    victim of long intrigue,
    assuming memory and mortal
    mortal fatigue.

As the sun rises, "falling into sight," it

sinks through the drift of bodies,
sinks through the drift of classes
to evening to the beggar in the park
who, weary, without lamp or book
    prepares stupendous studies:
    the fiery event
    of every day in endless
    endless assent.   [CP, 52]

Nature, patterned on rhetorical models, is reversed: sunrise becomes a
mortal fall from heavenly grace, sunset an endless "ascent." The poem is an
elegy, and its repetitions aim to set nature right: natural beginnings and
endings are reversed, without recourse to any faith outside of what the
poem's form and wordplays provide. Nature is not mastered but dissolves
into discourse when its motions come down to rhetoric and the play of
letters. In this Platonic detour, death is no longer a fact.

The late "Sonnet" effects a similar reversal:

Caught—the bubble
in the spirit-level,
a creature divided;
and the compass needle
wobbling and wavering,
undecided.
Freed—the broken
thermometer's mercury
running away;
and the rainbow-bird
from the narrow bevel
of the empty mirror,
flying wherever
it feels like, gay!   [*CP*, 192]

Given its age and near universality in European literatures, and its generic division into question (octave) and resolution (sestet), the sonnet form appears particularly suited to the large genetic subject—with its division into life and death—that Bishop addresses here. The alignment of generic and genetic sequences in fact raises the question whether forms or natural facts are the givens. Are art forms and other measuring instruments (level, compass, thermometer) prior to, and do they define the shape of, the nature they register and track, or is nature a prior force, shaping the instruments that would chart its course, measure its force? Standing the Petrarchan sonnet structure on its head—here the sestet or resolution precedes the octave or question—amounts to more than a formal experiment and enables Bishop to reverse the alignment of life with freedom and death with necessity. Life is caught in the resolution of the sestet; dying is a freeing into the question of the octave. This dissolution of the genetic issue into generic discourse may be small compensation—on the order of rainbows in mirror bevels—but it does exceed the limits of nature and of mere mirroring.

"One Art" not only effects such poetic reversals but exposes them as affected. Bishop's choice of a villanelle, a traditional form of repetition that promises to make "art" out of "losing," seems to support the opening assertion, but the negatives cast doubt on the project at the outset:

The art of losing isn't hard to master;
so many things seem filled with the intent
to be lost that their loss is no disaster.   [*CP*, 178]

Yet the title tells us that the art of writing and the art of losing are one, and the requirements of the form serve to render loss certain from the start. The third line already gives us the last word of the poem—the word she means to deny but is fated to write:

—Even losing you (the joking voice, a gesture
I love) I shan't have lied. It's evident
the art of losing's not too hard to master
though it may look like (*Write* it!) like disaster.   [*CP*, 178]

Writing and losing are one art because the formal repetition of loss, which promises mastery, simultaneously finalizes disaster: "(*Write* it!) like disaster." Repetition duplicates and divides, both masters and loses, and thus makes for "disaster." The division-by-duplication of the "aster" *is* the ill star that governs poets.

The disaster of "One Art" is foreshadowed by two major earlier poems. "Paris, 7 A.M." draws a spatial map of time: "Time is an Etoile" because the hours circle the center of the clockface, the way the twelve avenues of Paris spread out from the Etoile, light radiates from a star, or one's life disperses from its origin—the "star-splintered hearts of ice," the "ammunition" of snowballs in the "childish snow-forts, built in flashier winters." The architectures and geometries that delineate the history of cities and people, the rectangles that house the "circles" of "introspection" and "retrospection," contain and enclose a central "star," the lost source of time and space:

When did the star dissolve, or was it captured
by the sequence of squares and squares and circles, circles.
Can the clocks say.   [*CP*, 26–27]

Time gathers around a starlike center and takes shape as a city, an architecture, or a life history. Yet the center, which appears to dissolve in the process, is not necessarily a natural origin. The star might be just an asterisk; as Emily Dickinson puts it, "what are Stars but Asterisks / To point a human Life?"[8] The center of one's history, like that of a poem or monument, may be a creation of the structuring itself; the inside may be only what the enclosure posits. And if the center builds exactly as the peripheral accumulation builds up, the two "adequately" reflect each other. For example, the arrangement of odd bits and pieces that make up the monument may or may not have something within it:

It may be solid, may be hollow.
. . . .
But roughly but adequately it can shelter
what is within (which after all
cannot have been intended to be seen).[9]   [*CP*, 24–25]

In "Paris, 7 A.M." the star—seen only in the distance its light has traversed, measured only by disaster—may represent the beginning of time, a source of light already dead. Or it may be a figure of birth or childhood—a personal origin. But it may stand also for "the still point of the turning world,"[10] the eruption of the timeless into history. As we see in "Over 2,000 Illustrations and a Complete Concordance," the Nativity is another source star lost beyond recall: "far gone in history or theology," "everything" is "only connected by 'and' and 'and,'" and there are no origins or epiphanies. "Open the book," Bishop writes, "(The gilt rubs off the edges / of the pages and pollinates the fingertips.)" (*CP*, 57, 58.) The gilt on the illustrated concordance to the Bible is the "guilt" of history. Here, too, "disaster" is the dispersal of the star, the mangling of Spirit in the letter—"a grim lunette, / caught in the toils of an initial letter." The initial C becomes a grim reaper, the Christian star is caught in a Muslim crescent, and the Nativity itself can only be reconstructed through the toil of "2,000 Illustrations," each with discrete, *engraved* lines that, "granted," will "resolve themselves" into a picture. As the ambiguity of the final lines implies, we cannot see the "old Nativity," for its luster would be blinding; it can only be said that we "looked and looked." Thus Bishop defines history—natural, personal, cultural, and religious—as loss, as a radiation from a center that may be strictly conceptual. In such a diaspora, however, loss is gain. Just as in representations the distance from nature generates meanings, the gilt of the book "pollinates" the fingertips, for the "dust" is fertile and multiplies.

Thus the course of Bishop's wandering persona traces a detour through discourse, pursuing "Questions of Travel."[11] Questions, the rhetorical analogues of quests, center in a "de-centering"—in the dislocation between knowledge and ignorance. The generic question, then, is naturally prompted by the boundary line of death:

> Oh, is it
> freedom at last, a lifelong
> dream of time and silence,
> dream of protection and rest?
> Or is it the very worst,
> the unimaginable nightmare
> that never before dared last
> more than a second?   [*CP*, 73–74]

The central question that posits the extremes of absolute knowledge or home and absolute illusion or exile generates history itself:

The acuteness of the question
forks instantly and starts
a snake-tongue flickering;
blurs further, blunts, softens,
separates, falls, our problems
becoming helplessly
    proliferative.   [*CP,* 74]

The original questioning, fall, and proliferation of questions are already recorded; we can only repeat this generic history of loss. And it is only the question that we register, record, and are recorded by. For, of course, "there is no way of telling" the answer; "the eyes say only either." Absolute knowledge coincides with absolute ignorance beyond the spectrum of wavelengths we can register.

"At the Fishhouses" reiterates this point. The water is

Cold dark deep and absolutely clear,
element bearable to no mortal.   [*CP,* 65]

One can only contemplate what contact with the water would be like, if one should dip one's hand in it. And Bishop's description fails to describe:

your bones would begin to ache and your hand would burn
as if the water were a transmutation of fire.   [*CP,* 65–66]

This would be absolute, apocalyptic knowledge of "fire and ice" at once, and therefore "bearable to no mortal." Thus the water is

    like what we imagine knowledge to be:
dark, salt, clear, moving, utterly free,
drawn from the cold hard mouth
of the world, derived from the rocky breasts
forever, flowing and drawn, and since
our knowledge is historical, flowing, and flown.   [*CP,* 66]

Knowledge bearable to mortals is possessed only in imagination and memory, in representations and repetitions, "as if" and *as* it is lost. For "there is no way of *telling* it," either (emphasis mine).

"In the Waiting Room," then, properly tells or narrates the "growth of a poet's mind." The poet originates in the recognition of her separation from, and identity with, her world, at once finding and losing her "self." Her birth or awakening comes with a scream from inside the dentist's office that is also the voice of the child in the waiting room, since "inside" says "either." When the child produces her explanation, she is a poet:

How—I didn't know any
word for it—how "unlikely" . . .   [*CP*, 161]

To explain an identity in nature, she finds the word "unlikely"; the perception of sameness is unlikely, because it is more than a likeness or likely. If all
accounts of phenomena are likely stories only, the breach that gives birth to
the poet is an origin that both *is* and is unlikely. This is also the breach of
metaphor—unlikely identities. The scream, which is not "like" the child's
voice but *is* hers all the same, signals a birth into natural identity and an
unlikely language. For one's identity, one's sameness with and difference
from others and objects, comes to be adequately revealed in the unlikely
likenesses of metaphoric language. If there is an "inside" or a primal source
that is glimpsed in the child's vertiginous insight, it is covered up or "framed"
by the conspiracy of common sense, "objective" facts, and grammar—of
nature and poetry: "You are an *I*, / you are an *Elizabeth*, / You are one of
them." And the source disclosed in the grammatical cleavage of "you are an *I*"
is not a luminous star but nothingness itself, "cold, blue-black space," split by
a cry—"an *oh!* of pain"—that might have been ours.

Part Three

Chapter Seven

The Coinciding Leaves of Walt Whitman

From fibre heart of mine—from throat and
    tongue—(My life's hot pulsing blood,
The personal urge and form for me—not
    merely paper, automatic type and ink,)
Each song of mine—each utterance . . .
        "Now Precedent Songs, Farewell"

Walt Whitman begins by promising to begin again:

Have you practis'd so long to learn to read?
Have you felt so proud to get at the meaning of poems?
Stop this day and night with me and you shall possess the origin of all poems,

· ·

You shall no longer take things at second or third hand, nor look through the
    eyes of the dead, nor feed on the spectres in books . . .[1]

Appealing neither to Poe's ravenous past nor to the self-authorizing authority of poetic form that Emerson invokes, Whitman permits "Nature" to speak with "original energy" (*LG,* 29). The origin that his oracular utterance discloses is available to all; his speech is therefore communal—"These are really the thoughts of all men in all ages and lands, they are not original with me" (*LG,* 45)—and even common—"What is commonest, cheapest, nearest, easiest, is Me" (*LG,* 41)—because the "origin" is identity:

I celebrate myself, and sing myself,
And what I assume you shall assume,
For every atom belonging to me as good belongs to you.

To make sure that "atom" is not read figuratively, Whitman adds:

My tongue, every atom of my blood, form'd from this soil, this air,
Born here of parents born here from parents the same, and their parents the
    same.   [*LG,* 29]

"I" and "you" do not owe their identity to the liberties of metaphoric or
"poetic" language; such language is itself licensed by the given, physical
identity of "I," "you," and all else. As Whitman elaborates in "Crossing
Brooklyn Ferry," all seen identities are "struck" from a "float forever held in
solution" (*LG,* 162), and all process and change are sustained in this synchronic matrix of identity, so that "time nor place—distance avails not" (*LG,*
160).

Since past, present, and future coincide in a synchronic identity, nature is
not a blank slate for Whitman but a palimpsest. It is a tissue or fiber woven
through the ages that even now conveys actual conversions and metamorphoses of all ages and forms. Whitman sees the human body, for example, as a palimpsest of evolutionary codes:

I find I incorporate gneiss, coal, long-threaded moss, fruits, grains, esculent
    roots,
And am stucco'd with quadrupeds and birds all over,
And have distanced what is behind me for good reasons,
But call anything back again when I desire it.   [*LG,* 59]

Thus the "omnigenous" (*LG,* 60) poet encompasses nature, and it is in vain
that the plutonic rocks, snakes, or buzzards try to evade him. The identity of
humans with organic and inorganic nature, which evolutionary science substantiates, underwrites Whitman's poetic leaps and connections. The poet is
licensed to go backward as well as forward in time and to "tally" other forms
and lives in the same breath, for the story he tells is the story that tells him.
Language itself is isomorphic with this story, and the given connections,
identities, and isomorphisms that compose nature are inscribed in poetic
language, rendering it naturally metaphoric. "The science of language,"
Whitman observes, "has large and close analogies in geological science, with
its ceaseless evolution, its fossils, and its numberless submerged layers and
hidden strata, the infinite go-before of the present. Or, perhaps Language is
more like some vast living body, or perennial body of bodies."[2] In writing
that he incorporates plutonic rocks, for example, the poet discloses another,
isomorphic evolution in the body and etymology of his words, and thereby
proves that it *is* "in vain the plutonic rocks send their old heat" against his
"approach" (*LG,* 59).

The given or inherently metaphoric nature of language enables the poet to
speak in continuous double-entendres:

If I worship one thing more than another it shall be the spread of my own body,
   or any part of it,
Translucent mould of me it shall be you!
Shaded ledges and rests it shall be you!
Firm masculine colter it shall be you!

. . . .

Root of wash'd sweet-flag! timorous pond-snipe! nest of guarded duplicate eggs!
   it shall be you!
Mix'd tussled hay of head, beard, brawn, it shall be you!
Trickling sap of maple, fibre of manly wheat, it shall be you!   [*LG*, 53]

Whitman's originally metaphoric language is a hieroglyph, in which nature
and the human body are superimposed as isomorphic transparencies. Thus it
is indeed impossible to worship one more than the other. Language becomes
the universal ritual in which oracle and oratory, revelation and rhetoric,
coincide. Section 5 of "Song of Myself" is Whitman's most remarkable
palimpsest. Superimposing body and soul, sexual awakening and mystical
possession, he discloses an origin that opens simultaneously to natural and
supernatural energies, for the poet who carries tokens of his animal past
(section 32) also bears tokens of the gods: he touches "all laws" and tallies "all
antecedents" (*LG*, 240). And his "inspired" or "animated" language likewise
faces two ways, for his natural "leaves of grass" also amount to a palimpsest of
all past representations of divine power:

Magnifying and applying come I,
Outbidding at the start the old cautious hucksters,
Taking myself the exact dimensions of Jehovah,
Lithographing Kronos, Zeus his son, and Hercules his grandson,
Buying drafts of Osiris, Isis, Belus, Brahma, Buddha,
In my portfolio placing Manito loose, Allah on a leaf, the crucifix engraved,
With Odin and the hideous-faced Mexitli and every idol and image,

. . . .

Accepting the rough deific sketches to fill out better in myself, bestowing them
   freely on each man and woman I see.   [*LG*, 75]

Thus an original language, which physically channels natural energy and is
modeled on other biological processes like alimentary and respiratory translations between an outer and an inner nature, at the same time constitutes a
text of texts.

The generative process in Whitman consists not of the natural cycle of
death and rebirth, which poetry by analogy invokes to naturalize its metaphors, but of the recycling of nature and poetic texts, of leaves of grass and

Leaves of Grass. For writing, no less than speech, is a patterning passage of force through form. At the same time the "omnivorous" poet devours the world and transmutes natural energy into *Leaves of Grass,* his words are recycled into natural energy, inscribed in the ground as leaves of grass underfoot (*LG,* 89) and recorded in the "carols vibrating through the air" he "leaves" (*LG,* 131). "Leaves of grass," then, is a hieroglyph in which the categories of words and things coincide, inscribing the original identity of "struck" identities. Thus Whitman's poetic invokes the fully empowered Logos, at once the word and the world. He pronounces not only that the word is flesh—"This is the meal equally set, this is the meat for natural hunger" (*LG,* 46)—but that flesh is the word or "human bodies are words" (*LG,* 219). He repeatedly scorns a figurative use of language and calls for *"no ornamental similes at all—not one: perfect transparent clearness* sanity, and health are wanted—*that* is the *divine style"* (*LG,* 764). And when he employs metaphoric language, it always comes with a disclaimer: "(For the sake of him I typify, for the common average man's sake, your sake if you are he,)" (*LG,* 241). Just as each fact is identical to the whole and always points to more than itself, the whole is identical to each fact and always points to less than itself.

"Song of Myself" most closely approaches such an original and apocalyptic language, wherein symbolic and literal usages are the same. The kind of symbolism that operates without the duality of symbol and symbolized, vehicle and tenor, is anagogic symbolism. As Northrop Frye describes it, "In the anagogic phase, literature imitates the total dream of man, and so imitates the thought of a human mind which is at the circumference and not at the center of its reality."[3] Thus this "total dream" is indistinguishable from total actuality. For Whitman, the mind and nature are not related analogically, as they are for Emerson; instead, thought and nature are identical, superimposed as an apocalyptic hieroglyph. And such anagogic poetry is neither contained by nature nor measurable by the limits of natural plausibility. Frye elaborates: "When we pass into anagogy, nature becomes, not the container, but the thing contained. . . . Nature is now inside the mind of an infinite man who builds his cities out of the Milky Way. This is not reality, but it is the conceivable or imaginative limit of desire, which is infinite, eternal, and hence apocalyptic." Anagogically, "poetry unites total ritual, or unlimited social action, with total dream, or unlimited individual thought." This union of the outer and the inner, of form and force, in a Logos that is both *praxis,* or creative action, and reason characterizes the figurative mode of the Scriptures or apocalyptic revelation and of those literary works—Frye cites *Paradise Lost* and the *Divine Comedy;* we could add *Leaves of Grass* and the

Cantos—that constitute the definitive myths or "analogies of revelation" in their civilizations.[4]

In anagogy, metaphoric language becomes explosive, unbound and un-bounded: "Here we are dealing with poetry in its totality, in which the formula 'A is B' may be hypothetically applied to anything, for there is no metaphor, not even 'black is white,' which a reader has any right to quarrel with in advance."[5] Classifying Whitman's symbolism as anagogic—as exteri-or to classification—helps us to comprehend his originally metaphoric lan-guage, whose figuration is not an "eccentric" troping but a superscription revealing identities at the core. The metaphor of "leaves of grass," a figure contained in "Song of Myself," becomes the container, which titles and entitles Whitman's life work, because it authorizes his anagogic equation of nature and language. Section 6 of "Song of Myself" shows the "leaves-of-grass" figure to be the omphalos of his project, centering both his world of continuous process and his oracle. For grass is at once a fact and symbol of nature, with its generative and regenerative translations and transmutations, and of language—of all strategies and theories of signifying. To catalogue Whitman's catalogue: the grass is a "flag" of his hopeful "disposition," an objective sign of a subjective or psychological nature; it is a "remembrancer" of the Lord, a token "designedly dropt" from above, to signify divine imma-nence and sanction; it is a tautological answer to the questioner, the "pro-duced babe of the vegetation" mirroring the "child"; it is the "uncut hair of graves," or death absorbing and transforming all meanings into nature; it is language both as a physiological process—nature's oral music of "so many uttering tongues"—and as writing, a "uniform hieroglyphic"; and, like any theory of language, it implies a politics, for its universal literacy underwrites democratic equality, since it sprouts alike among the unlike "Kanuck, Tucka-hoe, Congressman, Cuff."

Yet this anagogic symbol, which defines the conceptual limits of the mind and language, is at the same time a pun. What licenses Whitman's poetic language, then, is itself licensed by poetic language. Nature grants authority to the poet's "leaves" in a play on words, itself a drastic yoking of linguistic force and form that is isomorphic with the grass blade's embodiment of the life force. Moreover, the pun is not capricious or accidental; the poet's language is etymologically inscribed with a history of associations of writing with leaves—from papyrus through folios to paper manufactured from trees. No ordinary metaphor, these leaves "infolding all life" (*LG,* 668) superimpose, "ply over ply," the facts and processes of language and nature, of history and thought. Whitman roots his poetic language in a coincidence that dissolves the dualities of a symbolism of correspondences like Emerson's.

Whitman's "orbic" project thus pivots on its wording. Not only does his breath tally spirit and nature in speech, but his leaves tally writing and nature. In other words, the inspired poet is at the same time a scribe, and the oracular revelation of the life force coincides with the oratorical patterning of language. Whitman insists on the physical presence of the man who is his book by stressing the voice: "Vocalism, measure, concentration, determination, and the divine power to speak words" (*LG*, 383). The divine life force is conducted by an "electric voice" (*LG*, 496), and elsewhere he writes of "screaming electric, the atmosphere using" (*LG*, 505). Harold Bloom argues that the trope of vocalism or voice is Whitman's transumptive trope: by insisting on the voice, Whitman transumes his antecedents in original writing.[6] Yet the trope of voice would seem to transume itself, for Whitman also insists on "con-fusing" speech and writing. He writes:

So I pass, a little time vocal, visible, contrary,
Afterward a melodious echo . . .   [*LG*, 505]

The echo is to the voice what the poet's leaves are to the "seed" he has "sought to plant" in his songs (*LG*, 501). The leaves are only what the poet leaves behind him as he passes "through Space and Time fused in a chant" (*LG*, 501):

Only these Souvenirs of Democracy—In them—in all my songs—behind me
    leaving,
To You, whoever you are, (bathing, *leavening* this *leaf* especially with my
    breath—pressing on it a moment with my own hands;
—Here! feel how the pulse beats in my wrists!—how my heart's-blood is
    swelling, contracting!)
I will You, in all, Myself, with promise never to desert you,
To which I sign my name,
        Walt Whitman   [*LG*, 498; emphasis mine]

The leavings/leaves of the poet's passage are leavened by breath. And the pun tells: the leaves are inspired by the poet's breath, but they are also made leaves thereby. Writing is the will of the passing poet, signed by his name and named by his signature. The intercourse of the soul and nature courses through the voice, which leavens the poet's leaves. In this leavening, the man's breath, his will and life force, tallies with the book's "strain musical flowing through ages and continents, now reaching me and America" (*LG*, 496).

The poet's passing and his passing "forward" (*LG, 496*) a charge that is at once "electric" and literary are both channeled through his signature, in his leaves. Thus Whitman's poet is master at once of the Logos and of the Scripture, leveling in himself the hierarchy of Father, Son, and Holy Spirit/Scripture. The poet-child who is autochthonous, who reemerges or goes "forth" and ingests his world "every day," devours his own father and is devoured, in turn, by the writing he fathers:[7] "His own parents . . . they became part of him," Whitman writes, and a final line, dropped in 1867, reads, "And these become of him or her that peruses them now" (*LG, 365*). The synchronic hieroglyph of "leaves of grass" channels this personal history of the poet as well as the history of nature and writing.

"Leaves of grass," then, is a key to Whitman's cosmos, a web of interlocking identities:

A vast similitude interlocks all,
All spheres, grown, ungrown, small, large, suns, moons, planets,
All distances of place however wide,
All distances of time, all inanimate forms,
All souls, all living bodies though they be ever so different, or in different
    worlds,
All gaseous, watery, vegetable, mineral processes, the fishes, the brutes,
All nations, colors, barbarisms, civilizations, languages,
All identities that have existed or may exist on this globe, or any globe,
All lives and deaths, all of the past, present, future,
This vast similitude spans them, and always has spann'd,
And shall forever span them and compactly hold and enclose them.   [*LG, 261*]

And the key to the similitude is similitude itself or the fact that one key unlocks "all." Whitman sometimes calls this key only a clue, a mere hint, for the truth is at once directly available and never to be encompassed:

Why even I myself I often think know little or nothing of my real life,
Only a few hints, a few diffused faint clews and indirections
I seek for my own use to trace out here.   [*LG, 8*]

Appropriately, Whitman's preferred spelling, "clew," also means a "thread"—specifically, the thread that guided Theseus out of the labyrinth. Again, ·textuality intersects with experience. The clew that the poet's lines spin becomes the key to the entire fiber-fabric, the warp to the weft of the universe, and hints at a cosmic coherence: "The threads that were spun are gather'd, the weft crosses the warp, the pattern is systematic" (*LG, 438*). If the mind and nature, words and fact, together weave this web, the cosmos is also a "kosmos." "Kosmos" appears to be the subjective isomorph of the cosmos; as Whitman defines it, "Kosmos, noun masculine or feminine, a person who[se] scope of mind, or whose range in a particular science, includes all, the whole known universe."⁸ And the poem "Kosmos" tells us that such a mind follows the clews of poetic figures; here, a kosmos is he or she

Who, out of the theory of the earth and of his or her body understands by
    subtle analogies all other theories,
The theory of a city, a poem, and of the large politics of these States.
                                                                    [*LG*, 392–93]

The cosmos interlocks in a "vast similitude," and the poet who is a kosmos holds the key (*LG*, 714) to its cipher and can unlock its secrets: "All are written to me, and I must get what the writing means" (*LG*, 47).

     Whitman's search for such clues to the underlying identity of writing and nature guides his development into a poet of death. "The Sleepers," which is coeval with "Song of Myself," already hints at what Whitman will make explicit in "Democratic Vistas"—that the poets of democracy will have to be great poets of death.⁹ For traffic with nature courses two ways, and to invoke Eros, the compositional, creative life force Whitman also terms "attraction" and "adhesiveness," is also to invoke Thanatos. In Whitman's vision, when the "great coming literatus" composes "the great poem of death," "man" will "take his right place, prepared for life, master of fortune and misfortune. And then that which was long wanted will be supplied, and the ship that had it not before in all her voyages, will have an anchor" (*PW*, 421). In "The Sleepers," poetic similitudes and attractions have their anchor in an actual similitude in nature. As the poet descends into the unconscious—the poetic or "likening" night—he makes connections to archetypal and generic likenesses such as the unconscious, night, death, the sea, and the womb. At the same time that he enters into his equalizing medium of poetic language with its archetypal identities, he enters nature and discovers a natural equality. Contemplating the "solemn" sleepers "stretch'd and still" (*LG*, 424), he writes:

I swear they are averaged now—one is no better than the other,
The night and sleep have liken'd them and restored them.   [*LG*, 431]

If "Song of Myself" celebrates diversity by relying on a faith in a central identity, "The Sleepers" pays homage to that identity; if "Song of Myself" is politically aggressive and celebrates the "teeming nation of nations" (*LG*, 711), "The Sleepers" sends all the immigrants back home, saluting "common mortality and death, man's great equalizers" (*PW*, 547). For if Eros is the constructive principle of physical phenomena, poems, and the polis alike, and if it can allay metaphysical, epistemological, and political doubts,[10] it can anchor itself only in and as death. In "Scented Herbage of My Breast" (1860), Whitman appeals directly to the basic identity of death to authorize his own "show of appearance":

Emblematic and capricious blades I leave you, now you serve me not,

.   .   .   .

Give me your tone therefore O death, that I may accord with it,
Give me yourself, for I see that you belong to me now above all, and are folded
    inseparably together, you love and death are,

.   .   .   .

For now it is convey'd to me that you are the purports essential,
That you hide in these shifting forms of life, for reasons, and that they are
    mainly for you,
That you beyond them come forth to remain, the real reality,
That behind the mask of materials you patiently wait, no matter how long.

                                                            [*LG,* 114–15]

The echo of "Crossing Brooklyn Ferry" (1856)—"You have waited, you always wait, you dumb, beautiful ministers" (*LG,* 165)—marks the change: the synchronic matrix that sustains all diachronic identities and metamorphoses and constitutes their "real" identity is now defined as death.

In "Out of the Cradle Endlessly Rocking" Whitman is in full possession of this new key—this basic fact *and* the "delicious word," "the word final, superior to all" (*LG,* 252)—that unlocks another vast similitude. The shared experience of love and loss links all creation together and empowers the emerging poet to tally birdsong, his own troubling emotions, and the vast background of nature and authorizes him to "translate" them in personifications and narratives. Whitman's new key gives him access to a broader range of rhetorical and literary devices while enabling him to maintain his anagogic conception of poetic language. Without the narrative that frames the "reminiscence" of the poem, the poet could not work back to the key word, the word that unlocked nature and natural similitudes for him. Without possessing the key word that authorizes his language, however, he could not frame his narrative, for the very narrative—its temporal "syntax"—is made possible by the knowledge of loss. The structure of the story and its purport— that all true stories end in death—are mutually empowering forces that make the poem's equilibrium.

Moreover, the key is now also a "clef"—a variant Whitman sometimes uses, as in "On the Beach at Night Alone"—for it sets the key for song. Poetic music, too, superimposes a "struck" identity and an identity at base, the language of the poet-child and the base rhythm of the mother-sea, the "aria" of individual loss and the backdrop of "the undertone, the savage old mother incessantly crying" (*LG,* 251). The poet can join a community of loss and adequately translate the bird's loss into words only if he can also translate his words into nature. For poetic meaning and music are empowered by the very force that would negate them. Whitman's language counterpoints the two isomorphic poetries: the "aria"—ordered, "crafted"—and the "dirge" of the sea, which echoes the base rhythm of Whitman's cadences, the cosmic music of loss inscribed in poetic language. And the "death" of this rhythm eternally counterpoints the "loved" of articulation, whether in communal, narrative, or grammatical "adhesions."

"Death, death, death, death, death" is thus the key line in the poem; it superimposes not only a word and a fact but a meaningful phoneme and a meaningless sound. Its superscription marks the limits of language, for language is reduced to nature here, as when a word repeated too many times loses its meaning and becomes mere sound. Conversely, the line marks the limits of nature, for death is reduced to a mere word repeated in a basic five-stress line of poetry.[11] Here, the epistemological boundary of language and the physical bounds of nature coincide. The irreducible, tautological reality and the impenetrable phoneme are one: "death" is death, sound is meaning, form is content. Against the backdrop of this maternal, synchronic identity play the "struck" identities or "adhesive" forces of similitude and metaphor, love and syntax, memory and narrative, loss and song. "Death," the "word up from the waves" (*LG,* 253), is the only word nature speaks in the poem, for all other words are presented as tallied. And "death" authorizes the poem's narrative and rhetoric, for it is the word that links language to nature; it is the omphalos of language.[12] The word of transubstantiation, "death" is "sweet" and "delicious"; it plays on the tongue and is the bread and the wine that inspire the breath of poetry.

But it is still a word, and "As I Ebb'd with the Ocean of Life" spells out the doubts that must shadow the poetic dream-desire of "Cradle." "As I Ebb'd" deconstructs the natural language that "Cradle" celebrates. In "Cradle," nature is the beginning and the end of poetic language, and in between darts the poet's musical shuttle, weaving together beginning and end, love and death. In "As I Ebb'd," however, the poet's dream of merging with the world, of being taken up again in the sea's "cradle," is shown to be only a dream. The interlocking similitude seems to be broken, as "the real Me" remains untouched by words, "untold, altogether unreach'd" (*LG,* 254); natural objects are no longer "dumb, beautiful ministers" but "debris"; and the poet's words, if they survive him, will not inscribe nature's hieroglyph on the very ground and air but remain more "chaff." The poet walks the Paumanok shoreline, seeking "types" or connections between nature and spirit. Without such "types," the poem's writing or type—letters, signs, and lines—is also merely a "*trail* of drift and debris," a few "dead *leaves*," a "little wash'd-up *drift*," a few "*lines* underfoot" (*LG*, 253–55; emphasis mine).

The words Whitman uses here all have double meanings, referring at once to an unredeemed nature and to an unauthorized poetry. For when the link between natural facts and spirit is broken, not only nature but the poet's language is reduced to chaff—useless husks and idle chatter. The life-giving, incarnate spirit seems "withdrawn far" (*LG*, 254); it is only a "phantom" (*LG*, 255), a disembodied ghost. The phantom may also allude to the "Phantom," "the genius of poets of old lands," which Whitman begins *Leaves of Grass* by simultaneously invoking and challenging (*LG*, 2). In this case, the poet's failure is basic, for if language cannot also be the hieroglyph of nature, it will be reduced to a mere "text," mere "writing."[13]

Yet Whitman confesses his failure to comprehend nature by using the very devices that would signify his understanding of it. In other words, he mourns his inability to discover the "types" capable of recharging his dejected body and his lines alike by using puns. But these are neither capricious nor willed. If language fails nature, it is itself not to be encompassed; its innate metaphoric structure, its natural plenitude, its given meaningfulness and connectedness all mark its isomorphism with nature, as Whitman's series of double-entendres underscores. The poet "wends" (from "to turn," "to change") a "shoreline" that is both natural and linguistic, "con-versing" and "converting." The shoreline demarcated by the drift of his life and words divides and joins his life and death, land and sea, a language of similitudes and given identities. In his double passage, he leaves behind him lines of poetry, dead leaves, just as the ocean leaves sea drift—which also links motion and meaning. Thus likenesses constitute the line that rims the known and the unknown and seem to be basic—to inhere in language, to structure it below faith, ideology, or rhetoric. Consolation is built into the failure, then. The poem calls to mind those astounding moments of revelation in the *Cantos* when Ezra Pound raises his head from his all-absorbing work and experiences an epiphanic recognition of his failure, which is at the same time his success, for it gives him a glimpse of what *does* cohere, even if his "notes" do not:

We, capricious, brought hither we know not whence, spread out before you,
You up there walking or sitting,
Whoever you are, we too lie in drifts at your feet.   [*LG*, 256]

It is impossible to fail in this project, for whether or not the poet can always articulate it, the center does hold, and "it is not chaos or death—it is form, union, plan" (*LG*, 88).

THE FORM

Speech is the twin of my vision,
  it is unequal to measure itself
        "Song of Myself"

Whitman's faith in a basic identity shapes every feature of his poetry. This belief yields, for example, an ethic of sympathy, and such a "natural" morality licenses the psychology of identification and projection, justifying the patternless patterns of his poems. The poet is able to move in and out of other lives, for all people feel and think alike, share the same desires, and make the same connections, because we are all constructed alike.

Section 11 of "Song of Myself" is a parable of this faith: the young men bathing, the woman, and the poet all wade in one psychic pool. Thus the poet's desire, which inspires figurative cohesions and adhesions and gives birth to poems, is isomorphic with the woman's desire, which inspires her psychological projection and links her to what she is separated from. The poet can ingest the world in "omnivorous" lines that declare, "All this I swallow, it tastes good, I like it well, it becomes mine, / I am the man, I suffer'd, I was there" (*LG*, 66), and can ask, "We understand then do we not?" (*LG*, 164), because we are woven of the same natural fiber and our desires weave the same text. Since identity backs up difference, order and disorder are not antithetical or even distinct, and poetic composition is no longer subject to the authority of such a hierarchy. Another formal implication of Whitman's faith is that beginnings and ends must not be privileged but should be treated as "arbitrary" moments plucked out of a continuum. Indeed, Whitman rejects the mediation of *a priori* structurings, whether formal or theoretical, in order to present the drift of the force gathering in words and disclosing a whole larger than what they encompass.

The perceiver and reporter of the unities and identities running through dualities, contraries, and varieties becomes, in Whitman's term, an *ensemblist*. As an example of such a thinker, he cites Hegel and distinguishes him from Schelling, whose thinking is analogical:

According to Hegel the whole earth, (an old nucleus-thought, as in the Vedas, and no doubt before, but never hitherto brought so absolutely to the front, fully surcharged with modern scientism and facts, and made the sole entrance to each and all,) with its infinite variety, the past, the surroundings of to-day, or what may happen in the future, the contrarieties of material with spiritual, and of natural with artificial, are all, to the eye of the *ensemblist*, but necessary sides and unfoldings, different steps or links, in the endless process of Creative thought, which, amid numberless apparent failures and contradictions, is held together by central and never-broken unity—not contradictions or failures at all, but radiations of one consistent and eternal purpose. [*PW,* 259]

In his poetic incarnation, the *ensemblist* is both an "assembler" and a "semblance-maker." Such a poet, who links things quantitatively and qualitatively, can say all and thereby All. The axes of metonymy and metaphor, by which Roman Jakobson designates the compositional procedures of prose and poetry, now coincide.[14] The "kosmic" poem is realistic as well as mythic, both a collage and an "orbic," autochthonous whole. This conception of poetry accounts for Whitman's stylistic peculiarities. Since the microcosm and the macrocosm are one and the same, Whitman can go to the limits of fragmentation to realize his purpose of unity; he can both insist that he speaks the "origin of all poems" and make his language locally and historically specific with slang, lists of proper names, and the use or misuse of foreign words. Not surprisingly, his stylistic impurities proved to be as offensive to some nineteenth-century readers as his enumerating the parts and functions of the body was to others. Here, too, Whitman violates a certain decorum of literary language in presenting the body of language *as* body in order to reveal its soul. He uses slang, for example, not so much for realism as for the "realization" of language, the resuscitation of its creative power by "breathing into its nostrils the breath of life" (*PW,* 577). Spoken language, whether defined physiologically by emphasizing the voice or sociologically with an emphasis on slang and Americanisms, is a local usage that discloses the universal creative force running through all usages.

Similarly, Whitman's much-lamented fondness for foreign phrases, including his misappropriations and abuses, hints at an isomorphism of languages and suggests that the fragmentation of Babel might be reversed by violating the sanctities of separate languages, whether English or "poetic." In "The Primer of Words" Whitman writes: "A great observation will detect sameness through all languages, however old, however new, however polished, however rude. —As humanity is one, under its amazing diversities, language is one under its. —The flippant, reading on some long-past age, wonder at its dead costumes, its amusements, &c.; but the master, understands well the old, ever-new, ever-common grounds, below those animal growths" (*DN,* 730). And in "Slang in America" Whitman calls language "a sort of universal absorber, combiner, and conqueror. The scope of its etymologies is the scope not only of man and civilization, but the history of Nature in all departments, and of the organic Universe, brought up to date; for all are comprehended in words, and their backgrounds" (*PW,* 572).

Finally, "the extraordinary jumbles and strings of names, places, employments, which deface his pages,"[15] are especially necessary, exhibiting in the same breath the coincidence of a historically specific yet universal natural language. The axis that is "without name" ("I do not know it—it is without name—it is a word unsaid, / It is not in any dictionary, utterance, symbol" [*LG,* 88]) is coded in names. One example is his use of Indian names:

The red aborigines,
Leaving natural breaths, sounds of rain and winds, calls as of birds and animals
    in the woods, syllabled to us for names,
Okonee, Koosa, Ottawa, Monongahela, Sauk, Natchez, Chattahoochee, Kaqueta,
    Oronoco,
Wabash, Miami, Saginaw, Chippewa, Oshkosh, Walla-Walla,
Leaving such to the States they melt, they depart, charging the water and the
    land with names.   [*LG,* 26]

Although this is a particularly masterly example, the principle at work here is the principle that authorizes Whitman's specificity in general. Names inhere in or pierce nature; they superimpose facts and language. For instance, when Whitman asks for "something specific and perfect" for his city—something specific and complete—"Whereupon lo! upsprang the aboriginal name," "Mannahatta":

Now I see what there is in a name, a word, liquid, sane, unruly, musical, self-
    sufficient,
I see that the word of my city is that word from of old,
Because I see that *word nested in nests of water-bays,* superb,
Rich, hemm'd thick all around with sailships and steamships, an island sixteen
    miles long, solid-founded.   [*LG,* 474; emphasis mine]

The poem ends with "City nested in bays! my city!" and thereby completes the equation of name and place. Whitman's notebooks reveal the source of his interest in aboriginal names: "*Names of cities, islands, rivers, new settlements, &c.* These should/must assimilate in sentiment and in sound, to something organic in the place, or identical with it" (*DN,* 705). Thus names are privileged, absolute words: "There are people who say it is not important about names,—one word is as good as another, if the designation be understood.—I say that nothing is more important than names. . . . Great clusters of nomenclature, is [*sic*] a land" (*DN,* 753–54). Hence the necessity for *American* names—for places, cities, states, days, and months. "*All lies folded in names,*" Whitman announces (*DN,* 755), and suggests that names infold a future as well as a history; they are both records of growths and predictions: "Names are the turning point of who shall be master" (*DN,* 756).

Names in particular[16] and words in general constitute for Whitman a grid along which history runs and patterns itself. "What a history is folded, folded inward and inward again, in the single word I" (*DN*, 733), he marvels. And if human history is inscribed in and courses through the channels of words, changes in history and grammar, politics and poetics, are isomorphic. Indeed, the "inscription" that retroactively inaugurates *Leaves of Grass* superscribes a new poetics and a new politics and marks an historical intersection that locates both the politics and the poetry:

One's-Self I sing, a simple separate *person,*
Yet utter the *word* Democratic, the *word* En-Masse.   [*LG*, 1; emphasis mine]

Political reasons dictate the necessity of forging a poetic language that conjoins persons and words: in the absence of any racial, historical, or geographical basis for a national identity, America needs poetry to make it cohere. The nation's history originates as a violent break with history, beginning with the revolutionary sloughing of the past and repeated with every immigration; it demands an original and autochthonous poetry that divorces authority from history. Americans are not a "race" but "the race of races" (*LG*, 713), "a teeming nation of nations" (*LG*, 711), and America coheres only in such hyperboles. Its political ideology is defined in paradoxes and oxymorons ("One's-Self I sing, a simple separate person, / Yet utter the word Democratic, the word En-Masse"); its unity in diversity turns on metonymy and synecdoche. And the language that tallies this politics—that takes account of and accounts for it—becomes politicized in turn. Its poetic figures become more than rhetorical ornaments; oratory coincides with oracular revelation, disclosing qualitative as well as quantitative equivalencies at the origin of the life of the polis and the language of the poem. For "these grand cosmic politics of ours" (*PW*, 391) are another ply or leaf of the Whitmanic "ply over ply" cosmos-kosmos.[17]

   Just as Whitman's political faith is inscribed with poetic tropes, his poetics imply a politics. The isomorphism of the political and the poetical appears in Whitman's form as well. For example, the speaker of "Song of Myself" does not speak a privileged, subjective language any more than he speaks a special poetic or figurative language. His speech amounts to a revision of a politics encoded within language, especially the language codified by "ultramarine" grammarians (*DN*, 810). Northrop Frye has noted a central segment of this code: "The word 'subject' in English means the observer of the objective, and it also has the political meaning of an individual subordinated to the authority of his society or its ruler, as in 'British subject.'"[18] Whitman's political faith in a rule without subjects—in a coincidence of law and freedom, as he spells it out in "Democratic Vistas"—entails a psychological and epistemological revision of the subject as an inner observer subjected to an authoritative, "objective," observed world. If we fail to register this political and historical process enmeshed in his grammar and language, Whitman and his "equations" will appear "facile."[19] In his equation of subject and object, political hierarchies and psychological dualities disappear concurrently. As a result, generic categories likewise break down. For example, how is "Song of Myself" to be classified? Is the poem a lyric or an epic; is its "I" the observed or an observer; and does the poem unify a fragmented objective experience, or does it fragment a unified subjective state?[20]

In Whitman's orbic whole, then, formal and political changes are isomorphic: "political liberty, which is the animus of all liberty" (*LG*, 729), underwrites a concurrent urge in the arts to "make it new" and directs the shaping of the "new free forms" (*LG*, 719). Whitman's speaker is not only a literary and biological "filter" but a political one. Through him flows the spirit that animates facts and history, that shapes bodies and geography, poems and cities, myths and civilizations. Thus his "revisions" and irregularities are fully licensed: "The Real Grammar will be that which declares itself a nucleus of the spirit of the laws, with liberty to all to carry out the the the [*sic*] spirit of the laws, even by violating them, if necessary" (*DN*, 735). And he reiterates that "real grammar, vast, deep, perennial, has plenty of room for eccentricities and what are supposed to be gaucheries.—and violations.—" (*DN*, 810).

Whitman's free verse similarly grows out of his "purports." His somewhat paradoxical eagerness to legitimize his "barbaric yawp" (*LG*, 89)—symptomatic of being a belated autochthonous poet, of the vicissitudes of being "both in and out of the game" (*LG*, 32)—led him to append Emerson's letter of praise to the second printing of *Leaves of Grass* and thus publicly to forge a link that it has become habitual to affirm. Whitman has consistently been seen in the shadow of Emerson—as a follower, a disciple, or an uncanny incarnation of Emerson's prophecy of the "American Poet"—despite their subsequent disowning of each other. In the confusion engendered by this link, Emerson's formalism has been ignored and Emerson reduced to an unsuccessful practitioner of his own proto-Whitmanic preachings, and the nature of Whitman's poetic discovery has been obscured by being seen within the conceptual framework of Emerson's poetic theory.

However one interprets it, Emerson's "metre-making argument" preserves meter in poetry and maintains the duality of form and force or argument. Emerson only reverses the presumed order of operations: instead of meter determining the argument, he insists, the argument ought to determine—as it invariably will—the meter. His understanding of meter never strays far from the framework of English measures, and his most radical break with the norm of blank verse consists simply of a return to an older English meter—a two-stress or a two-part, four-stress line. Because Emerson's theory has been so consistently interpreted according to Whitman's practice, Emerson's "metre" has never been taken to mean meter. Whitman would not have made this mistake. When he uses the term "meter," he is always clearly referring to traditional English meters; the word is not used in connection with his own poetry. For Whitman does away with the very distinction between meter and argument that Emerson depends on. Just as Whitman's symbolism denies the hierarchical duality of "seen" form and "unseen" significance, of vehicle and tenor, his verse form rejects the invidious dualism of meter and argument—the significance or inner truth housed in mere meters. For Whitman, the inner and the outer coincide, and his argument is no more an "argument" than his meter is a "metre"—a merely formal, quantitative measurement or, at least, a quantifying qualitative feature of verse.[21]

Thus Whitman can at the same time regard *Leaves of Grass* as only a "language experiment" and make such a statement as "the words of my book nothing, the drift of it every thing" (*LG*, 13).[22] These two pronouncements appear contradictory only if form and content are seen as distinct and opposed. If we accept both statements as accurately describing Whitman's aims in *Leaves of Grass,* we see how his form and drift are one. To begin with, his very rejection of conventional metrical measures constitutes an argument. To subscribe to a metrical system would render American literary language dependent on English literary history, and such a subjection to formal mediation and deputation would violate both the metaphysical and the political principles underwriting Whitman's poetry. Moreover, nonmetrical verse itself seems to communicate certain values or content. For example, the free verse of "Song of Myself" seems, in Paul Fussell's words, "virtually to determine that the theme of the poem will be 'freedom' and flux as distinguished from the enclosing 'houses and rooms' of traditional metrical lines and poetic forms."[23] "Freed" from convention, such verse can, by extension, tap other "freedoms"; thus Whitman's metrically free, end-punctuated and syntactically independent lines and the loose "federated" arrangement of his line-groups and stanzas may be read as embodying his political and metaphysical "purports."

At the same time, his verse revitalizes conventional forms as well, for even as he relinquishes English meters, Whitman renders them effective expressive devices. When the occasion demands, he can use a perfect iambic pentameter line almost as an allusion. In "When I Heard the Learn'd Astronomer," Whitman clinches his argument for the superiority of poetic vision to the astronomer's measurements by countering the long labored lines describing the astronomer's procedures—"When I was shown the charts and diagrams, to add, divide, and measure them"—with a regular final line: "Look'd up in perfect silence at the stars" (*LG,* 271). Curiously, the iambic pentameter substantiates the poet's claim to superior vision with an allusion to a formal measurement and the poetic authority encoded in English meters. Such a move is not inconsistent with Whitman's poetics, because here, too, a certain content, value, or argument is shown to inhere in a certain form—at least when that form is chosen and used as an expressive or rhetorical device rather than as a mere convention. Whitman's use of other conventional devices such as alliteration, internal rhymes, and assonance has the same rationale.

All of Whitman's formal choices are open to such interpretation, for his form is always already an argument. Such a coincidence of form and content is part of his project of autochthonous poems. The specific poetic devices he uses to replace English meters derive from his paradoxical precedent for autochthonous writing, the Bible.[24] From the start, Whitman's readers have observed that his work is fashioned after Old Testament verse with its determining device of parallelism, which Gay Wilson Allen was the first to analyze.[25] The Bible provided the most appropriate model for Whitman partly because his project of writing the "New Bible" (*LG,* 765) could only benefit from alluding to the authorized King James version his readers relied upon for their history, prophecy, and wisdom. But the Bible also offered an example of writing that was more than literature—that was both a history and a metaphysic infusing the history with meaning. Most important for Whitman's form, the same fusion of fact and meaning informed the linguistic structure of Biblical writing. For Biblical verse is measured according to the rhythm of thought, which closely corresponds to syntactic rhythms. Unlike meter, which measures the physical properties of words and thereby posits a mutually affecting dialogue with a nonphysical semantic content, the parallel structure of Old Testament verse recognizes no such duality. Biblical verse structures lines on the basis of phonetic, syntactic, *or* semantic parallelism, which includes contrasts and modifications as well as repetitions and elaborations. The lines are units of thought, and all or any of these linguistic features may be used, together or interchangeably, to mark verse units. The device of parallelism enables Whitman to wed his sense to his verse structure; it enables his argument to integrate with and to "measure" his words. As he writes, "Speech is the twin of my vision, it is unequal to measure itself" (*LG,*

55); thus the distinction between quantity (measure) and quality (vision) dissolves.

Just as purely formal elements function rhetorically in Whitman's verse, syntax also plays more than a formal role. His use of periodic sentences in the opening lines of "Out of the Cradle" and in "When Lilacs Last in the Dooryard Bloom'd" to establish continuity and cyclicality is one example; another is his use of inversions, as in "Song of Myself":

Here and there with dimes on the eyes walking,
To feed the greed of the belly the brains liberally spooning,
Tickets buying, taking, selling, but in to the feast never once going,
Many sweating, ploughing, thrashing, and then the chaff for payment receiving,
A few idly owning, and they the wheat continually claiming.   [*LG*, 77]

Here, too, meaning inheres in syntax, for the inverted order is isomorphic with the perversions of human nature the lines describe. Such devices tend to bring poetic and prose composition closer together, and once again Whitman's practice approaches the writing of the Old Testament. In his study of Biblical verse, James L. Kugel effectively denies any clear-cut distinction between poetry and prose in the Bible and considers such a distinction to be a Hellenistic dualism imposed on Biblical writing. According to Kugel, parallelism is not a trope but *the* trope of Biblical language, structuring it at all levels; he characterizes this inherent structure as a "natural reflex" of the language. Prose and poetry do not constitute two distinct modes but form a continuum that runs from the least to the most marked use of various parallelistic devices. When the parallelism becomes more insistent and regular, a heightened rhythm emerges, and such a heightening marks a rhetorical or emotional emphasis and is closely allied to the development of content.[26]

This idea is useful for understanding Whitman, who distinguishes between prose and poetry—his prefaces, notes, and essays come in prose, his poems in verses—yet lifts segments of prose from his prefaces and writes them out, largely unchanged, in verse.[27] Accordingly, while he makes a distinction between poetry and prose, he does not establish a hierarchy of higher and lower modes. In his 1876 preface he proposes that the two "veins, or strata" of the book—"politics for one, and for the other, the pensive thought of immortality"—account for its double structure, "the prose and poetic, the dual forms of the present book" (*LG*, 748). Just as "politics" and "the thought of immortality" are distinct yet mark points on one continuum of "kosmic" identities, poetry and prose are distinct insofar as they designate points on the continuum of written language—the phonetic, syntactic, and semantic patterning that shapes all language. Poetry and prose are not mutually exclusive categories, as the distance of English metrical verse from nonmetrical prose might suggest:

In my opinion the time has arrived to essentially break down the barriers of form between prose and poetry. I say the latter is henceforth to win and maintain its character regardless of rhyme, and the measurement-rules of iambic, spondee, dactyl, &c., and that even if rhyme and those measurements continue to furnish the medium for inferior writers and themes, (especially for persiflage and the comic . . .) the truest and greatest *Poetry,* (while subtly and necessarily always rhythmic, and distinguishable easily enough,) can never again, in the English language, be express'd in arbitrary and rhyming metre, any more than the greatest eloquence, or the truest power and passion. [*PW,* 519]

Thus it appears that autochthonous poems must regather the historical diffusion of the authority of language into poetry (metrical) and prose (nonmetrical). Whitman's "measures" cross poetry and prose by appealing to the structural properties of language; he tallies form and force or argument in the compositional drift of language. And by aligning semantic, phonetic, and syntactic patterns and structures, he grounds phonetic repetitions in the substantial equivalencies of his content and bases semantic parallels on the rhetorical predisposition of syntactic structures. To cite only one example:

I am the poet of the Body and I am the poet of the Soul,
The pleasures of heaven are with me and the pains of
      hell are with me.   [*LG,* 48]

The syntactic parallelism of the first line underwrites the argued equivalence of "Body" and "Soul"; the second line reinforces the syntactic pattern with a phonetic patterning. A formal equivalence appears in the body of language (syntax and the alliteration of *p*s and *h*s) and is isomorphic with the argument or content of the lines. Thus the lines are autochthonous: for proof, they need only point to themselves.

Whitman's originality, then, comes into focus. Seeking a language in which "Nature" may speak with "original energy," he rejects English meters and their conceptual basis and turns instead to the Bible—an "original" literature—for a model of how the inherent, structural properties of the English language might be formally emphasized in order to let language "speak."[28] While a dualism of sound and sense shapes English poetry as a dialogue between meter and argument, Whitman attempts to disclose an identity of sound and sense—to offer a glimpse of a fecund, generative matrix of language out of which different senses and sounds are "struck." His leaves infold this identity, at once disclosing the "origin of all poems" and discoursing in words, lines, and tropes. Thus his language is at once oracular and oratorical. His nonmetrical verse alludes to the rhythms of public speech, wherein emphasis is determined not by meters but by argument and follows upon context, sense, and syntax, so that quantitative stress coincides with qualitative emphasis. His techniques for structuring his lines—repetition or anaphora that favors syntax and chiastic caesuras that formalize speech or thought rhythms—are all oratorical devices. Yet such devices also character-ize the rhythms of oracular verse, as in the Bible or the Koran. According to Northrop Frye, an "oracular or associational rhythm, the unit of which is neither the prose sentence nor the metrical line, but a kind of thought-breath or phrase," stands between poetry (metrical rhythm) and prose (discursive rhythm) and can characterize both poems ("free verse") and prose ("stream of consciousness").[29] Thus the coincidence of politics and metaphysics shapes the form as well as the figuration of Whitman's oratorical/oracular poetry. And since this "infolding" language is self-generating and self-autho-rizing, even the poet is not master of what he says; even he cannot contest his words. For example, Whitman challenges his own words:

> . . . you conceive too much of articulation,
> Do you not know O speech how the buds beneath you are
>   folded?
> Waiting in gloom, protected by frost,
> The dirt receding before my prophetical screams.   [*LG*, 55]

Yet his challenging of "articulation" is made possible by his own authorizing articulation—the pun of "leaves of grass," the folded "buds" beneath speech—and his question amounts to an affirmation. It is impossible to challenge a language both contingent and absolute, for its "identities" infold all difference, making "the whole coincide" (*LG*, 21).

Chapter Eight

*E*zra Pound's Hard Currency

> The root is thru all of it,
> a tone in all public teaching:
> This is not a work of fiction
> nor yet of one man:
>
> . . . .
>
> The whole tribe is from one man's body,
> what other way can you think of it?
>
> *Cantos,* 99

Ezra Pound wrote in 1933, "Mr. Eliot and I are in agreement . . . in so far as we both believe that existing works form a complete order which is changed by the introduction of the 'really new' work." But he offered a qualification that measures the radical "disagreement" between the two poets: "'Existing monuments form an ideal order among themselves.' It would be healthier to use a zoological term rather than the word monument. It is much easier to think of the *Odyssey* or *Le Testament* or Catallus' *Epithalamium* as something living than as a series of cenotaphs. After all, Homer, Villon, Propertius, speak of the world as I know it."[1] For Pound, the tradition is not "a set of fetters to bind us" (*LE,* 91), and it is not an archaeology: "We do NOT know the past in chronological sequence" of "anesthetized" data; "what we know we know by ripples and spirals eddying out from us and from our own time" (*GK,* 60).

Pound's is a "live tradition," and it can be "gathered from the air" (81:522). "The best of knowledge is 'in the air'" (*SP,* 23), he insists, and the kind of learning he values is "knowing that is in people, 'in the air'" (*GK,* 57). *Paideuma,* "the gristly roots of ideas that are in action" (*GK,* 58), is a term he borrows from Leo Frobenius, who is one of Pound's models: "His archaeology is not retrospective, it is immediate," Pound writes; it "goes not only into past and forgotten life, but points to tomorrow's water supply" (*GK,* 57). Pound's own "immediate" archaeology would be similarly pro-jective, weaving both backward and forward, ranging farther—in Whitman's words—to "nearer bring."

Whitman begins such a "living" tradition[2] in America. The nation, Pound writes, "wanted a tradition like other nations, and it got Longfellow's 'Tales of a Wayside Inn' and 'Hiawatha' and 'Evangeline'" (*SP,* 124). By contrast, Whitman sounds "our American keynote" (*SP,* 123): he "established the national *timbre,*" and "it is in the air, this tonic of his" (*SP,* 124). Concluding his essay "Patria Mia," Pound explicitly aligns himself with Whitman and thereby proves that poetry is a "living art," "changing and developing, always the same at root, never the same in appearance for two decades in succession" (*SP,* 114): "It is a great thing, reading a man to know, not 'His Tricks are not as yet my Tricks, but I can easily make them mine' but 'His message is my message. We will see that men hear it'" (*SP,* 146).

For Pound, one force informs nature and texts alike, and this identity provides the basis for a living tradition:

> "We have," said Mencius, "but phenomena."
> monumenta. In nature are signatures
>   needing no verbal tradition,
> oak leaf never plane leaf.   [87:573]

Pound's American precedent here is Whitman, who also believes in "a tradition" that is "not mere epistemology" (87:573). Grounding the "signatures" of the "verbal tradition" in nature, Whitman writes in "Shakespere-Bacon's Cipher,"

> In each old song bequeath'd—in every noble page or text,
> (Different—something unreck'd before—some unsuspected author,)
> In every object, mountain, tree, and star—in every birth and life,
> As part of each—evolv'd from each—meaning, behind the ostent,
> A mystic cipher waits infolded.[3]

This "uniform hieroglyphic" (*LG,* 34) is the mystic meaning infolded in all "ostent" leaves, whether of books or grass, and

> O the blest eyes, the happy hearts,
> That see, that know the guiding thread so fine,
> Along the mighty labyrinth.   [*LG,* 228]

Pound, too, defines the "verbal tradition" as an inhering "cipher": writing does not represent[4] natural force but—like Plotinus's "body" that is "inside the soul" (98:685, 99:700, 113:788)—"in-heres" in it. And Pound's anagogic identification of writing with nature stems from the same root he shares with Whitman (*P*, 89)—the faith that "it is not chaos or death—it is form, union, plan" (*LG*, 88), and that the plan is pervasive:

The plan is in nature
rooted

[99:709]

Just as Whitman's grass bears God's "name" (*LG*, 33), Pound's grass seed, acorn, or cherry stone is "intelligent" (113:788), bearing the cipher or code that enables it to reproduce grass, oak trees, or cherries. This code, which writes the "nature of being oak or maple [that] extends to every part of the oak tree or maple," bespeaks an "indivisible . . . nature extending to every detail" (*SP*, 82). The name Pound gives this rooted intelligence, this "intimate essence," is "God" or *Theos* (*SP*, 49). He would agree with Whitman that

In this broad earth of ours,
Amid the measureless grossness and the slag,
Enclosed and safe within its central heart,
Nestles the seed perfection.

[*LG*, 226]

Although we are "utterly ignorant" (*SP*, 49) about this essence, we have a very real kinship to it: "I believe in a sort of permanent basis in humanity," Pound affirms. "Our kinship to the ox we have constantly thrust upon us; but beneath this is our kinship to the vital universe, to the tree and the living rock" (*SR*, 92). When Whitman asserts that he incorporates "gneiss, coal, long-threaded moss, fruits, grains, esculent roots" and is "stucco'd with quadrupeds and birds all over" (*LG*, 59), he affirms the same faith that "the soul or spirit transmits itself into all matter—into rocks, and can live the life of a rock—into the sea, and can feel itself the sea—into the oak, or other tree—into an animal, and feel itself a horse, a fish, or bird—into the earth—into the motions of the suns and stars."[5] Myths and poetry spring from this kinship: "We have about us the universe of fluid force, and below us the germinal universe of wood alive, of stone alive." Humans are isomorphic with nature, made up of "a few buckets of water, tied up in a complicated sort of fig-leaf," and a consciousness that in certain people is "germinal": "Their thoughts are in them as the thought of the tree is in the seed, or in the grass, or the grain, or the blossom. And these minds are the more poetic, and they affect mind about them, and transmute it as the seed the earth" (*SR*, 92–93).

Such a transmutation is what Whitman calls "translation" or tallying. Transmuting natural energy into verbal forms in effect reenacts the myths that codify our kinship to the vital universe by breathing life into them. Pound's "resuscitation" of dead languages (*P,* 187) is both literally a translation of texts and a passage of "air" through abiding patterns or codes.[6] The patterns are abiding not because they carry the authority of the past but because tradition only carries on the form/force that inheres in the nature of things. His use of a global tradition in the *Cantos* is neither an exoticism nor an archaism. It is meant to show that "'as a wind's breath / that changing its direction changeth its name'" (106:752), different languages, literatures, and ages variously name the same breath animating all life. Because the tradition records the shape of things, the poet's language is naturally allusive. Poetic ontogeny repeats phylogeny; organicism rewrites the tradition. In Whitman's words, "See—as the annual round returns the phantoms return" (*LG,* 299).

Such knowledge underwrites the chant of creaturely "humility" in canto 81:

Pull down thy vanity, it is not man
Made courage, or made order, or made grace,
　　Pull down thy vanity, I say pull down.
Learn of the green world what can be thy place
In scaled invention or true artistry   [81:521]

The pun on "scaled invention" is Pound's axis here: the poet bows before nature and scales down his pride before the artistry of scaled creatures, the "green casque" that has outdone his "elegance." Yet the entire canto 81, which reiterates "(To break the pentameter, that was the first heave)" (518), is also an extended homage to the scaled music of the English lyric tradition and indeed scales the very climax of its "awakening" to the pentameter:

What thou lovest well remains,
　　　　　　　the rest is dross
What thou lov'st well shall not be reft from thee
What thou lov'st well is thy true heritage.   [520–21]

In the same move, Pound scales his "vanity" to both nature and tradition yet concludes by reaffirming, in clear speech rhythms and diction, that his attempt to "make it new," to gather "from the air a live tradition," was not "vanity."[7] The *Cantos* extol such a community of nature, tradition, and the individual poet. The signatures in nature, the seeds that carry its mystic cipher, are borne on the wind, just as the verbal tradition is borne on the breath. And just as the "whole tribe is from one man's body" (99:708), its whole long tale is from one "man's" breath. The poet's respiration and inspiration, both his life and his song, partake of the same breath—in Whitman's words, "the common air that bathes the globe" (*LG,* 45).

This pervasive, life-bearing breath or spirit launches the poet on the journey of the *Cantos:*

> and winds from sternward
> Bore us out onward with bellying canvas,
> Circe's this craft, the trim-coifed goddess.   [1:3]

The life that Pound as Odysseus breathes into the verbal tradition, descending into the textual-chthonic underworld in order to begin the journey once again, is the same breath that carries on nature's reproductive processes, the same art or "craft" that bears on with bellying sail:

> "This wind roars in the earth's bag,
>   it lays the water with rushes."   [4:15]

Thus the *Cantos* can freely superimpose natural and textual patterns. For example, the Homeric story of a descent into the underworld is one of the "seeds" carried in the air of the *Cantos,* a germinal code that patterns more than one story of passage. The first canto proposes that this narrative pattern is abiding and informs, among others, the *Odyssey,* the *Aeneid,* the *Seafarer,* and the *Cantos.* It is also a natural pattern governing the daily or seasonal tropic cycles of the sun's descent and return and informing the array of vegetation myths that repeat:

> The light has entered the cave. Io! Io!
> The light has gone down into the cave,
> Splendour on splendour!
> By prong have I entered these hills:
> That the grass grow from my body,
> That I hear the roots speaking together,
> The air is new on my leaf,
> The forked boughs shake with the wind.
>
> . . . .
>
> By this door have I entered the hill.   [47:238]

And the new air of Pound's leaf—"measured" by "this gate" (47:237)—tells the old story Whitman tells, similarly identifying natural and human reproductive/productive processes.

For the pattern is not a "fiction" of "one man" (99:708): "by no man these verses" (49:244). It is not even a fiction of man: "ΟΥ ΤΙΣ / ΟΥ ΤΙΣ / 'I am noman, my name is noman'" (74:426). Just as "ΟΥ ΤΙΣ, ΟΥ ΤΙΣ? Odysseus / the name of my family" (74:425) is heard also in "the swallows crying: / 'Tis. 'Tis. Ytis!" (4:13–14), the "infant" ("without speech") wasp of canto 83 journeys after the same knowledge Odysseus seeks:

> The infant has descended,
>   from mud on the tent roof to Tellus,
> like to like colour he goes amid grass-blades
>   greeting them that swell under XTHONOS XΘONOΣ
> OI XΘONIOI; to carry our news
> εἰς Χσονιους to them that dwell under the earth,
> begotten of air, that shall sing in the bower
>   of Kore,   Περσεφονεια
> and have speech with Tiresias, Thebae   [83:533]

Our news does not need words; the imperative "Day by day make it new" (53:265) is itself "begotten of air," drawn from the sun's "tradition." Thus the verbal tradition is alive because it speaks of the living world, and when the poet finds himself in the "hell" of the Army's Disciplinary Training Center at Pisa—"OY TIΣ / a man on whom the sun has gone down" (74:430)—he begins to make it new dawn after dawn, to make Zeus rise again from Ceres's bosom (81:517). The sun's cycle, Adonis's myth, Odysseus's tradition, Brother Wasp's nature, and Pound's personal history all follow the same pattern and trace one "periplum." Pound composes his poem not only by superimposing isomorphic texts and "rhyming" historical periods; he also superimposes textual and natural patterns, bearing witness to an extratextual plan that underwrites intratextual isomorphisms and authorizes intertextual "rhymes."

Canto 2 presents a matrix of natural metamorphoses as a backdrop for the metamorphosis or evolution of the tradition the first canto embarks on. The first canto authorizes not only a metamorphic or changeable hero but a historically resonant language that sounds the "ages' and ages' encrustations" (*LG,* 544)[8]—the composite record of the poet-hero's changes—to show that

> The two, the past and present, have interchanged,
> I myself as connector, as chansonnier of a great future, am now speaking.
>   [*LG,* 299]

Accordingly, canto 2 authorizes a naturally metamorphic language by staging "perpetual transfers and promotions" (*LG,* 87), the ongoing transmutations of natural force. The *Cantos* transfer energy both through time, threading it from text to text, and through space, making it "flow thru" (116:797) form to form.[9] In canto 2, Ovid's story of Dionysus changing Acoetes's ship into a rock and his crew into fish underwrites such language as ends the canto—words compounding, changing, and evolving other words, etymologizing nature and bodying forth the birds', fauns', and frogs' "rewriting" of Odysseus's metamorphoses:

Glass-glint of wave in the tide-rips against sunlight,
　　pallor of Hesperus,
Grey peak of the wave,
　　wave, colour of grape's pulp,

Olive grey in the near,
　　far, smoke grey of the rock-slide,
Salmon-pink wings of the fish-hawk
　　cast grey shadows in water,
The tower like a one-eyed great goose
　　cranes up out of the olive-grove,

And we have heard the fauns chiding Proteus
　　in the smell of hay under the olive-trees,
And the frogs singing against the fauns
　　in the half-light.
And . . .   [2:10]

In this "half-light," natural and supernatural creatures cohabit in one matrix, appearing and disappearing, emerging and submerging into the fluid background. Here Pound presents a primal energy that patterns itself variously and steals into many forms, disguising and revealing itself over and over. He uses metamorphic compounds ("fish-hawk"), similes ("the tower like a one-eyed great goose"), puns ("cranes"), mythical metamorphic creatures ("fauns"), and actual metamorphic creatures ("frogs") to fashion a protean language that is isomorphic with the natural matrix of transformation. This passage, which inspires the poetic of a postmodernist like Gary Snyder, illustrates Pound's idea of metaphor not as analogy but as metamorphosis, a shift between different manifestations of one pervasive, Dionysian energy. The "wave, colour of grape's pulp," a "wine-red glow in the shallows" (2:7), in particular bears witness to the animating presence of Dionysus: it accounts at once for the shape of nature—the "wine-red algae" (2:9) off the coast of "Scios"—and for the tradition. "Scios" or Chios is an Aegean island claimed to be Homer's birthplace, and Pound's line traces Homer's "wine-dark sea" back to its pre-text, a natural landscape "written" by Dionysus. The "gods"—the immortal energy that Dionysus's many names name—inscribe the sea and underwrite the tradition. Thus nature and Pound's "live tradition" alike are "alight" (4:14) with gods:

The Gods have not returned. "They have never left us."
> They have not returned.
Cloud's processional and the air moves with their living.   [113:787]

As canto 2 presents it, right metaphor is a transfer of energy. Pound's ideogrammic figuration is indebted to Ernest Fenollosa's study of Chinese written characters. "Metaphor," Fenollosa proposes, "is at once the substance of nature and of language," for both "think" or "create" by transferring power, force, or energy, revealing vital links between phenomena. Fenollosa points out that the "two things added together" in Chinese compounds "do not produce a third thing but suggest some fundamental relation between them." He also insists that "the primitive metaphors do not spring from arbitrary subjective processes. They are possible only because they follow objective lines of relations in nature herself. Relations are more real and more important than the things which they relate. The forces which produce the branch-angles of an oak lay potent in the acorn. Similar lines of resistance, half curbing the out-pressing vitalities, govern the branching of rivers and of nations. Thus a nerve, a wire, a roadway, and a clearing house are only varying channels which communication forces for itself. This is more than analogy, it is identity of structure."[10] Such a vital, interconnected universe—what Hugh Kenner terms a universe of "patterned integrities"[11]—grounds a language that is "more" or "less" than rhetoric and works above or below the horizontal grid on which mere analogies are plotted. The kind of figuration that reveals structural identities is neither "explanatory metaphor" (*SP,* 374) nor mere "fustian and ornament" (*LE,* 162)—"false metaphor, ornamental metaphor," the business of the "rhetorician" (*SP,* 374)—and sometimes Pound calls such language "beyond metaphor" (*SR,* 33, 158). Laszlo Géfin, who considers Pound's "image," "vortex," and "ideogram" just different names for his abiding "juxtapositional" method, defines his stance as "antimetaphoric" and remarks that it rests on the "fundamental insight that the universe in all its manifestations is isomorphic."[12]

Relying on such a fundamental design, Pound can focus on discrete facts—the "luminous details" that "govern knowledge as the switchboard governs an electric circuit" (*SP,* 23)—and yet can hope to present the "intelligence of a period" (*SP,* 22), its *paideuma.* As Herbert Schneidau points out, "Pound's use of the principle of discontinuity . . . does not rest on a shallow appeal to the *Zeitgeist*—which for him is only the froth that obscures the *paideuma.*" Instead, Pound was reacting against "the canons of closure, unity, formalist coherence: the so-called metaphysical complicity of literature."[13] Yet the grounds of his reaction are less deconstructionist than mystical, attesting to the faith that the origin is "now"—that, in Whitman's words, "there was never any more inception than there is now" (*LG,* 30). A belief in an interconnected universe also entails a particular compositional method. In Pound's words, "Energy creates pattern"; in poetry, "emotion causes pattern to arise in the mind" (*SP,* 374). Thus "emotion is an organiser of form," and "form" includes imagery and timbre (*SP,* 375). Pound's "transformational" forms[14] identify emotion and pattern, force and form, nature and rhetoric. It is in this identification that we experience "freedom from time limits and space limits" (*LE,* 4), and the "sudden growth" that Pound's image offers is a clarity at once natural and transcendent. This is Pound's idea of "style, that is to say, limpidity, as opposed to rhetoric."[15]

The image that offers liberation from time limits in fact has a temporal or transitive structure that is isomorphic both with nature's own successive processes and with the processes of perception and thought. Natural process is a transformational or metamorphic passage, and such passage constitutes Pound's central poetic value: "The thing that matters in art is a sort of energy, something more or less like electricity or radioactivity, a force transfusing, welding, and unifying" (*LE,* 49). Good art effects a transference of energy and works like an ideogram, a coin with two faces, or a pun: it can flash one aspect or another ("fish-hawk"; "salmon-pink") and coheres empirically like the two sides of a coin or a pun. Such figuration approximates Chinese compounds with their "visible" metaphors and "visible" etymologies.[16] The reverse is a frozen art, an obstruction of the "flow," a petrification of energy, and its proper "anti-muse" is Medusa, ancestor of Geryon.[17] Accordingly, Pound's syntax is transitive. "Nature herself has no grammar," Fenollosa writes. "All processes in nature are inter-related; and thus there could be no complete sentence . . . save one which it would take all time to pronounce." Pound's energy flows through sentence fragments, by-passing grammar in order to follow the vital "lines of force" "pulsing" through the universe. Such transitive writing rids itself of what Fenollosa calls "the dead white plaster of the copula," so that "words crowd upon words, and enwrap each other in their luminous envelopes until sentences become clear, continuous light-bands."[18] This vision approaches Pound's "radiant world where one thought cuts through another with clean edge, a world of moving energies" (*LE,* 154). A world of light and clarity, where "Gods float in the azure air" (3:11), calls for a language patterned after the gods': "by hilaritas: gods; / and by speed in communication" (98:690). Of its very nature, such language radiates transparencies—"ply over ply" (4:15) of "plura diafana" (83:530).[19]

The perceptual basis of Pound's figuration and rhythm is likewise a vision that is metamorphic rather than one-directional or perspectival; it is a seeing and being seen, a changing and being changed:

A fat moon rises lop-sided over the mountain
The eyes, this time my world,
> But pass and look *from* mine
>> between my lids
>>> sea, sky, and pool
>>> alternate
>>> pool, sky, sea,

morning moon against sunrise
like a bit of the best antient greek coinage   [83:535]

The "antient" coinage is of the same "coin" as the *ming* ideogram, superimposing the sun and moon signs, coining the passage of time, turning the solar cycle, and flashing forth time's passage. Pound defines the *ming* ideogram as "the sun and moon, the total light process, the radiation, reception and reflection of light; hence, the intelligence. Bright, brightness, shining."[20] The ideogram superimposes not only natural time and timeless time but perception and understanding, for its meaning is both literal and figurative. In the ideogrammic vision of the above passage from canto 83, morning and night, sun and moon or the two "eyes" of the universe, and "inside" and "outside" "interpass, penetrate" (81:520). Like an ideogrammic compound or a pun, the "stance between the eyes" superimposes and alternates two images in order to focus a unified vision—both sight and *eidos.* Thus the physiology of sight is isomorphic with the *ming* ideogram, superimposing the two "eyes"— of the subject and the universe—at a central point of vision or light. Seeing is an ideogrammic process, and a poetic "image" that works by superposition is isomorphic with that process. The metamorphic "stance" between the two components of the one-image poem—of which "In a Station of the Metro" has become the paradigm—renders it more than a "bilateral" "contraposition" (*SP,* 452–53); it makes for a vision that transcends its components and offers, again, "sudden growth" and "freedom" (*LE,* 4). For in such a superimposition, mysticism and naturalism coincide. "All things that are are lights" because our eyes—through which we see and are seen—answer to light. "Man, earth: two halves of the tally" (82:526) are separated and linked by the eye. The space between the sun and the moon measures the sky's arch and coincides with the "stance between the eyes, / colour, diastasis"—giving rise to vision, perception of color, and "manifest" light. The brain's "dome" and the sky's exactly coincide, and this coincidence or "hypostasis" (81:520) is tallied by the eye.

In Pound, the eye's tallying the light of the mind and that of the sun replaces the tallying of metaphors. He insists that analogy is useless for seeing into the "intimate essence" of the universe, the *Theos:* "Confusion enters argument the moment one calls in analogy" (*SP,* 51). And he "speculates" on the reflective nature of analogy: "Religions have introduced analogy?" (*SP,* 51). Analogy cannot disclose anything of the intimate essence, which is not of the nature of human consciousness (*SP,* 49); it can only "speculate" a divinity in its own image, claiming further knowledge by comparison to something already known. Moreover, substitutive rhetorical strategies displace and defer force rather than transferring it and concur with other intransitive poetic structures like the teleological forms of grammar, narrative, and formal closure. The "theological" cognate of such a poetic is a religion of deferral, which postpones presence and holds out a "painted paradise" (74:436) at the end.

For Pound, however, "nor began nor ends anything" (114:793), and paradise is not artificial, nor does it wait at the end of time. It is a "jagged" paradise that is "in the air":

> Le Paradis n'est pas artificiel
>   but spezzato apparently
> it exists only in fragments unexpected excellent sausage,
>   the smell of mint, for example   [74:438]

When the gods are immanent and paradise can spring up in mint scenting the air, the poet's proper interest is in "equity / not in mere terminology" (97:680). "Equity" stresses the solid or net value of any currency, and "coin is the symbol of equity" (105:748). Equity in language consists of right naming, precision in wording: "The function of poets [is] to new-mint the speech" (*SP,* 361). And the pun on "mint" suggests that right naming links the poet to nature—"oak leaf never plane leaf"—and insures his part in the productive continuity of the earth:

> Wisdom lies next thee,
>   simply, past metaphor.
> Where I lie let the thyme rise
>   and basilicum
>   let the herbs rise in April abundant   [82:526]

"Wisdom" is not metaphor but passage and transformation; here, it is the metamorphosis of the human into the earth, so that his "lies" or false-hoods—his time, basilica, and mintage—translate to the truth "past meta-phor" in the earth, "by thy herbs menthe thyme and basilicum" (74:435). The literary isomorph of the reproductive/productive "coitu inluminatio" (74:435) is an understanding, by the light of the mind, past metaphor, past

symbolism, past the "capricious blades." Such a union is more than metaphoric, as the radiance of the above passage with its fertile puns testifies.

Significantly, the second usury canto (51) ends with the *cheng ming* ideogram, which denotes "precise verbal definition,"[21] for precise definitions in
economic and linguistic currency or script are cognates. For Pound, rhetorical and formal strategies of abstraction, absenting, and deferral mark a credit
economy, and credit is the temporal deferral of money: "The difference
between money and credit is one of time. Credit is the future tense of
money" (*SP,* 308). And, unlike a figuration backed up by "equity" or empirical coincidences, analogical metaphor is usurious: it creates excess "truth" or
value "out of nothing" or *ex nihilo.* Just as the creations of "vanity" (root:
"empty, nothing") cannot compare with poems made "out of a mouthful of
air" (*GK,* 152), usurious increase is a mockery of the gods' creating "out of
nothing":

> And, out of nothing, a breathing,
>   hot breath on my ankles,
> Beasts like shadows in glass,
>   a furred tail upon nothingness.
> .   .   .   .
>
>   void air taking pelt.
> Lifeless air become sinewed   [2:8]

Following Dante, Pound represents usury by "Geryon (fraud) of the mar-
vellous patterned hide" (*LE,* 211). Geryon, whose "craft" moves "backward,
backward" and carries Dante and Virgil deep into hell, is represented as a
fraudulent mimic of the real thing: "That filthy effigy / of fraud" wears the
face of a "just man, / so gracious was his features' outer semblance," and
justice signifies equity, whether in rhetoric or economy. Geryon's twisting,
serpentine body—again, a fake of the evil-vital life force—has a richly
patterned back: "No Turks or Tartars . . . nor had Arachne ever loomed such
webs." But his "patterned" hide hides the true pattern, the rooted plan. It
reproduces and falsifies the truth; it counterfeits nature's "craft" or breath:

> circling in eddying air; in a hurry;
> the 12: close eyed in the oily wind
> these were the regents; and a sour song from the folds
>   of his belly
> sang Geryone; I am the help of the aged;
> I pay men to talk peace;
> Mistress of many tongues . . .
> I am Geryon twin with usura   [51:251]

Geryon is indeed the proper guide to the lowest levels of Dante's eighth circle, where we meet frauds—falsifiers of persons (impersonators), precious metals (alchemists), coins (counterfeiters), and words (liars)—who could all boast "'how apt I was at aping nature.'" Dante equates the counterfeiting of money and words: "If I spoke false, you falsified the coin," one lost man accuses another.[22] Pound likewise links usury to a failure of right naming, the illusion and fraud purveyed and perpetrated by false metaphor or analogy:

Money is not a product of nature but an invention of man. . . . Metal is durable, but it does not reproduce itself. . . . The vegetable leads a more or less autonomous existence, but its natural reproductiveness can be increased by cultivation. The animal gives to and takes from the vegetable world: manure in exchange for food.

Fascinated by the lustre of a metal, man made it into chains. Then he invented something against nature, a false representation in the mineral world of laws which apply only to animals and vegetables. [*SP,* 346]

The equivalent danger of false representation in the arts is clear. By false analogies, humans leave their "root" in nature; indeed, they erect institutions that deny, pervert, and destroy the vital universe and its natural productivity. Again: "The error has been *pecuniolatry,* or the making of money into a god. This was due to a process of denaturalisation, by which our money has been given false attributes and powers that it should never have possessed. Gold is durable, but does not reproduce itself—not even if you put two bits of it together, one shaped like a cock, the other like a hen. It is absurd to speak of it as bearing fruit or yielding interest. Gold does not germinate like grain. To represent gold as doing this is to represent it falsely. It is a falsification. And the term *'falsificazione della moneta'* (counterfeiting or false-coining) may perhaps be derived from this" (*SP,* 348–49).

Nature's productivity is Pound's standard of value in politics and poetry as well as in economics. "The sick part of our philosophy is 'Greek splitting,'" Pound writes (*SP,* 85). "Greek philosophy, and European in its wake, degenerated into an attack on mythology and mythology is, perforce, totalitarian . . . . [It] tries to find an expression for reality without over-simplification, and without scission" (*SP,* 87). In these terms, "The Confucian is totalitarian. When the aims of Shun [2255–2205 B.C.] and Wan [1231–1135 B.C.] were set together, though after a thousand years interval, they were as two halves of a tally stick" (*SP,* 85). Such a total or totalitarian system of values bespeaks a basis in an abiding natural order: "That things can be known a hundred generations distant, implied no supernatural powers, it did imply the durability of natural process which alone gives a possibility for science" (*SP,* 86). The reason the Confucio-Mencian system appeals to Pound is that "at no point does . . . [it] splinter and split away from organic nature" (*SP*, 87), and by staying close to the organic universe, "honest men" will repeatedly come up with the same answers in ethics (*SP*, 89). The same axis centers poets in *their* tallying, which locates and brings together the "two halves" joined in their nature: "man, earth : two halves of the tally" (82:526). The ideograms *fu* and *chieh* are translated both as "halves of a tally stick" (77:476) and as "halves of a seal" (77:468). Such sound symbolization—and Kenner informs us that the Greek *symbol* also goes back to "tally sticks"[23]—is authorized or backed up by the permanence of organic nature and can underwrite, vouch for, or measure the soundness of economic, political, and ethical systems.[24]

In Pound's world, the golden light that gods "rain" down to impregnate the earth (4:15–16) also sets a "gold standard" of esthetic, political, and economic value. The imperative "Day by day make it new" derives from this standard of value—light and its dissemination. And the poet can work to further the process, to make "it flow thru" (116:797), for light answers to light like two halves of a tally. The light that "rains" and "pours"—"The liquid and rushing crystal / beneath the knees of the gods" (4:15)—also bespeaks "the reality of the *nous,* of mind, apart from any man's individual mind, of the sea crystalline and enduring, of the bright as it were molten glass that envelops us, full of light" (*GK,* 44); it is

> this light
> > as a river
> in Kung; in Ocellus, Coke, Agassiz
> > 'ρεῖ, the flowing
> > this persistent awareness   [107:762]

The light, of which all things that are are, is composed and bodied forth in the earth's breath:

> this breath wholly covers the mountains
> > it shines and divides
> it nourishes by its rectitude
> does no injury
> overstanding the earth it fills the nine fields
> > to heaven   [83:531]

The "final good" of the poet is to tally with his own breath "this breath" that fuses heaven and earth:

> I have tried to write Paradise
> Do not move
> > Let the wind speak
> > that is paradise   [120:803][25]

"Ego scriptor," "a lone ant from a broken ant-hill" (76:458), tries "to make Cosmos" (116:795)—to "make a paradiso / terrestre" (117:802), to "write" a paradise of the cosmic process:

in this air as of Kuanon
enigma forgetting the times and seasons
but this air brought her ashore a la marina
with the great shell borne on the seawaves
      nautilis biancastra
    By no means an orderly Dantescan rising
but as the winds veer

. . . .

    as the winds veer and the raft is driven

. . . .

      as the winds veer in periplum   [74:443]

His "craft" or "raft" is borne on the winds that "veer" in "periplum," following a central plan that is "in nature / rooted" (99:709). So that, if the poet loses his "center" (117:802)—if he is a mere "leaf in the current" (81:519) and "cannot make it cohere" (116:796)—he is sustained by the knowledge that "it coheres all right / even if my notes do not cohere" (116:797). If the poet is now "a blown husk that is finished," still

    the light sings eternal
a pale flare over marshes
    where the salt hay whispers to tide's change
Time, space,
    neither life nor death is the answer.   [115:794]

Since "nor began nor ends anything" (114:793), only process is the answer, and if the poet has breathed something of this process that is not manmade, that makes "men" and all else, his work has not been "vanity." He has "furnished" his "part" toward the "soul" (*LG*, 165); he has delivered his "seed,"

. . . the record
      the palimpsest—
a little light
    in great darkness—

. . . .

And as to who will copy this palimpsest?
    al poco giorno
        ed al gran cerchio d'ombra
But to affirm the gold thread in the pattern

. . . .

A little light, like a rushlight
       to lead back to splendour.   [116:795, 797]

The gold thread's allusion to Ariadne's thread and Theseus's labyrinth make more sense if we see that Ariadne originally is linked to Aphrodite as an earth goddess.[26] The wind-borne, sea-born procreative force that she represents is the clew, the thread, "the silk cords of the sunlight" (99:694) that will lead out of the "great darkness" where we are imprisoned:

      pure Light, we beseech thee
    Crystal, we beseech thee
Clarity, we beseech thee
                from the labyrinth ["Addendum for C": 799]

Moving "with the seed's breath" (83:531), the goddess will "lead back" to the "seed of light," that "great acorn of light bulging outward" (106:755). Or, to let the tradition that is in the air speak, "the gold thread in the pattern" is the clew that will lead out of the "mighty labyrinth" of history to the "seed perfection," for

From imperfection's murkiest cloud,
Darts always forth one ray of perfect light,
One flash of heaven's glory.   [LG, 227]

Thus the poet of the Cantos can hope to "confess wrong without losing rightness" (116:797): "Tho' my errors and wrecks lie about me" (116:796), "to have done instead of not doing / this is not vanity." "Here error is all in the not done" (81:521–22), for "there is no substitute for a lifetime" (98:691).

Chapter Nine

Frank O'Hara: The Speech of Poetry

two parallel lines always meet
except mentally
            "Poem V (F) W"

"Great art," Frank O'Hara insists, "is seldom about art"—"except in ba-
roque periods." Its insights may be so compelling and so pervasive that they
can be applied to art as well, but its true subject is the "structure" of nature.
In de Kooning's work, for example, "structures of classical severity" grant
"insight into the structure of man's identification with nature and the play of
forces which it involves." Similarly, "to think that late Mondrian is 'painting
about painting' is a grievous error," and "when Keats wrote, 'Beauty is truth,
truth beauty,'—it is a grievous error to think that he was writing about
writing poetry"; instead, he was stating his "insight into the structure of
human sensibility." O'Hara acknowledges another kind of art, however,
"which *looks* to be about nature but is lacking in perceptions of it": "the real
subject is not nature, but portraying nature, and while it may be very
beautiful it is less grand to observe the structure of artistic effort as a
metaphor for the structure of nature itself."[1] To translate O'Hara's distinction into poetic terms, observing the structure of artistic creation as a
metaphor for the structure of nature would make one a poet of analogies, but
an anagogic poet—for whom "parallel lines always meet"—sees nature,
human sensibility, and poetic form as isomorphic.

From Whitman's leaves, which identify humans and nature in the patterning drift of poetic language, to Pound's image or vortex, where energy creates
pattern and emotion organizes form,[2] the work of O'Hara's predecessors
attests to the "implacable identifications of man with nature" (*SS,* 42). Their
vision of the identity of nature and human sensibility cannot be reduced to an
insight into the structure of language, for the insight that is revealed in poetic

language has also patterned the language of the poem itself. Such an insight exceeds the terms of language; as Pound claims, the imagist poem of the "super-position" of the outward or objective on the inward or subjective offers "freedom from time limits and space limits."[3]

A language that discloses and is informed by the structure of nature and human sensibility does not subscribe to the codings of the ego, which include the dichotomies of subjective and objective, conscious and unconscious minds, space and time, foreground and background, past and future. According to O'Hara, too, "great art" transcends these distinctions in a coincidence or superimposition of total subjectivity and total objectivity. Consequently, he can insist on "a clearheaded, poetry-respecting objectivity" (*SS,* 35) and, at the same time, allow that great art offers transcendence—in his words, "Well, great painting does make one feel like God" (*SS,* 41). O'Hara attributes to Jackson Pollock the achievement of just such a total subjectivity/objectivity: "It is the physical reality of the artist and his activity of expressing it, united to the spiritual reality of the artist in a oneness which has no need for the mediation of metaphor or symbol."[4] The poetic analogue of this kind of art would be a writing more than writing and more than "style"—a writing that would identify nature and sensibility, the physical and the spiritual.

O'Hara's search for an anagogic writing for his time begins with a species of surrealism, a rejection of the mediating structures of figurative rhetoric, representation, and logical or grammatical progression. "Second Avenue" exemplifies this phase, about which O'Hara writes: "To put it very gently, I have a feeling that the philosophical reduction of reality to a dealable-with system so distorts life that one's 'reward' for this endeavor (a minor one, at that) is illness both from inside and outside" (*SS,* 37). Although Pound could be more clinical about this "illness," O'Hara is referring to the same "economy," the same debased "currency," the same "disease." His concluding remarks about the poem suggest a possible cure: the "verbal elements," he writes, are "intended consciously to keep the surface of the poem high and dry, not wet, reflective and self-conscious" (*SS,* 40). Yet, since a "high and dry" surface can signal a species of estheticism—promising "to destroy something but not us" (*CP,* 149)—it does not make for the objectivity or transcendence of "great" art, and the question becomes how to deepen the surface so that the "nature" of language can keep pace with its "sensibility."

One way to give language such depth is to write in a measure that responds to "breath" or the physiology of writing. In an interview O'Hara remarks, "It seemed to me that the metrical, that the measure let us say, if you want to talk about it in Olson's poems or Ezra Pound's, comes from the breath of the person just as a stroke of paint comes from the wrist and hand and arm and shoulder and all that of the painter. So therefore the point is really more to establish one's own measure and breath in poetry, I think, than—this sounds wildly ambitious since I don't think I've done it but I think that great poets do do it—rather than fitting your ideas into an established order, syllabically and phonetically and so on." He adds that the painters inspired the poets in this project of trying to "be the work yourself" (SS, 17). "Adherence to nature, indifference to conventions" (SS, 43) guide O'Hara's emphasis on "breath" as a compositional force.[5] The poet can do without the mediation of conventions if he can manage to reveal the passage or flow of energy that is the nature or structure of his medium. And O'Hara's description of Pollock's "spiritual clarity" suggests that such a "state" is the poet's goal as well: "In this state all becomes clear. . . . This is not a mystical state, but the accumulation of decisions along the way" (AC, 25).

In such a "strange ascent," it is technical engagement that opens up the "limitless space of air and light in which the spirit can act freely and with unpremeditated knowledge" (AC, 26). The "light" of Whitman's "Crossing Brooklyn Ferry" and Pound's spectrum of lights—the "measureless seas and stars, / Iamblichus' light" in which the gods move; the sunlight/moonlight of the ming ideogram, which depicts the stillness at the center of natural time; and the final "little light, like a rushlight / to lead back to splendour"—are isomorphs of O'Hara's "light."[6] At the end of "Biotherm"—which O'Hara believed he was able to keep "'open' and so there are lots of possibilities, air and such"[7]—a transcendent light shines through the elements into which the speaker dissolves:

as I wave toward you freely
the ego-ridden sea
there is a light there that neither
of us will obscure
rubbing it all white
saving ships from fucking up on the rocks
on the infinite waves of skin smelly and crushed and light and absorbed.

[CP, 448]

O'Hara's submergence in Whitman's and Pound's process, which takes him beyond surrealistic negativity and culminates in his identification with his poem in "Biotherm," begins in "In Memory of My Feelings," where he contrasts two kinds of memory and two kinds of poetry. The kind of art into which pain may be converted reifies forms and is exemplified by statuary. Such a conversion means forgetting one's temporality, "loves," and "feelings" (*CP*, 257), and this choice of forgetfulness makes for the recorded history of Western art. It is what the "mountainous-minded Greeks" chose when they could "speak / of time as a river and step across it into Persia, leaving the pain / at home to be converted into statuary" (*CP*, 254). The metaphoric elision of time and the formal conversion of pain into stone are versions of the same choice, O'Hara suggests, and adds, "I adore the Roman copies," extending the tradition through and beyond Rome to other examples of "supreme lucidity, / humanism, / the mere existence of emphasis" (*CP*, 254),[8] to end with the romantic apotheosis of a sublime "mountain-mindedness":

> At times, withdrawn,
> I rise into the cool skies
> And gaze on at the imponderable world with the simple identification
> of my colleagues, the mountains. Manfred climbs to my nape,
> speaks, but I do not hear him,
> > I'm too blue.   [*CP*, 253]

Peoples outside the Western humanist tradition—Hittites, American Indians before history, and the Arabs "racing into sands, converting themselves into / so many" *(CP*, 254)—offer an alternative to such memorializing and forgetful art. "Sands," suggesting the erosion of mountains and statues, are not "cool"; nevertheless, the desert inhabitant remains protected:

> Rising,
> he wraps himself in the burnoose of memories against the heat of life.   [*CP*, 255]

At the conclusion of the poem, O'Hara calls such possession of one's temporality history; unlike art, history offers remembering. By history he means not a forgetful, codified, and "counted" history but the project of being in and of one's time.

In this project, Whitman remains O'Hara's guide, as his explosive catalogue of "sordid identifications" (*CP*, 256) acknowledges. The spatial and temporal expansion of this section recalls the later sections of "Song of Myself," where Whitman traces the phylogeny of the systems of thought inscribed in the convolutions of his brain, as he had earlier traced the phylogeny inscribed in his physiology.[9] Such a "repetition" on the poet's body, psyche, and tongue constitutes a "re-membering," a true "re-collecting" of spatial and temporal dispersal and variety; at the same time, however, it is destructive of the "ego," shattering the grid of space/time on which distinct lives are plotted, and dispersing the self into grains of sand, waves of light, leaves of grass. Yet O'Hara affirms that it is a

                              Grace
to be born and live as variously as possible.   [CP, 256]

In the sequence of identifications that follows, O'Hara is "afoot" with his vision and travels through time and space, dissolving the categories of inside and outside. For O'Hara no less than for Whitman, the self is not a conceptualization of physiological, psychosexual, and psychosocial processes but a literal body, the stage on which such processes, dramas, and metamorphoses are played out. Thus O'Hara's series of identifications appears also to be triggered physiologically by alliteration, consonance, internal rhymes, and so on. While a series such as "I am a baboon eating a banana / I am a dictator looking at his wife I am a doctor eating a child / and the child's mother smiling I am a chinaman climbing a mountain" (CP, 256) is open to psychological and sociological interpretation, the passage refuses to be reduced to an ulterior meaning. No such danger exists, because O'Hara's is a "deep" surface, which is itself the structure of the interpenetration of subject and object, mind and matter.

    The "Grace" that precipitates O'Hara's catalogue is the fulcrum of the poem. Not unlike Whitman's "leaves," "Grace" is O'Hara's saving name, his Logos that redeems all the other proper names strewn through his pages and renders their dispersal a grace indeed. "Second Avenue" already hints at the transforming power of the word in a description of a Grace Hartigan painting:

                        . . . Grace destroys
the whirling faces in their dissonant gaiety where it's anxious,
lifted nasally to the heavens which is a carousel grinning
and spasmodically obliterated with loaves of greasy white paint
and this becomes like love to her, is what I desire
and what you, to be able to throw something away without yawning
"Oh Leaves of Grass! o Sylvette! oh Basket Weavers' Conference!"   [CP, 149]

The same name-word appears in "Poem (Khrushchev is coming on the right day!)." The turbulent, windy day, complete with atmospheric foreshadowings of an apocalypse or a second coming, is a day of "cool graced light" that miraculously "saves" or redeems the darkness of other names ("Purgatorio Merchado, Gerhard Schwartz") and other lives ("François Villon, his life, so dark"), if only in passing:

and the light seems to be eternal
and joy seems to be inexorable
I am foolish enough always to find it in wind   [CP, 340]

—which is an unexpected and unmerited grace after all, what with still being "close to the fear of war and the stars which have disappeared" (*CP*, 210). "Poem" also alludes to "Grace Hartigan's / painting *Sweden,*" for in the superimposition of "Grace" and "grace"—of a proper name, a part of one's time and "loves," and the word that signifies divine love or transcendence of historical contingencies—lies the grace/Grace of an immanent Logos or light that can regather its temporal and spatial dispersal. And this one grace granted the poet is a pun, an accidental gift.

While "In Memory" retains both an autobiographical past and a narrative syntax, "Biotherm" aspires to forgo all such mediation and to *be* a poem of immanence. More academic than either long poem, "Essay on Style" outlines the difference between them, for it spells out the conditions of an "intimate" language. Here, O'Hara renounces subject matter and all other contingencies—mothers and their social-familial network, as well as the mediations of syntactic and grammatical connectives—that threaten to come between him and intimacy with his mother tongue. Likewise, "lettrism" is exposed in the metaphor it rides on—"treating / the typewriter as an intimate organ why not? / nothing else is (intimate)" (*CP*, 394). Just as the poet will probably not eat alone for the rest of his life, however, he will probably continue to make use of *and, but, also,* and "NEVERTHELESS (thank you, Aristotle)" (*CP*, 437). In "Biotherm," O'Hara relinquishes as much as possible syntactic orders, subordinations, and hierarchies—all analogues of the social-familial relationships that repress the intimacy of the mother tongue—in order to sound a language intimate and intense, purified of "rhetoric." "Biotherm" engages the "serpent" of "In Memory" in action: shedding the orders of the self, all perspectives, calendars, histories, geographies, and even articulation itself, we uncover "the ardent lover of history . . . / tongue out" (*CP*, 255).

O'Hara's last major poem, "Biotherm" can serve as a focal point for a study of his entire career, which in a sense is a countdown for this final explosion. The poem tests the limits of his conception of poetry as speech that informs the body of his work. From the beginning, the temporal line of speech is O'Hara's principle of organization, underlying his surface coherence. Yet his speech cannot be regarded as simply "chatter" or "conversation," which would reduce his poems to mere surface. O'Hara's description of Pollock's achievement—"The scale of the painting became that of the painter's body, not the image of a body" (*AC*, 34)—provides a painterly analogue of his own deep surface. The "scale" of "Biotherm" is the poet's tongue, not a language that is the image of the tongue's activity. The tongue in all its functions is primary for O'Hara. It is the organ of speech, an erotogenic organ, and, as Webster's puts it, "an important organ in the ingestion of food." "Biotherm" is written in the impure language of the tongue performing all its functions, sometimes simultaneously; in these lines, for example, O'Hara speaks, drools over the words, and chews them up, all at once:

no flesh to taste no flash to tusk
no flood to flee no fleed to dlown flom the iceth loot[10]

Still, the lines are consciously "poetry," complete with echoes of "The Rime of the Ancient Mariner." Although such impure speech appears in many other O'Hara poems, nowhere is the flow of words so torrential, so exhilarating and terrifying, as in "Biotherm." It is a *journal intime* that places us inside language as it is being spoken, and returns us to the root connection of "intimate" and "intestine" ("in time" of the body). The energy and excitement that charge the poem derive from an infantile wholeness predating the differentiation of the functions of the tongue. Freud writes that sexual activity first "attaches itself to functions serving the purpose of self-preservation and does not become independent of them until later"; thus the erotogenic nature of the mouth grows out of the pleasurable sensation of "the warm flow of milk."[11] It is this infantile mouth that speaks the fleshly speech of "Biotherm."

O'Hara's consumption of language—which is impersonal, synchronic or ahistorical, and grammatical—in speech that is of the flesh of his body determines not only the texture of the words but the organizing principle of "Biotherm." His method is not that of a dream if, following Freud, we define a dream as "a mutilated and altered transcript of certain rational psychical structures," to which it has a metonymic or metaphoric relationship.[12] "Biotherm," however, cannot be resolved or translated back into a rational "metatext" of explainable sequences, for O'Hara constructs *his* sequences over the void of interpretation, the void that would connect the metatext to the text it would explain. For example, he writes:

then too, the other day I was walking through a train
with my suitcase and I overheard someone say "speaking of faggots"
now isn't life difficult enough without that
and why am I always carrying something
well it was a shitty looking person anyway
better a faggot than a farthead
or as fathers have often said to friends of mine
"better dead than a dope" "if I thought you were queer I'd kill you"
you'd be right to, DAD, daddio, addled annie pad-lark (Brit. 19th C.)

The "analysis and synthesis of syllables"—the "syllabic chemistry" that Freud describes in *The Interpretation of Dreams*[13]—is no more gratuitous here than in a dream. The alliteration ("faggot," "farthead," "fathers," "friends"), though it parodies the use of such a poetic device, still manages to be quite significant. Similarly, the sequence of words ending in verbal disintegration ("dead," "dope," "DAD, daddio, addled annie pad-lark") is a palpably significant sequence; yet any interpretation would be gratuitous. Either the sequence is related as a surface, or it is not related at all. For in the final two lines the chemistry of the words takes over and makes the words into things. When the tongue composes the line, the referentiality of the words appears all but irrelevant, and the very project of interpretation is challenged. The distinction between the surface and what hides behind it becomes untenable, for the surface is now a depth. The inner is turned inside out, giving us an intimate surface.

"Biotherm" is full of verbal improvisations that deepen its surface, for O'Hara's verbal play always has an emotional, psychic, and/or sexual undertow. Yet interpretation remains beside the point, since it is primarily the tongue that is playing with language. The various "translations" in the poem, for instance, are strictly lingual. *Vitalità nell' arte* is played into "vitality nellie arty," which, as O'Hara himself hints, is far from an insignificant phrase: "ho ho that's a joke pop." The passage playing with "balls" in two languages is another example of a kind of *Ursprache* of the tongue—a universal, physical human speech. Emphasizing the tongue as the poetic organ is one way of combating the alienation of language. At its inception, language seems to be distanced from its physical source. Edward Sapir tells how language is not a biological function, "for primary laryngeal patterns of behavior have had to be completely overhauled by the interference of lingual, labial, and nasal modifications before a 'speech organ' was ready for work. Perhaps it is because this 'speech organ' is a diffused and secondary network of physiological activities which do not correspond to the primary functions of the organs involved that language has been enabled to free itself from direct bodily expressiveness."[14] This is the first kind of displacement or "difference" that O'Hara tries to undo by stressing the multifunctional nature of the tongue.

The intimate connection between words and food, between using language and eating in the infantile erotic/nourishing sense, provides O'Hara with a secular version of the "Word made flesh" and accounts for the overwhelmingly alimentary nature of his imagery, including his imagery about poetry. "Biotherm" contains a full range of images of questionable

edibles, inedible edibles, and edible inedibles, for here O'Hara resists the
merely edible just as he resists a transparently referential language that
reduces words to currency:

first you peel the potatoes
then you marinate the peelies
in campari all the while playing
the Mephisto Waltz on your gram
and wrap them in grape leaves
and bake them in mush ouch
that god damn oven delicacies
the ditch is full of after dinner

And:

oh god what joy
you're here
sob and at the
most recent summit
conference they
are eating string
beans butter
smootch slurp
pass me the filth
and a coke pal
oh thank you

And:

perhaps
marinated duck saddle with foot sauce and a tumbler of vodka

And even:

(MENU)
Déjeuner Bill Berkson
        30 August 1961

Hors-d'oeuvre abstrait-expressionistes, américain-styles, bord-durs, etc.
Soupe Samedi Soir à la Strawberry-Blonde
Poisson Pas de Dix au style Patricia
Histoire de contrefilet, sauce Angelicus Fobb
Le réunion des fins de thon à la boue
Chapon ouvert brûlé à l'Hoban, sauce Fidelio Fobb
Poèmes 1960–61 en salade

Fromage de la Tour Dimanche 17 septembre
Fruits de Jardins shakspériens
Biscuits de l'*Inspiration* de Clarence Brown

Vin blanc supérior de Bunkie Hearst
Vin rouge mélancholique de Boule de neige
Champagne d'*Art News* éditeur diapré
Café ivesianien "Plongez au fond du lac glacé"
                    Vodka-campari et TV

Food becomes a metaphor for everything one takes in and processes; from the most physical to the most spiritual, all things are converted into energy, body heat, "biotherm." The alimentary imagery, metaphors, and "sound effects" that turn words into food and food into words serve to redefine poetry as speech. This kind of speech is an activity of the whole person: it converts matter and motion; it recycles impressions, feelings, memories, emotions, hopes, loves, foods, drinks, poems, books, magazines, movies, languages. "Biotherm" is a "secular" microcosm of the *Cantos:* instead of Pound's patterning mind we have O'Hara's kind of patterning digestive system, and what we experience while reading it is the sense of the passage of time *through* the man writing it. Everything is in flux—ingested, processed, and voided by the poet's body. And if a poem is not the process of this passage, it is inert and alien—waste or excrement.

In "Personism: A Manifesto," O'Hara takes credit for finishing literature off and adds, "For a time people thought that Artaud was going to accomplish this, but actually, for all their magnificence, his polemical writings are not more outside literature than Bear Mountain is outside New York State" (*CP,* 499). Of course, neither are O'Hara's poems, for whatever one writes is forever turning into "Art," always freezing into form on "one / after another filthy page of poetry" (*CP,* 277), and the problem remains that one cannot destroy literature except in literature. This is what Jacques Derrida calls the "fatal complicity" of the destructive discourse, which must inhabit the structures it would destroy.[15] O'Hara is trapped along with Artaud, and there is a basic affinity between them. Artaud promises an art of total presence—in Derrida's words, "an art which no longer yields works, an artist's existence which is no longer a route or an experience that gives access to something other than itself; Artaud promises the existence of a speech that is a body, of a body that is a theater, of a theater that is a text because it is no longer enslaved to a writing [i.e., a script] more ancient than itself, an ur-text or an ur-speech."[16] For if one's speech is not the breath, if the body is not the

text or the theater of life, then the excreted, fragmentary, lifeless "work of
art" is indeed "Pig-Shit," as Artaud calls it.[17]

To conceive of writing as the physical activity of speech, as body chemistry
and not its product (unless it be body heat or biotherm), has important
implications for poetic forms.[18] First of all, in Artaud's words, "when we
speak the word 'life,' it must be understood we are not referring to life as we
know it from its surface of fact, but that fragile, fluctuating center which
forms never reach. And if there is still one hellish, truly accursed thing in our
time, it is our artistic dallying with forms, instead of being like victims burnt
at the stake, signaling through the flames."[19] The repeatable, "static" structures posited by forms are beside the point, since the center of life is
elsewhere:

The best thing in the world but I better be quick about it
better be gone tomorrow
                              better be gone last night and
                        next Thursday better be gone
    better be
                  always

These lines open "Biotherm" and give fair warning that the poet is going to
be "quick," because the present disappears as it occurs. In order to inhabit
the fluctuating center of life, one has to keep up with time. Conventional
formal devices, however, do not inhabit destructive real time; they only
represent it by abstracting it into a repeatable time. Thus, while William
Carlos Williams may be "better than the movies" (*CP,* 498), his "measure
shmeasure" must be rejected nonetheless, for measure surfaces the fragile,
fluctuating center of life, the biological depth of words, by abstracting speech
into a pattern. O'Hara attempts to destroy the concept of measure by
undoing the word with "shmeasure"; yet such a gesture affirms his faith in
word magic, which remains the basis of poetry.

O'Hara's parody of Williams—he has in mind the ending of Book Five of
Paterson—continues:

measure shmeasure know shknew
unless the material rattle us around

The phrase "know shknew" suggests the second major formal implication of
a poetic of speech. Seen as a physical activity, speech is total presence, and
this conception of literature implies more than a rejection of narrative,
syntactical, and metrical forms; it rejects signification altogether. Since
words can be things only at zero-degree referentiality, signification can be

achieved only at the cost of "presence"—only through the symbolic distancing of a word, which is "the murder of the thing."[20] Like grammar or meter, referential word use reduces language to a currency one can use and be used by. The analogue of O'Hara's emphasis on words as things is his transformation of monetary units, another currency, into color values ("the dime so red and the 100 dollar bill so orchid / the sickly fuchsia of a 1 the optimistic / orange of a 5 . . . / the magnificent yellow zinnia of a 10")—all so that when he adds two and two, he does not have to get four: "now this is not a tract against usury it's just putting two and two together / and getting five." The gibe at Pound reminds us that here, too, O'Hara's play is serious, for Pound and Williams are his acknowledged predecessors in this project. Williams also asks "for relief from 'meaning'" and admonishes:

—never separate that stain
of sense from the inert mass.   Never.
Never that radiance
                    quartered apart,
unapproached by symbols

Extracting "meaning" from the "mass" leaves behind dead matter or inert "lead," whether the husk of the signifier whose "soul" has been "stolen" by the signified, or the earth itself, which has become "an excrement of some sky."[21] Pound attacks the same excremental, usurious "economy" of signification, which steals, absents, and defers life itself.

   Again, however, O'Hara's attempt to undermine the currency of referential language is doomed to failure, since it must be carried out in referential language. He confronts once more the fatal complicity of destructive discourse in what it would demolish, and the desire for "presence" remains just that—a desire signifying a lack. Yet there is a way out, which is also a way in; and that way madness lies. Jacques Lacan defines psychotic language as a language of "regression"—of treating words like things: to the psychotic, "all the Symbolic is Real." As a result, his discourse is "composed of nothing but words, rather than of the Word"; it is "incomprehensible" discourse.[22] If symbolic or referential word use is "sane," defines "sanity," and upholds the verbal arrangement called "reality," a confusion of the symbolic relationship between words and things represents a total derangement of reality, including a derangement of the words "world" and "I." But poets can work in this ground between word and thing. While the madman is caught in the "sliding" relationship between signifier and signified,[23] a poet like O'Hara chooses to inhabit that slippery ground, asserting his freedom both from the convention of language as symbolic word use that cuts us off from things, and from the tyranny—the totalitarianism—of a world where signifier and signified are literally identical.

Madness and poetry meet in a writer like Artaud, for whom words are wholly body. Gilles Deleuze discusses Artaud in terms of the schizophrenic's experience of language and the body as all depth and no surface: "Freud emphasized this schizophrenic aptitude for perceiving the surface and the skin as if each were pierced by an infinite number of little holes. As a result, the entire body is nothing but depth." And "as there is no surface, interior and exterior, container and content no longer have precise limits; they plunge into universal depth," and language gets lost in "the vertigo of the bodies' depths and their alimentary, poisonous mixtures." Artaud's language, "articulating, insufflating, or palatalizing a word, causing it to blaze out so that it becomes the action of a partless body, rather than the passion of a fragmented organism," is a literary example of such language, in which the word is "still a sign, but one that merges with an action or passion of the body." In this state, the categories of both the signifier and the signified have disappeared, and "'speaking' has collapsed onto 'eating,' and into all the imitations of a 'chewing mouth,' of a primitive oral depth."[24]

O'Hara's use of words in "Biotherm" springs from these depths and tests the limits of an anagogic rhetoric. Once again, the title is telling: the suntan lotion Biotherm with plankton—"practically the most health-giving substance ever rubbed into one's skin" (*CP,* 554)—is food absorbed through the skin, which at the end of the poem becomes coextensive with the sea and swallows up the universe in a gaping innerness turned inside out. When the inside/outside dichotomy disappears, words lose their meaning. They may still retain a certain power of designation and signification, Deleuze argues, but this function is experienced as "empty," "indifferent," "false."[25] "Biotherm" stands on this threshold, for the unavoidable residual referentiality of O'Hara's language becomes almost "irrelevant." Thus the "non-sense" of "Biotherm" is neither a metaphysical puzzle nor a mimicry of nonsense like Lewis Carroll's "Jabberwocky"; O'Hara's is the "non-sense" of the language we use—of referential language seen inside out. Thus the poet's resistance to meaning, referentiality, and an impersonal language that "steals" his breath-speech and alienates his life in the form of someone else's "message" renders him "mad" at the source.

"Poetry," written some ten years earlier, presents the same complex of ideas and suggests what might have set in motion the poetic that culminates/bottoms out in "Biotherm":

The only way to be quiet
is to be quick, so I scare

you clumsily, or surprise
you with a stab. A praying
mantis knows time more
intimately than I and is
more casual. Crickets use
time for accompaniment to
innocent fidgeting. A zebra
races counterclockwise.
All this I desire. To
deepen you by my quickness
and delight as if you
were logical and proven,
but still be quiet as if
I were used to you; as if
you would never leave me
and were the inexorable
product of my own time.   [*CP*, 49]

In nature, time is inseparable from essence, while the poet can only desire
such presence. For the use of language places him in sequential time, so that
he experiences his essence—which is time—as alien. Time is not an "accompaniment" to the "innocent fidgeting" of speech; time is the fatal fidgeting of speech, which can only yearn for the wholeness of the praying mantis,
crickets, the zebra. All can race counterclockwise yet be of their "own time,"
for without speech their time is not sequential. The speech of poetry introduces the consciousness of an external time; this "mortal meaning," Lacan
writes, "reveals in the Word a center exterior to Language."[26] That center is
time, and while O'Hara does not always write a nonsequential, nonreferential
"speech," he is always conscious that the attempt to write as a mimesis of
speech—the attempt to undercut an impersonal language—introduces another kind of absence, a nonbeing at our source. Thus O'Hara is always
conscious of speaking "A Step Away from Them," for he knows that the
minute he begins to speak, he begins to thread his way to the dead. The
darkness that backs the surface shimmer of a poem like "A Step Away" marks
the essential O'Hara, whose dazzle of surfaces so full of life's clutter and
chatter is only so much "neon in daylight" (*CP*, 258).

Part Four

Chapter Ten

E mily Dickinson's Untitled Discourse

Who were "the Father and the Son"
We pondered when a child,
And what had they to do with us.

                    P–1258

Emily Dickinson's work represents an ironic comment on nineteenth-cen-tury poetics, for she plays against each other the rhetorics that implicitly or explicitly authorize other major nineteenth-century poets. She claims only the privilege of her "provincial" "discernment";[1] as she puts it in a poem about Thanksgiving Day,

Neither Patriarch nor Pussy
I dissect the Play   [P–814]

The lines "dissect" the laws of both nature and the powers that be, exposing the "Play" of "Patriarch" and "Pussy" alike through a writerly intrusion. The p- alliteration brings the two parties into proximity, touching each with a hint of the ludicrous, and puts them on the stage of her play. And the writerly practice of alliteration domesticates the Father as a more petulant "Pa-triarch" and Nature as a pettier "Pussy," technically subverting any claims they might have to authority over her "Play." Her dissection thus consists of writerly incisions performed by the stylus. Such a technically subversive poetic derives its authority precisely from the poet's distant relationship to prevailing authorities. Dickinson characteristically stands in the middle and juggles systems and alliterations, as in P–721 where her play dissects two rhetorics:

Behind Me—dips Eternity—
Before Me—Immortality—
Myself—the Term between—

.   .   .   .

'Tis Miracle before Me—then—
'Tis Miracle behind—between—
A Crescent in the Sea—
With Midnight to the North of Her—
And Midnight to the South of Her—
And Maelstrom—in the Sky—

Here, Christian and naturalistic terminologies are equally valid, for the "Miracle" and "Midnight" come to the same thing—the unknown that surrounds the "term between." The "term between"—words and time generating and dissecting systems—is the center, and once again alliteration lends an ironic touch to the sleight of hand that juggles miracles and midnights.[2]

Dickinson's ironic characterization of herself as the "Queen of Calvary" (P–348),[3] which dissociates her from the Christian model for poetic writing that it invokes, helps us to place her in her original dislocation. The Son begotten by the Father—"And the Word was made Flesh, and dwelt among us" (John 1:14)—provides a model of production without reproduction that authorizes the living word of poetic language through direct patriarchal entitlement. In translating the spirit into the spatially and temporally distancing medium of letters, the poet reenacts the sacrificial Christian drama, relinquishing presence in the process of "re-presenting" it. While this loss or "fall" is mourned by any lyric poet,[4] the "degree" of Dickinson's loss is made more "acute" by her alienation, as a woman, from the Christian drama that redeems the generic loss of poetic language. The "Queen of Calvary" is not the Son "sacrificed" as a temporal signifier in order to signify the absent One, the "Son of None" (P–721); Dickinson's gender displaces her from this patrilineal line of symbolic substitutions that authorizes poetry.

The poet who is modeled after Christ disperses his words legitimately, for they are underwritten by the Logos and will be regathered by the Father's right or writing hand. The Christian Logos is an identity that authorizes difference; it underwrites metaphoric substitutions and, therefore, signification:

God is a distant—stately Lover—
Woos, as He states us—by His Son—
Verily, a Vicarious Courtship—
"Miles," and "Priscilla," were such an One—

But, lest the Soul—like fair "Priscilla"
Choose the Envoy—and spurn the Groom—
Vouches, with hyperbolic archness—
"Miles," and "John Alden" were Synonym—   [P–357]

This metaphoric voucher, this hyperbole, constitutes the rhetoric of the
Logos, which identifies the model with the representation, the "groom" with
the "envoy," the spirit with the letter. Thus, if a "soulful" poet chooses the
"Son" that "states" us—or chooses temporal language over the immortal
Word—all is not lost, for he can still be pulled together or saved by the
Logos, the synonymy of the copy with the original. Without this faith, the
"envoy" is generically cut off from the source:

Upon the gallows hung a wretch,
Too sullied for the hell
To which the law entitled him.
As nature's curtain fell
The one who bore him tottered in,—
For this was woman's son.
"'Twas all I had," she stricken gasped—
Oh, what a livid boon!   [P–1757]

Without a symbolic backup system, the "boon" is "livid," for the pure
signifier, the mere "woman's son," is a gift of death. Since the "Son of God" is
begotten metaphorically upon a literal mother-flesh, the physical or literal
reproduction that brings the Logos into being is a mere repetition of the
primary production of conception or inspiration. The mother is mere matter—a connection etymology sustains—and does not matter. Or, in terms
of the writing authorized thereby, the spirit gives life, but the letter kills.
Thus the son of woman remains outside the law—outside heaven and hell,
outside signification—and the banker-father, who has the capital to underwrite projects, remains in power, resented though he may be.

Dickinson's exclusion from a patrilineal system of authorized deferrals and
substitutions, which her patronymic with its "-son" underscores, makes her
mistrust symbolic systems and turn to the letter of the law, the matter at
hand—the materials of writing.[5] Since her very identity depends on the
difference between words and things, she aims to short-circuit a transparent
or referential language by undermining the legitimate processes of articulating meaning. Dickinson's untitled, unauthorized work celebrates the deviation of a "slant" language and consists, in fact, of poems without titles and
often without authorized versions. She resists the Word directly authorized,
for to speak it would amount to an apocalyptic destruction of the mediation
of matter, by which she and her language exist:

To pile like Thunder to its close
Then crumble grand away
While Everything created hid
This—would be Poetry—

Or Love—the two coeval come—
We both and neither prove—
Experience either and consume—
For None see God and live—   [P–1247]

The "imperial—Thunderbolt" (P–315), the "divine rape" of direct inspiration, must be deflected in order to preserve life itself. She cannot be one of
the "saints" with "ravished slate and pencil" (P–65); she must favor the
"slate" and the "pencil," for not the unity of the Logos but the mediation of
"loved Philology" (P–1651) sustains her in her difference as a woman and a
poet. Her distance from the authority of the Logos grants Dickinson her
authority—if merely as a scribe of letters, syllables, and sentences.
Elsewhere, she describes her separation as

Easing my famine
At my Lexicon—
Logarithm—had I—for Drink—
'Twas a dry Wine—   [P–728]

The "Lexicon" and "Logarithm" deflect "Bolts of Melody" (P–505), locating
meaning in letters and rhythm in numbers. Dickinson's language marks her
painful abstinence, her resistence to possession and transubstantiation. Her
wine is not the wine of Emerson's Bacchus—the "blood of the world" that
will "quicken" the poet to "unlock / Every crypt of every rock"[6]—but the
dry wine of "Logarithm"; her bread is not the immanent "Word made Flesh"
but the script of the "Lexicon"—a text flat or unleavened and her only
companion.

In P–454, the present that "the Gods" hand the "little Girl" who would be
a poet is the authorizing or "emboldening" "difference" between names and
things:

I kept it in my Hand—
I never put it down—
I did not dare to eat—or sleep—
For fear it would be gone—
I heard such words as "Rich"—
When hurrying to school—
From lips at Corners of the Streets—
And wrestled with a smile.

Rich! 'Twas Myself—was rich—
To take the name of Gold—
And Gold to own—in solid Bars—
The Difference—made me bold—   [P–454]

The gift she keeps in her hand and guards so jealously is the gift of writing, the gods' present of the absent. For the difference between the "name of Gold" and the thing, the "solid Bars," is the word itself, the literal difference between the metaphysical and the physical—including the difference between "God" and "Gold," as in the pun of taking the "name of Gold," which turns on the letter *l*. Dickinson's location of meaning in the literal difference of words informs her esthetic:

To tell the Beauty would decrease
To state the Spell demean—
There is a syllable-less Sea
Of which it is the sign—
My will endeavors for its word
And fails, but entertains
A Rapture as of Legacies—
Of introspective Mines—   [P–1700]

"Rapture" springs from the failure to find the right word and is found in the "entertaining" language. "It" in line 4 means both the sea and the word *sea:* as the word *sea* is to the actual, "syllable-less" sea, the sea itself is to an invisible, eternal sea. The failure to reach beyond the words and the visible makes for poetry and its introspective vistas. Dickinson's words are mines that can be mined, they entertain as they are entertained, and their sense proliferates between the cracks of a syntax that does not "tell" or "state."

If the daughter lives outside the law of the Logos, her self-reliance puts her at the center of logic, which outlines the laws of difference. Dickinson is a master of division and difference, of dialect and dialectic; her dissecting language becomes a center productive of difference. She writes:

To fill a Gap
Insert the Thing that caused it—
Block it up
With Other—and 'twill yawn the more—
You cannot solder an Abyss
With Air.   [P–546]

Dickinson's "gap" or lack has been read in various ways, depending on the reader's theoretical bias. According to one's approach—whether psychological, humanist, feminist, autobiographical, or deconstructionist—it could represent a psychological, physiological, theological, or sociopolitical lack, a personal loss or a linguistic one. However, if we regard the poem as establishing the distinction between gaps or abysses and the things capable of filling them—between nonmaterial and material entities—we will see that the very idea of a gap is generated by the poem itself. Such a poem invites readings but rules out any authoritative reading. The structure of opposition lies at the heart of Dickinson's work, and thematic variants can be referred to this structure for analysis and anatomizing. Oppositions like immortal God and mortal human, the saved and the damned, the "wife" and the "girl," Paradise and Amherst are all interchangeable, and in fact she often blends within a single poem the passages of marriage, divine possession, death, and resurrection, which divide as opposites the states they would bridge.

Dichotomy not only informs Dickinson's themes but structures her rhetoric and form. To begin with, the brevity of her poems sensitizes us to the minutest literal details of her language by juxtaposing material or quantitative limitation with semantic, metaphoric, or qualitative expansion. "I dwell in Possibility – / A fairer House than Prose" (P–657) is the manifesto of this poetic, which stages the logic of poetic language. "Dwelling" in "possibility" both separates and joins the determined and the indeterminate, limitation and freedom, houses and nature, closure and expansion. Dickinson presents poetry as a house of words that closes to open and—as "spreading wide my narrow Hands / To gather Paradise" suggests—opens to close. Prose, by contrast, is simply closed:

They shut me up in Prose—
As when a little Girl
They put me in the Closet—
Because they liked me "still"—   [P–613]

Prose cannot sustain a dialectic of limitation and freedom, because such a dialectic is generated by playing formal elements, which emphasize the letter, against figurative features. And the same dialectic operates within metaphor itself, for describing one thing in terms of another constitutes a mutual redefinition that simultaneously limits and liberates. To describe a house as nature, for example, is to blow it apart:

Of Chambers as the Cedars—
Impregnable of Eye—
And for an Everlasting Roof
The Gambrels of the Sky—   [P–657]

Yet this description also defines and delimits nature as a house. For Dickinson, poetic language exposes the coeval emergence of the literal and the metaphorical, the material "seen" and the nonmaterial "unseen," the letter and the breath or spirit; in other words, she lays bare the logic of the Logos.

The subversive structure of Dickinson's poems precludes any harmony of form and content, any formalist or organicist illusion of their unity. For example, she establishes as her norm the hymn stanza, with its rigid metrical and syllabic requirements,[7] only to subvert it. The metric norm so severely limits the verse it empowers that the verse grows cryptic, crabbed, and idiosyncratic and resists communication itself, thus undermining the religious and social function of hymns that the form alludes to as authorization for her "dialect," her "New Englandly" tune. Under the guise of faithfully serving formal requirements, Dickinson violates the laws of agreement of antecedents, persons, numbers, and tenses. Thus she will drop—or add—a final *s* without regard for tense or number and will engage in impossible inversions of normal word order in the name of the rhyme scheme.[8] She will forgo auxiliaries, conjunctions, and even points of the argument itself to meet at all costs the demands of the syllable count and to make her meters regular.

The specifically textual features that aid in "crumpling" her syntax syncopate her semantics and her rhythm, working against both semantic transparency and metrical regularity. The writerly medium becomes an opaque presence emphasized by her distinctive typography and idiosyncratic punctuation. The dashes that "staple" the song (P–512) manipulate both rhythm and syntax, joining as they divide and dividing what they join. They insist on the poem as a literal artifact, as do her mid-sentence capital letters that resist sentencing and introduce disorder even while appealing to notions of hierarchy and order. They assert the sovereignty of written, literary language and mark its distance from realism and revelation alike. Subverting grammar, Dickinson undermines the Logos as reason or the orderly progression of meaning; subverting the conventions of writing, which standardize the transcription of the spoken word and legitimize writing by appealing to the prior authority of speech, she undermines the authority of the Logos as the living word.[9]

At the same time, however, her compressed deviant syntax opens up expansive, cosmic vistas and initiates another kind of commerce in its proliferation of meanings. Dickinson's choice of words, pressurized by the demands of syllabic economy, calls attention to etymology, spelling, and the agglutinative process by which syllables and morphemes add up to words. In exposing the historical and linguistic processes of articulation and composition, she reveals the creative word to be the *created* word that goes on reproducing, either legitimately by etymology, whose connections are historically sanctioned, or illegitimately by literal accidents, whose connections are capricious though irrepressible. Thus Dickinson's formal restraint and her emphasis on limits enable her concurrently to indulge in a "formless" or illicit multiplicity of meanings, which is a "bliss" *and* an "abyss" (P–340). As her containment of even this erotic and destructive indeterminacy within a rhyme suggests, however, both form and formlessness—bounds and boundlessness—come into play within the poems. Her poems are informed by the tension between the centripetal force of a repressive metrical norm and a cramped syntax and the centrifugal force of semantic expansion—the blissful/abysmal *excess* of meaning and suggestiveness made possible by formal and syntactic compression.[10] And Dickinson indulges herself fully in the multiple "inflections" of her "pen."[11] For example, she does not give her poems titles, which would limit the inflections by marking the borders of authorized readings. Similarly, her habit of revising poems by listing alternate words and letting the slate of candidates stand, sometimes without indicating which word was chosen, shows that she proceeded not by getting closer to some blueprint and controlling her inflections but by moving farther away from a center. Thus the line between logic and illogic, between the legal and the illegal production of meaning, and between the spoken Logos and the written "logarithm" becomes the very axis Dickinson's poems spin on.

II.

Ah, Necromancy Sweet!
Ah, Wizard erudite!
Teach me the skill,

That I instil the pain
Surgeons assuage in vain,
Nor Herb of all the plain
Can heal!   P–177

Dickinson's dissection of the "Play" of "Patriarch" and "Pussy" leaves her in the breach between Christian and naturalistic metaphysics. She traces this metaphysical opposition to the dichotomous structure of her medium—the way language produces meaning by division, by generating distinctions. Her poetic practice discloses, at every level of a poem's language, an aporia, an irreducible difference between the spirit and the letter. Rhetorically, she plays metaphorical senses against the literal meanings of words; formally, she plays the semantic axis of language against the apparatus of grammar, syntax, spelling, punctuation, capitalization, and so on. For example, she can cast doubt on the Christian faith in immortality by giving a literal reading of one of its supportive metaphors:

Those—dying then,
Knew where they went—
They went to God's Right Hand—
That Hand is amputated now
And God cannot be found—   [P–1551]

The violent juxtaposition of the metaphoric "hand" with a surgical term like "amputated" reduces the metaphoric to the literal and thus disarticulates the whole anthropomorphic myth of God, for a reduction of the metaphoric to the literal is in effect a loss of faith. Any system of belief rests upon the symbolic function of language: the believer enters into a contractual relationship with religious language and agrees to read "God's Right Hand" in a certain way. Dickinson, who traffics in such contracts, can choose to expose the point at which the literal becomes the metaphorical. And she has at her disposal a remarkably varied diction to aid her. "Hand," for example, is an Anglo-Saxon word with a concrete referent; it is "amputated" with a Latinate word, and the surgery displaces a central, historically authoritative language as much as a central, patriarchal mythology. Dickinson generally associates the symbolic function of language with authority. "Papa above!" (P–61) nicely demonstrates how she questions the authority of religious language by literalizing God the Father as "papa" and exposing the reductive figure of personification on which such language rests. Although her childlike persona can be trying, it accurately represents her position: her rebellion sounds childlike because it is the expression of a literalizing imagination.

Dickinson's literalizing imagination manifests itself most clearly in her dissection of words. She unglues long words in order to reveal the way meaning is generated. Her functional unit is the syllable, which is the borderline between articulation and disarticulation and mediates between sense and nonsense.[12] A primary unit of sound that becomes a unit of sense as well, the syllable links and separates sound and sense, nature and spirit—each of which, in its pure state, is syllableless. The creations of "Mother Nature" are material only;

The Veins of other Flowers
The Scarlet Flowers are

Till Nature leisure has for Terms
As "Branch," and "Jugular."

We pass, and she abides.
We conjugate Her Skill
While She creates and federates
Without a syllable [P–811]

Yet the syllables we conjugate as we pass *are* the leisure of Nature, without which she would not abide. Just as the "sheen must have a Disk / To be a sun" (P–1550), the syllableless needs syllables to be syllableless. Similarly, a nonmaterial or "syllable-less Sea" (P–1700) needs the demarcating shoreline of syllables to *be* a sea "Unvisited of Shores" (P–695).

In a number of poems, Dickinson focuses on the syllable as a building block in order to show how it adds meanings by introducing division into the syllableless:

If my Bark sink
'Tis to another sea—
Mortality's Ground Floor
Is Immortality— [P–1234]

The juxtaposition of "Mortality" and "Immortality" calls into question what the poem ostensibly asserts, for the very concept of immortality must be built upon the "Ground Floor" of mortality by adding the negative prefix *im*- to the root word, and not the other way around. The syllableless natural state or "mort" yields its antithesis, the syllableless eternal state or immortality, when the prefix *im*- introduces opposition. P–1503 likewise dissects the composition of sense:

More than the Grave is closed to me—
The Grave and that Eternity
To which the Grave adheres—
I cling to nowhere till I fall—
The Crash of nothing, yet of all—
How similar appears—

Life is nothing, because it is without eternity. Yet it is all; for all we know, it appears all we know. This "here," then, is nowhere; yet it is *now here:* the "now here" posits the "nowhere" of eternity, and vice versa. The grave's "ad-here-ing" to eternity makes here nowhere. Thus presence is defined by absence, and absence by presence (the "Grave" "adheres" to "Eternity"). And the defining line is the dividing line—the line that draws distinctions, whether between words or worlds.

Another example of Dickinson's method is found in P–1420:

Why Birds, a Summer morning
Before the Quick of Day
Should stab my ravished spirit
With Dirks of Melody
Is part of an inquiry
That will receive reply
When Flesh and Spirit sunder
In Death's Immediately—

Without the mediation of language and temporality, death's presence or immediacy will reply, but with silence; it will answer, but not *her* question. As she defines "Heaven" elsewhere,

And bye and bye—a *Change*—
Called Heaven—
Rapt *Neighborhoods* of Men—
Just finding out—what puzzled us—
Without the *lexicon!*   [P–246; emphasis mine]

The italicized words show that, in order to define "Heaven," we must rely on the guidelines of this world. In "Heaven," where words are things, there are no puzzles and no need for a lexicon. But because our questions are generated by our being outside "Heaven," by our lexicon and its slant relationship to the earth, "Heaven" is beside the point. Similarly, "Death's Immediately" cannot answer *our* questions about time, questions predicated by mediacy. Separation, then, is primary, and wholeness or "Immediately" is an idea, a fiction added on by a prefix. As Dickinson puts it elsewhere, we "infer" the existence of paradise "By its Bisecting / Messenger—" (P–1411). A whole unbisected by messages exists only in the inference of a bisecting messenger, a temporal language. Since the mediation of language introduces the distinctions it would bridge, Dickinson can say:

The Brain is just the weight of God—
For—Heft them—Pound for Pound—
And they will differ—if they do—
As Syllable from Sound—   [P–632]

"Syllable" and "Sound" are coeval, both different and the same, for articulation begins when a unit of sound is mentally perceived as a phoneme or a syllable—as a meaningful unit. Before the syllable, neither syllable nor sound exists.

At times, however, Dickinson descends below even syllables to the level of letters and graphemes and walks the line between the rational and the irrational, the "circumference" of what makes discourse discourse, as in P–1624:

Apparently with no surprise
To any happy Flower
The Frost beheads it at its play—
In accidental power—
The blond Assassin passes on—
The Sun proceeds unmoved
To measure off another Day
For an Approving God.   [emphasis mine]

This poem proposes a series of distinctions or different ideological positions and begins by distinguishing between nature's "accidental power" and God's planned procedures. This difference, however, is immediately subsumed by the larger distinction between the point of view of the observer-poet and the events observed and recorded. The opening "Apparently"—with its differing senses of "manifestly" and "ostensibly"—places the speaker with her doubt outside the system of the poem and in effect dissolves the issue. Whether nature rules directly by accident or God by proxy, the speaker is alien to both. From her perspective, the machine seems to work; only she is on the outside looking in, only she is "surprised" or "moved." "Apparently" asserts the speaker's rhetorical freedom: she is free to draw lines and introduce distinctions—such as the one between chance and determinism—and to see the events as she sees fit, interpreting their import for herself. Yet the difference between language and extralinguistic phenomena seems, in turn, to be subsumed by a third distinction between accidental and determined language. Apparently, the speaker's rhetorical freedom is belied by the literal pattern of the poem. The conscious speaker's distance from the processes of nature is only apparent, for "apparently" itself places the speaker in a naturalistic, physical, or literal pattern set up by the poem's language. In fact, the word relates the observer to all the other processes with the same literal construction: "apparently" is linked directly to "approving," and in between range happy flowers, accidental powers, and passing assassins. The question of whether this pattern signifies the poet's subordination to, or complicity with, natural laws is moot. The question of whether the sequence of words with the same structure is accidental or assassinating as planned by an "approving" poet cannot be answered, for it is itself generated by the poem's duality, the rift-bridge between its meaning and its literal shape. The letters of the poem free it from its metaphysical burden—the debate between chance and determinism, between naturalism and faith in a universe by design. At the same time, however, they liberate it from rationality into an irrational patterning that functions below permissible or legitimate ways of signifying—whether such patterning is unconscious or conscious, psychologically determined or formally chosen for, say, the purpose of alliteration.

The number of poems that "mean" by such "accidents" of lettering brings to the fore the issue of legitimate meaning. For example, in "There is a word / Which bears a sword" (P–8), the "cutting" word—any word that brandishes a "sword"—is disarmed by the literal insight that "sword," too, is a word; indeed, it bears a word. The lettering is an irrational staging of the rational argument. "Forgot" is the word that bears a sword and kills like the scythe of the Grim Reaper, Time. Yet the sword or time itself bears the word or language. An accident of lettering thus blunts the metaphoric threat of the "cutting" word. Likewise,

During my education,
It was announced to me
That *gravitation, stumbling,*
Fell from an *apple* tree!   [P–3]

"Gravitate" was coined by Newton from *gravitas,* meaning "heavy" or "grave." "Grave," however, announces still another fall: deriving from a different, Old English root that means "to dig" or "to scratch" and gives us "engraving," it signifies also a tomb. Both gravities—the Newtonian and Biblical falls, "fact" and "myth"—are joined *and* separated in the word "gravitation." The difference between fact and myth both arises from and dissolves in writing and is engraved in the word "grave"—in the fact that the same letters can spring from two different roots and mean two different things. Physics fell from myth; myth was grafted onto physics; and the grave is the ambiguous apple or the fruit of their union and their fall.

Here, the conceptual issues are inscribed in letters. The questions and answers of a conceptual universe break down to letters, but the letters that simultaneously generate and dissolve these issues are themselves the givens of language. Is such homophony an accident of language or an approved revelation—an annunciation—within language of the word of God? This question applies to other puns or homophones like "son" and "sun," on which the Logos itself turns. Thus poetic language draws the line between accidental and legitimate revelation, using the givens of language both to intimate and dissolve truths beyond language. Questions about accidents and revelations,

about demarcating the meaningless and the meaningful, are generic to writing, because they are generated only by writing.

Dickinson's juggling of letters and graphemes invites us to a play that may
well venture beyond the licit. I will take another chance with P–1330:

Without a smile—Without a Throe
A Summer's soft A*ssemblies* go
To their entrancing *end*
Unknown—for all the times we met—
Estranged, however intimate—
What a di*ssem*bling Fri*end*—   [emphasis mine]

"Assemblies" gives the lie to itself, since it contains *lies,* and points to
"dissembling," which, by balancing "assembling," no longer only "lies" but
also "decays," for it no longer "sembles" or "re-sembles." Thus summer's
"assemblies" *are* lies; "dissembling" is her true nature, just as the "end" is
contained within the "Friend," who is less than "intimate"—for all the
"times we met." The "dissembling" of nature is revealed in, or represented
by, the "assemblies" of letters, graphemes, and syllables.

In Dickinson, then, poetic language itself generates the oppositions that
make discourse possible; as such, poetic language is the paradigm of human
understanding:

The Zeroes—taught us—Phosphorous—
We learned to like the Fire
By playing Glaciers—when a Boy—
And Tinder—guessed—by power
Of Opposite—to balance Odd—
If White—a Red—must be!
Paralysis—our Primer—dumb—
Unto Vitality!   [P–689]

"Zero," which derives from "cipher," is a figure without content, yet it
designates a system of writing. It signifies nothing yet empowers signification
thereby; it is the "paralysis" that underwrites the "primer." "Zero," then, is
neither presence, since it signifies nothing, nor absence, since it is both a
number and a word; rather, it proposes a system of delineating and designating presence and absence. What it teaches us is "phosphorous," the "bringer
of light," from Greek *phōs,* light, akin to "phantasy"—"idea, notion, appearance." The pure cipher—the *O*—is the circumference between presence and absence, being and appearance, wherein lies Dickinson's business.
Dickinson's circumference has called forth a variety of readings, but all of
them adhere to the pure cipher or the circle, the traditional emblem of God

and eternity. Both a letter and a number, the cipher *0* is the key to writing and to counting—both indeed guarded by the Father, the Logos *and* the Banker, who backs symbolic transactions and who himself counts in order to teach the uncountable:

'Tis One by One—the Father counts—
And then a Tract between
Set Cypherless—to teach the Eye
The Value of its Ten—   (P–545)

According to such binary logic, One $+ \ 0 \ = \ $ 10, and the poet's business is properly a "logarithm" (Logos $+$ rhythm)—a lettering and an accounting, an engraving and a rhythm. The *0* that is a letter and a number connects the two systems; it is the quintessential cipher *and* a gap, a blank, a "cypherless" "tract." It adds nothing to "One" ("1" and "I"), infuses a self-contained presence with absence, and liberates it to create the world. Thus

By homely gift and hindered Words
The human heart is told
Of Nothing—
"Nothing" is the force
That renovates the World—   [P–1563]

Words are reduced to nothing; a transcendent absence stands behind and sustains human words and community. Yet nothingness itself is reduced to a word when put in quotation marks, and that *word* "renovates the World." Language adds its "nothing" to the presence of the world, infusing it with absence and resurrecting it from the "Atom's Tomb" (P–376), the "numb" silence that is its death, into "this smart Misery." For Dickinson's language does not create the world but slips an *l* into the word to call it the "World."

Chapter Eleven

H art Crane: Inscribing the Sublime

> Twice and twice
> (Again the smoking souvenir,
> Bleeding eidolon!) and yet again.
> Until the bright logic is won
> Unwhispering as a mirror
> Is believed.
>
> Then, drop by caustic drop, a perfect cry
> Shall string some constant harmony . . .
>   "Legend"

Taking on himself the oppositions that generate the discourse of literary history, Hart Crane assumes a sacrificial role in American poetry. Just as Emily Dickinson dissects Christian and transcendental poetics, Crane plays against each other his two major influences—an Eliotic formalism with its roots in French Symbolism, and a Whitmanic organicism.[1] Crane has been repeatedly judged a failure on the grounds that his Symbolist and Whitmanic visions are incompatible; less often, he has been defended on the same grounds. For example, Sherman Paul sees that the "'confusion' in Crane's work is not inadvertent, as Tate and others believe, but deliberate. . . . To those in quest of certainty, Crane's vision is disturbing because it is 'doubtful' or double; it is not a vision of either/or but of both/and."[2]

Crane's "doubtful" vision is a version of Dickinson's anomalous vision, and it informs every phase of his writing. Rhetorically, he centers his poetry in the breach or discontinuity of metaphoric equivalence. This discontinuity takes on epic proportions in *The Bridge,* where its philosophical implications are spelled out. If an epic assumes the immanence of meaning in history, *The Bridge* draws the line between history and meaning, for it anatomizes the bridging operations of language itself and thus exposes the rhetoric of epic poetry. Technically, Crane adopts Dickinson's subversive strategies, pitting the centripetal force of formal and literal limitation and syntactic compression against the centrifugal force of semantic expansion. The meaning of such poetry lies precisely in its articulating and disarticulating rhetoric and syntax, which preclude certainties and unequivocal readings. The diacritical interplay of fusion and diffusion in his poems places them at the source of linguistic articulation and constitutes an ironic dissection of both formalism and organicism.

Dickinson's disarticulating or "amputating" language is the prototype of Crane's poetic. The logical division of the Logos into letters constitutes her radical surgery, and the psychological territory her poetry marks and occupies is, appropriately, pain. To break discourse into syllables and letters is to reveal an aporia at the center of meaning, a gap that is the profane double of a transcendent absence. Meaning is thus shown to be a "con-fusion" of sense and nonsense, spirit and letter, syllable and sound. The mutilation of the word into "killing" letters bares pain, for Dickinson's zero-cipher that teaches "Phosphorous" teaches by lack or an "Element of Blank." Such an anomalous or ironic language marks the "Boundaries of Pain . . . Between Eternity and Time."[3] Heidegger identifies this painful crossing of "Eternity" and "Time" as the threshold of language, the "middle" where "world" (which "grants to things their presence") and "things" (which "bear world") interpenetrate: "The intimacy of world and thing is not a fusion. . . . In the midst of the two, in the between of world and thing, in their *inter,* division prevails: a *dif-ference.*" This "dif-ference" is pain: "But what is pain? Pain rends. It is the rift. But it does not tear apart into dispersive fragments. Pain indeed tears asunder, it separates, yet so that at the same time it draws everything to itself, gathers it to itself. Its rending, as a separating that gathers, is at the same time that drawing which, like the pen-drawing of a plan or sketch, draws and joins together what is held apart in separation. Pain is the joining agent in the rending that divides and gathers. Pain is the joining of the rift. The joining is the threshold. . . . Pain is the dif-ference itself."

Heidegger's concept of a "rift-design," which he variously describes as a threshold, doorway, bridge, brightness, or stillness,[4] helps in reading Crane as well as Dickinson, for he also understands poetic language as the pain-ful difference cleaving and joining "Eternity" and "Time." In his "silken skilled transmemberment of song,"[5] a surgical dismemberment or disarticulation of syntax is meant to effect the "re-memberment" and "trans-substantiation" of song. Crane measures his syllables and dismembers his sentences in order to "re-member" the Word. He alludes to the paradox of the Christian Word, which promises to regather in itself the historical and temporal dissemination of words; he regards the diffusion and the gathering as coeval, however, so that his "con-fusing" language traces the severing and joining line between the very concepts of the sacred Word and profane words.

"Lachrymae Christi" presents Crane's "Janus-faced" (*CP,* 25) poet. Referring at once to the Passion of Christ and a brand of wine, the title itself joins the sacred and the profane faces of poetic language. At the same time that this wordplay invokes the family resemblance of Dionysus and Christ, it identifies the two-faced poet as their dividing-joining center and thus is the paradigm of Crane's language. The poet invokes Dionysus and Christ as gods whose mutilation gives rise to resurrection or a healing whole. The violence the poem records is both natural violence—the "red perfidies" of early spring, the "compulsion of the year"—and the violence done to nature or the "grail / Of earth" by history, the industrial machinery of mills where only a "sill / Sluices its one unyielding smile" (*CP,* 19). The poet modeled on the mythic paradigm of the Savior would redeem the perfidies of both nature and history; yet the linguistic violence in the poem subsumes the larger, mythic patterns, including the poet's identification with Dionysus/Christ.

The poem's language is exceptionally anarchic, even for Crane. The extreme syntactic compression and ellipses, the network of syllabic associations and echoes that both underlie and interrupt the drift of the poem, the semantic indeterminacy that follows from the emphasis on isolated words, and the "excess" of meaning—the connotations that overwhelm the denotation—render parts of the poem all but incoherent. Thus the poet as the sacrificial figure who would make whole the division and heal the mutilation—specifically, who would integrate pagan and Christian myth with history and machines—is master only of a disintegrating idiom and ends up "mangled" by the lexicon, while projecting the image of the whole god, mysterious and beguiling, just above or below the words:

> Thy face
> From charred and riven stakes, O
> Dionysus, Thy
> Unmangled target smile.   [*CP,* 20]

Dionysus is targeted to be mangled not only seasonally in his physical body and historically in the mills that mangle more than cotton or wood, but also in the poet's script, for another meaning of "mangle" is to garble a text. Thus the tears of Christ are cognate with both "the year's / First blood" *and* the "tearing" or rending of the world into words:

Names peeling from Thine eyes
And their undimming lattices of flame,

Spell out in palm and pain
Compulsion of the year, O Nazarene.   [*CP,* 20]

The would-be mythic poet is necessarily mangled or crucified by the alphabet and the lexicon in order to point to a targeted whole. Crane's identification with Dionysus/Christ functions not thematically but technically. His articulation proceeds by disarticulation and deconstructs the mythic paradox, revealing it to be created in the image of the operations of language. Crane strikes the pose of a poet inspired or possessed by Bacchus's wine, yet he works from the dictionary, sending readers to their lexicons to research etymologies and discover the multiple meanings of his words. For Crane is interested in the structure of linguistic meaning as the crossing of the axes of physical limits and semantic and rhetorical expansion. These axes designate the profane and sacred faces of language, and Crane centers in the gap between them, rhyming the tears of the Nazarene with "benzine / Rinsings" and balancing Dionysus's "target smile" with the "unyielding smile" of a "sill." Joseph Riddel discusses Crane's "alleged visionary" style: "That Crane presumes to be an orphic poet, in the profoundest mythical sense, is one thing; the self-consciousness with which he goes about playing that role, and creating its style, is another."[6] His analysis of this central disjunction in Crane is valid; Riddel does not credit Crane with full consciousness of his "presumption," however, so that he is reduced, once more, to a "failed Whitman." Yet Crane's expansive, Whitmanic gesture—his possessed, sublime, ecstatic excess—is always calculatedly cut short by the limits of writing.

Insisting on an opaque syntax and the self-imposed formal pressures of metrical and syllabic reckoning, his poems occupy the same ironic, diacritical ground Dickinson first clears. He dwells in the Dickinsonian gap or "wound" that marks the intersection of a transcendent vision and the mechanism of poetic composition, of the infinite spirit and the finite letters of poetry. "Paraphrase" compares iambic rhythm to the "steady winking beat between / Systole, diastole" (*CP,* 17). This "record" is "wedged" in the "soul," just as the poetic beat is wedged in the "soul" of language. In time, these measures of temporal and spatial dispersion destroy the soul or the life they enable; the systematic repetitions of stress patterns and heartbeats, as well as other "records," "feet," "integers," and "brackets," tear apart the "unmangled target" or the whole they project. The "winking beat" is the dividing center that gives life as it deals death; it is "that Eternity possessed / And plundered momently in every breast."[7] A rhythm of "systole" (to draw together or gather) and "diastole" (to push apart or disperse) makes poetic language, and Crane emphasizes equally the limits of the poem as formal artifact and the expansive, transcendent nature of its meaning. His tortured syntax is in part a response to metrical requirements, yet it liberates words from assigned syntactic functions that would limit the range of applicable readings. Such a poem that centers between freedom and limitation, between its transcendent vision and its temporal nature, offers a "winking" vision, as much as it measures a "winking beat" (*CP*, 17)—a "great wink of eternity" (*CP*, 36), as Crane puts it in "Voyages II." His is always a mocking insight engendered by an artifact, a pulsating paraphrase of vision. The poem "Paraphrase" demarcates the circumference between vision—the dread, apocalyptic "antarctic blaze"—and dead letters, the "white paraphrase" of the "hollowed" skull.

"The Broken Tower" again draws the line between the two coordinates of language. Once more, a "record" is "wedged" in the "soul," and the "bells break down their tower":

The bells, I say, the bells break down their tower;
And swing I know not where. Their tongues engrave
Membrane through marrow, my long-scattered score
Of broken intervals. . . . And I, their sexton slave!

. . . .

And so it was I entered the broken world
To trace the visionary company of love, its voice
An instant in the wind (I know not whither hurled)
But not for long to hold each desperate choice.

My word I poured. But was it cognate, scored
Of that tribunal monarch of the air
Whose thigh embronzes earth, strikes crystal Word
In wounds pledged once to hope—cleft to despair?   [*CP*, 193]

The poet is at once the "sexton slave" of the bells and charged to "trace the visionary company of love." The question is whether his word is "cognate" with the "crystal Word," whether his music is "scored" "Of that tribunal monarch of the air"—of the Law/Logos, Zeus/God whose thigh wound gives birth to Dionysus, whose wounds are the rebirth of Christ. Or is the poet's word cognate only with the bell that "gathers God"? Writing or engraving is a wound, but is it a wound "pledged . . . to hope," to a healing whole godhead, or "cleft to despair," "scored" to the cleft hoof of the metrical foot, to division, loss, and time:

The steep encroachments of my blood left me
No answer (could blood hold such a lofty tower

As flings the question true?)—or is it she
Whose sweet mortality stirs latent power?——

The rhetorical question ending the stanza gives the answer: the "sweet mortality" of blood both erects and breaks down the "tower" and is cognate with love and the poet's words, which pulse to the same systole-diastole rhythm. "Tracing" the "visionary company of love" becomes at once a joining and a severing, drawing the line that divides what it joins. Likewise, "company" (L. *com-*, with + *panis*, bread) is targeted by the "companiles" that precede it, and the "visionary company" of the divinity of love, the sharers of the divine bread-flesh, is "mangled" by "each desperate choice," "scoring" to the tune of the bells. Poetry is another cognate, both "pledged" to hope and "cleft to despair." The Word of Transubstantiation and its transmemberment—its re-memberment and dismemberment—constitute mutually defining axes and are cognate with the Logos and the lexicon, the Love and the "scoring."

Crane's logic of metaphor seems to designate this crossing. The "logic of metaphor," he claims, "antedates our so-called pure logic, and . . . is the genetic basis of all speech, hence consciousness and thought-extension" (*CP*, 221). Such a claim suggests that he is talking not about metaphoric rhetoric but about the diacritical dynamics of all linguistic meaning. His logic is not Emerson's logic of analogy or resemblance, which puts one on an equal footing with nature and enables one to "climb" on metaphor, in Robert Frost's analogy, as on a ladder; nor is it the logic of Poe and Eliot, an allegorical expression or representation of a prior referent. Neither does Crane mean a way of proceeding through metaphoric associations rather than logic. His "explication" of "At Melville's Tomb" for Harriet Monroe hints at the illogic of his logic: "You ask me how *compass, quadrant and sextant 'contrive'* tides. I ask you how Eliot can possibly believe that 'Every street *lamp* that I pass *beats* like a fatalistic *drum!*'" (*CP*, 236). Crane appears oblivious to the difference between his metaphor and Eliot's. Eliot's terms maintain a logical relationship to each other and to the whole: drums and street lamps are alike because they both "beat" at measured intervals and, therefore, "fatalistically." In Crane's metaphor, however, the measuring devices or instruments do not record but contrive natural time, mechanically extend it or render it knowable. His logic is that of Dickinson, for whom a measuring instrument like writing contrives, changes, and makes a knowable nature itself. Such logic posits at once a literal measuring and a "tide" that the "compass, quadrant and sextant" cannot contrive. "It is my hope," Crane writes, "to go *through* the combined materials of the poem, using our 'real' world somewhat as a spring-board, and to give the poem *as a whole* an orbit or predetermined direction of its own" (*CP,* 220). The "orbit" of the poem is its distance from "our 'real' world," so that it can be "at least a stab at a truth" (*CP,* 220). Ideally, this "stab at a truth" is "a single, new *word*" the reader is left with, a word "never before spoken and impossible to actually enunciate, but self-evident as an active principle in the reader's consciousness henceforward" (*CP,* 221).[8] He also defines his goal as creating a state of "'innocence' (Blake)." "Innocence" (L. *in* + *nocens,* harmful, from IE *necro,* death) means freedom from the wrongs of time and experience. The "stab" at truth is a word that is "absolute" and exists outside sequential, temporal structurings, whether of enunciation or paraphrase.

Crane's crumpled syntax, oxymoronic logic, synesthetic imagery, and mixed metaphors are all ways of short-circuiting rational, paraphrasable wording in order to project the unspeakable Word, which can be glimpsed as single and whole only by mangling the conventions of discourse. His logic "stabs" at a truth by dissecting grammar and analogy, cutting through the rational to the irrational. While ordinary logic follows grammatical laws, the "bright logic" of metaphor breaks the rules of agreement and sequentiality, and Crane works with fragments, unclear referents, syntactic discontinuities, and ambiguous subjects. Such illogical logic is meant to be both a violation and a revelation; it is a cut that heals, an ellipsis that links. Crane's emotional excesses, his cultivation and simulation of states of crisis (Gk. *krisis,* from *krinein,* to separate, to cut), are analogues of his stylistic paradigm. Like Dickinson, whose poems about pain make more sense as psychological cognates of her diacritical poetics than as autobiography, Crane gives us the emotion of art and not an art of emotion. His "abysses" are "ellipses," and his emotional intensities are impossible to distinguish from his stylistic derangements. Crane is not a failed Transcendentalist but a mannered one. His poetry depends on a conscious distancing from experience—whether realistic or mystical, naturalistic or transcendent. Dickinson, Crane, and John Ashbery are all conscious that poetry does not signify a primal, primary, or even prior experience, perception, or conception; it refers to writing itself— to the structures of poetic form and rhetoric, the strategies of articulation and representation, and the intensities and plateaus of poetic sensation.[9]

"Voyages" exemplifies the generation of such esthetic emotions that arise from the opposition of the poem's "scoring" and the unspeakable Word. Words retain their isolated presences in "Voyages," and the barely paraphrasable network they weave is a parody of connection. The poem adheres to what Roland Barthes describes as the "lexical basis" of modern poetry, whose unit is the word. Such poetry "retains only the outward shape of relationships, their music, but not their reality. The Word shines forth above a line of relationships emptied of their content, grammar is bereft of its purpose, it becomes prosody and is no longer anything but an inflection which lasts only to present the Word. Connections are not . . . abolished, they are merely reserved areas, a parody of themselves."[10] Yet Crane's tone is not parodic. For his linguistic anatomizing and dispersal aim to leave us with an inkling of the transcendent word—posited by its very absence—that would regather the diffusion and bespeak the timeless identity of love, death, and song; of blood, sea, and ink; of phallus, oar, and quill. This synchronic word is "impossible to actually enunciate," just as the "signature of the incarnate word" (*CP,* 38) cannot be scored or written. The transcendent "imaged Word"—the "unbetrayable reply / Whose accent no farewell can know" (*CP,* 41)—is projected by the betraying image, the natural "accents" of language. The "Sea, whose diapason knells / On scrolls of silver snowy sentences" (*CP,* 36), both "tests the word" (*CP,* 50) and harbors the "Belle Isle," "The imaged Word . . . that holds / Hushed willows anchored in its glow" (*CP,* 41). The "Belle Isle" that Crane's voyager seeks to shore up nature, writing, and time is but the "white echo" of his "oar" (*CP,* 41), which throughout the poem is associated with other blades that cut, engrave, write.

The motion of the oar-pen, in whose wake the "unbetrayable reply" rises, is the center of Crane's poem, which rests in a stasis *within* its motion—*between* a purposive, entropic motion and a transcendent stillness. His emphasis on the etymologies, connotations, and multiple meanings of words, together with his syntactic indeterminacy, thickens the synchronic axis of "Voyages" and resists a linear progression of meaning to create a "freedom" that "stays" (*CP,* 45) in its motion. This "erotic double"—in Ashbery's phrase—of a transcendent timelessness is the real end of Crane's parabolic voyage: discovering a timeless "insular Tahiti" equally removed from natural and supernatural consummations. Like Dickinson, he seeks a "bright impossibility / To dwell—delicious—on" and, in "so sweet a Torment," to deflect the "Bolts of Melody" that would "stun."[11] Emphasizing formal containment, Crane subverts or slants the transcendence that is the ostensible goal of his fiction; freeing his "meaning" from its denotative and grammatical underpinnings, he escapes the natural fate that is his actual origin and end. Thus he is able to locate the "wound" at his center, the "bright logic" where the Immortal Word still bleeds to death and the word still "bleeds infinity" (*CP,* 117). "Madly meeting logically in this hour," the poet can sing "this mortality alone / Through clay aflow immortally to you" (*CP,* 38). Whitmanic in its ecstatic surrender to love and death, "Voyages" is not Whitmanic in its language, and this formal difference is crucial: Crane is no more a failed

Whitman than Dickinson is a failed Transcendentalist. His formalism dissects and measures the unformed, the transcendent and/or naturalistic "formless." It does not morally or metaphysically "justify" the ways of the unformed; it only justifies literally, setting its margins so as to dwell between them or "in possibility."

This possibility goes undefined; as in Dickinson, the unformed may be God or only an "unsponsored" nature. It may be "miracle" or "midnight,"[12] for either is but an inflection of the poet's pen. Thus "Belle Isle" has its double in the "Carib Isle," the other face of the static ecstasy, the linteled sublime, or the lettered Word of "Voyages." The paradise of words that the "fervid covenant" (*CP,* 41) of poetry grants the poet, as reimbursement for the scoring, is itself reflected and reversed in the Satanic island with its pilgrim "for slow evisceration bound" (*CP,* 157). And the Word, "Whose accent no farewell can know," is echoed in a language that is a shell emptied of breath or spirit—a "carbonic amulet / Sere of the sun exploded in the sea" (*CP,* 157).[13] Now language is a deadly script, a legend or inscription indifferently captioning the legend or myth of the transcendent word:

The tarantula rattling at the lily's foot
Across the feet of the dead, laid in white sand
Near the coral beach—nor zigzag fiddle crabs
Side-stilting from the path (that shift, subvert
And anagrammatize your name)—No, nothing here
Below the palsy that one eucalyptus lifts
In wrinkled shadows—mourns.   [*CP,* 156]

On this "doubloon isle," the wind in fact stifles the poet's impulse to breathe life into the "crypt" of writing:

To the white sand I may speak a name, fertile
Albeit in a stranger tongue. Tree names, flower names
Deliberate, gainsay death's brittle crypt. Meanwhile
The wind that knots itself in one great death—
Coils and withdraws. So syllables want breath.   [*CP,* 156]

A "fertile" tongue—the creative word that names or speaks life—is robbed of its breath by a "literalism" as of "zigzag fiddle crabs," death's "crypt" or the cipher-code of letters and syllables. In such language, the names that would breathe life only "maim" (from the same root as "mangle")—a telling rhyme with "name" that Crane uses in "A Name for All." Being "struck free and holy in one Name" and being maimed by a name "pinioned" to the body mark the opposition (*CP,* 164) of Belle Isle and Carib Isle (whence "cannibal"). The isles of life and death, ruled by two different "Captains," designate the two axes of writing: the letters "pledged . . . to hope" and "cleft to despair."

Without the benefit of Dickinson's generic eccentricity, Crane fully assumes the cross of poetic language. He is torn between hope and despair, ecstatic and elegiac by turns, subscribing to the Word and "conscripted 'o" (*CP,* 23) the "accents" of words. *The Bridge* is his most ambitious attempt to hold the healing design and the rending rift in a tensile balance. The poem has been considered a failure because of a division or disjunction of one kind or another—between a Symbolist style and Whitmanic aims, between a lyric talent and an epic theme, between means and ends. And the harshest judgment of the poem is that it lacks an intellectual center.[14] If we regard Crane's center as a crossing of the forces of fusion and diffusion,[15] however, *The Bridge* offers yet another dramatization of his poetic and the task it assigns to the discoverer-poet:

> Remember, Falcon-Ace,
> Thou hast there in thy wrist a Sanskrit charge
> To conjugate infinity's dim marge—   [*CP,* 92]

The "wrist" has a pulse, charged by writing ("a Sanskrit charge") and charged to write ("to conjugate"). And the pulse has a "grammar," which conjugates and temporalizes the infinite and conjugates or unites with it. The double-entendres of "charge" and "conjugate" suggest that the charge or spark results in duty, law, and "conjugation." The rhyme of "charge" and "marge" also suggests that the unmeasurable infinity and the measuring are coeval and trace the circumference delineating them.

In *The Bridge,* the physiological and mechanical measuring is expanded to include historical time. The cut of the "timber torn / By iron, iron—always the iron dealt cleavage" (*CP,* 66) has ruptured the continent's Edenic, timeless space, which Crane depicts in the circle drawn by Pocahontas-Eve "wheeling" "naked as she was, all the fort over" (*CP,* 53).[16] And the arc of the iron bridge—the product of a history committed to entropic time ("shorter hours, quicker lunches, behaviorism, and toothpicks" [*CP,* 232])—is also the "terrific threshold of the prophet's pledge" (*CP,* 46) and projects a redemptive circle, a healing whole that might "pardon" history and time (*CP,* 116). The bridge, then, is a historical embodiment of the rift-design that structures the poetic word. As such, a bridge represents a generic symbol—as Heidegger, in fact, argues[17]—spanning the spatial and temporal cleavage that it deals. Thus the grammar that "conjugates" timeless space, dispersing in declensions and syllables, can also be a

. . . Choir, translating time
Into what multitudinous Verb the suns
And synergy of waters ever fuse, recast
In myriad syllables,—Psalm of Cathay!
O Love, thy white, pervasive Paradigm . . .   [*CP*, 115]

The "Psalm" that is a "pervasive Paradigm" is not only a model or representation of "Love" but a temporal "declension" of it, since a second meaning of
"paradigm" is a model of grammatical conjugation or declension. The systole-diastole of such a language as Crane's constitutes a generic-genetic pulse
that coheres and disperses as it records "time's rendings, time's blendings"
(*CP*, 64).

The "incognizable Word"—God's "parable of man," of which Christ is
the paradigm—follows in *The Bridge* a parabolic path between a timeless
center and a linear, naturalistic, or entropic time. Spanning stasis and motion,
the bridge is an analogue of Crane's stylistic resistance to diachrony. It
represents an "unfractioned idiom" (*CP*, 46) that builds on the ground floor
of "fractions" and "idioms" to become a "palladium helm of stars," by which
the stars themselves steer. Such a bridge-language is "one arc synoptic of all
tides below" (*CP*, 114). It mediates between the one God and His "teeming
span" (*CP*, 51); between the "woman" whose "namelessness" "is / God" (*CP*,
98)—"Whose depth of red, eternal flesh" is "our native clay" (*CP*, 88)—and
her declension and conjugation through history:

We found God lavish there in Colorado

.   .   .   .

    And glistening through the sluggard freshets came
In golden syllables loosed from the clay
            His gleaming name.   [*CP*, 76]

The parable of the nameless God's declension remains equidistant from a
lyric center and a narrative history. Crane's gloss of "Powhatan's Daughter"
offers a grammatically coherent narrative version of the lyric history that the
poems tell, and gathers their dispersal. The lyric-epic discrepancy that the
poem's early critics denounced is, in fact, the crux of Crane's project, as the
visible gap between the two stories, styles, typefaces, and columns indicates.
Crane employs both lyric and epic idioms in order to play them off each
other, just as he invokes generic and grammatical requirements in general
only to subvert them, so that we can "dream" "beyond the print that bound
her name" (*CP*, 66), "*knowing her / without name*" (*CP*, 67).[18] By displaying the
division of literary idioms, the poem prophesies an "unfractioned idiom":

Always through blinding cables, to our joy,
Of thy white seizure springs the prophecy:
Always through spiring cordage, pyramids
Of silver sequel, Deity's young name
Kinetic of white choiring wings . . . ascends.   [*CP,* 116]

    The gap between the artifact of stone and steel and the "Bridge of Fire" is the same gap that links letters and the words they articulate, words and the Word they project. A poetic language whose paradigm is a bridge is double at the source, both a "stammering" "through the pangs of dust and steel" and the "circular, indubitable frieze / Of heaven's meditation" (*CP,* 115). It is a temporal idiom or dialect that pierces and punctuates the clarity of vision that it enables:

Sheerly the eyes, like seagulls stung with rime—
Slit and propelled by glistening fins of light—
Pick biting way up towering looms that press
Sidelong with flight of blade on tendon blade
—Tomorrows into yesteryear—and link
What cipher-script of time no traveler reads
But who, through smoking pyres of love and death,
Searches the timeless laugh of mythic spears.   [*CP,* 115]

Crane's epic does not surrender to time and history; it is not empowered by a faith in immanence and the coincidence of "The Epos of a life" and "of The Lands, identical."[19] In fact, *The Bridge* deconstructs the Whitmanic identity of whole and part and the consequent coincidence of the epic and lyric idioms. In Crane, whole and part, epic and lyric are two distinct idioms ironically juxtaposed, as are his Whitmanic faith and his formalist language.[20] For Crane's faith is only the internal, logical coordinate of his conjugating and scoring language; he proposes an identity we can only "infer" from its "Bisecting / Messenger."[21] Or, in his compass metaphor, "A needle in the sight, suspended north,— / Yielding by inference and discard, faith" (*CP,* 51). Like Christopher ("bearing Christ") Columbus, the poet of *The Bridge* does bring the "incognizable Word / Of Eden" (*CP,* 51); but, like Dickinson's "stories" of timeless states and experiences that are functions of the very operations of language, Crane's is the timeless story of the generation of time and eternity in poetic script. It recites in epic guise the generic poem Crane writes over and over: the timeless account of the birth/death of the sacrificial Word, told now in the "antiphonal" whispers (*CP,* 117) of the "bound cable strands," those "arching strands of song" "veering with light," "as though a god were issue of the strings." (*CP,* 114).

Chapter Twelve

John Ashbery:
Parodying the Paradox

All life
Is as a tale told to one in a dream
In tones never totally audible
Or understandable, and one wakes
Wishing to hear more, asking
For more, but one wakes to death, alas,
Yet one never
Pays any heed to that, the tale
Is still so magnificent in the telling
That it towers far above life, like some magnificent
Cathedral spire, far above the life
Pullulating around it (what
Does it care for that, after all?) and not
Even aiming at the heavens far above it
Yet seemingly nearer, just because so
Vague and pointless . . .

"Litany"

"Steeped in the nostalgia of a collective past,"[1] John Ashbery's poetry exhibits a greater range of stylistic influences than Dickinson's or Crane's. Yet his rhetorical strategies are Dickinsonian, for he also places himself "between" the "big, / Vaguer stuff," the grander schemas that constitute "the tradition" (*HD*, 34).[2] Or, as he writes elsewhere,

I no longer have any metaphysical reasons
For doing the things I do.
Night formulates, the rest is up to the scribes and the eunuchs. [*AWK*, 91]

More discursive than Dickinson or Crane, Ashbery takes on the larger formulas of articulation, dismantling the "syntax" of their rhetoric. He

divests the rhetorical and grammatical formulas of discourse of their epistemological authority and insists that he intends his poems to communicate
something—but nothing previously known or subsequently relatable. Similarly, he distinguishes the rhetoric and style of "the process of philosophic
inquiry" from any specific philosophical concepts or positions; he isolates the
rhetoric or "forms of autobiography" from the idea of a consistent, definable
ego with special experiences; he strips the rhetoric of the lyric of its fiction of
timeless presence, just as he divests the rhetoric of narrative of its teleological
order. Finally, he divests the rhetorics of meditation and prayer of their
metaphysical and theological implications.[3] And in the interstices of the
dismantled and demystified structures of articulation appear inklings of
transcendence, auras of grace, shadows of light, oddly recalling what has
been lost in the rhetorics that Ashbery exposes. The revelation of such
"meaninglessness" at the heart of "meaningful" structures of formulation is
his amazing grace. Much like Dickinson's and Crane's, Ashbery's diacritical
language marks the threshold between sacred and profane language and
entertains, in its metaphysical destitution, a spiritual/erotic excess of meaning.

In "Litany" Ashbery announces, "*I want to write / Poems that are as inexact as
mathematics*" (*AWK,* 46). The "inexactness" of mathematics is radical, the
"natural" basis for its methodological or rhetorical exactions. Thus it would
share something of the beauty Ashbery ascribes to experimental art and
religion—the "recklessness" of their position, "the strong possibility that
they are founded on nothing."[4] Ashbery dwells in this possibility. Just as
Dickinson keeps disarticulation in synchrony with articulation, and Crane
aims for a "steady beat" both rending and rendering the whole, Ashbery
attempts to keep random "dispersal" in step with meaningful "gathering."
Reminded by an interviewer that "as randomness increases, meaningfulness
decreases," Ashbery responds that he tries to "keep meaningfulness up to the
pace of randomness. . . . I really think that meaningfulness can't get along
without randomness."[5] Logically, the two concepts are coeval, and Ashbery's
work beguilingly traces their diacritical path in order to maintain a balance of
forces resting on nothing. On the one hand, his poems attract us with their
gesture of "meaningful" discourse in the manner of Wallace Stevens—the
meditative pace of the syntax and the memories and expectations of meaningfulness that it evokes, the careful use of qualifiers, the precisions and
surprises of the diction. Yet "the pattern that may carry the sense" stays
"hidden" (*HD,* 34), and these technical features do not "add up," because
they are accompanied by violations of grammar and logic. Ashbery is fond of
the phrases "add up" and "connect up" because they spell out the hierarchi-

cal and teleological assumptions that underwrite meaningful discourse, prescribing what should be put in or left out and how the parts should be arranged to answer to some "*sense of accomplishment*" that "*haloes*" them "*from afar*" (*AWK*, 67). He alludes to meaningful discourse—nostalgically and satirically by turns—yet subverts it, exposing its political and metaphysical assumptions. The traces of narration and the allusions to coherence that his verse retains become ineffectual parodies of their own presumptions and register only as centripetal impulses against the concurrent drive to randomness.

One model of Ashbery's compositional strategy is a convex mirror, which doubles the inherent distortion of representation. It both gathers and disperses light, so that there is "no / False disarray as proof of authenticity" (*SP*, 69). Rather, the "disarray" is generic, as in Parmigianino's self-portrait:

> . . . the chaos
> Of your round mirror which organizes everything
> Around the polestar of your eyes which are empty,
> Know nothing, dream but reveal nothing.   [*SP*, 71]

Parmigianino's painting questions Renaissance perspectivism from within by a meticulous application of perspectival techniques, coupled with the distortion of a convex representation. Specifically, this distortion magnifies the painter's organizing hand as the centripetal focal point of the dispersal that speeds up at the periphery of the convex mirror. Here, a technique is played up to question a metaphysic. Ashbery's strategy is similar: in his "convex" composition, a "near-sighted" focus on successive present moments of attention disperses the past and the future, "the thoughts / That peel off and fly away at breathless speeds" (*SP*, 71).[6] His interchangeable pronouns contribute to the same end: "The personal pronouns in my work very often seem to be like variables in an equation. 'You' can be myself or it can be another person . . . and so can 'he' and 'she' for that matter and 'we.'"[7] The equation stands above such variables as subject matter and persons. Stripped of these contingencies, the syntactic and rhetorical structures of communication or expression emerge as absolute forms of human discourse that rise "far above" realism and its metaphysics. Yet Ashbery also suggests that his technical discontinuities produce a polyphony of voices, which is "a means toward greater naturalism."[8] Just as Parmigianino's self-portrait lies "between" realism and "a *bizarria*" (*SP*, 73), Ashbery's technique falls "between" naturalism and mannerism. Such anomalous works as Parmigianino's painting and Ashbery's poem alike aim to remain

                    stable within
Instability, a globe like ours, resting
On a pedestal of vacuum, a ping-pong ball
Secure on its jet of water.   [*SP*, 70]

Ashbery's version of Orphic poetry, then, attempts to "correct" its innate, temporal erring—"the error that incites us / To duplication" (*AWK*, 67), the duplicity and dissembling of being in time—not by an Emersonian "intercourse" with "truth" but by doubling its error. This "sublime that is not sublime" is the proper esthetic of a language and nature infected by difference:

All that we see is penetrated by it—
The distant treetops with their steeple (so
Innocent), the stair, the windows' fixed flashing—
Pierced full of holes by the evil that is not evil,
The romance that is not mysterious, the life that is not life,
A present that is elsewhere.   [*AWK*, 74]

Instead of engaging his rhetorical medium with a nonrhetorical fate, Ashbery proposes to duplicate the error in the hope that two wrongs might make a right,

                    So in some way
Although the arithmetic is incorrect
The balance is restored because it
Balances, knowing it prevails,
And the man who made the same mistake twice is exonerated.   [*SP*, 11]

Ashbery begins by "supposing that you are a wall / And can never contribute to nature anything / But the feeling of being alongside it" (*AWK*, 23). Thus distancing himself from the romantic sublime and its intercourse with nature, Ashbery exposes its "duplicitous" rhetoric:

It goes without saying that
To have it make sense you
Would have to belong to all who are asleep
Making no sense, and then
Flowers of the desert begin, peep by peep,
To emerge and you are saved
Without having taken a step, but I
Don't know how you're going to get
Another person to do that.   [*AWK*, 55]

"You" have to get "another person" to "do that"—to die into nature and not make "sense" in order to authorize "you" to make sense. Ashbery rejects this model and proposes instead to flatten out time and space, to fragment and gather at once, to "make no sense" and "make sense" concurrently. According to this diacritical logic, the operations of linguistic articulation internalize the drama and dialectic of romantic poetry:

> We must first trick the idea
> Into being, then dismantle it,
> Scattering the pieces on the wind . . .   [*AWK*, 79]

The process of "scattering" entails more than deconstruction and accounts for the peculiar feel of Ashbery's poetry. He suggests that the "pathos and liveliness of ordinary human communication"—"the way we talk and think without expecting what we say to be recorded or remembered"—is "poetry" to him.[9] Grammatical subversion and the resultant irreducible difficulties create the illusion of such "throw away" language and account for the "pathos" of Ashbery's version of Orphic poetry, which attempts to keep the "will to endure" well "hidden" (*SP*, 79) and intimates there may not be a future to "re-member" it.

Ashbery himself dates his analytic/synthetic method from "Clepsydra" in *Rivers and Mountains:* "After my analytic period, I wanted to get into a synthetic period. I wanted to write a new kind of poetry after my dismembering of language. Wouldn't it be nice, I said to myself, to do a long poem that would be a long extended argument, but would have the beauty of a single word?"[10] Ashbery's account approaches Crane's view of his intention to create a new state of consciousness, to communicate something not previously known, "as though a poem gave the reader as he left it a single, new *word,* never before spoken and impossible to actually enunciate, but self-evident as an active principle in the reader's consciousness henceforward."[11] Crane conceives of his word that "bleeds infinity" as a wound; Ashbery also images his unspeakable "word" as a gap or a "central crater," around which gather "all the things that have names" (*AWK*, 55). His "namelessness" is a profane version of Crane's "It is / God—your namelessness":[12]

> Meaningless syllables that
> Have a music of their own,
> The music of sex, or any
> Nameless event, something
> That can only be taken as
> Itself.   [*AWK*, 4]

This "meaningless" or "nameless" state is erotic, as it is in Dickinson's "Wild Nights" or Crane's "Voyages." Such a language has, in Ashbery's terms, an "anti-referential sensuousness,"[13] for the synchronic or semantic axis is so layered that reading becomes an erotic lingering between multiple meanings.

Ashbery plays the two axes of discourse against each other, and the gathering forces of syntax and form not only oppose semantic, allusive, and figurative dispersals but are double-crossed from within by segments of discourse that do not "course," bits of syntax that do not synthesize, and residual forms—"what Wyatt and Surrey left around" (*SP*, 19)—that have forgotten their original force or purpose. Subverting the centripetal laws of grammatical agreement of tenses and persons that govern meaningful discourse, Ashbery undermines sequential time in an attempt to approximate "*this* thing, the mute, undivided present" (*SP*, 80). Such a present at least "has the justification of logic" (*SP*, 80), which is the parodic double of the Emersonian "justice" of truth. Ashbery does not "rhyme" rhetoric and fate; he only balances intratextual forces so that they cancel each other out to offer a "pure / Affirmation that doesn't affirm anything" (*SP*, 70). Ashbery neither has a "homestead" nor is at sea but dwells, as on a houseboat, in possibility:

>   . . . To praise this, blame that,
> Leads one subtly away from the beginning, where
> We must stay, in motion.   [*HD*, 39]

Thus a discourse that is "random" (from the root "to run," from IE *er-*, "to set in motion," whence "origin") is "stable," and its motion resists diachrony, purposefulness, and progress, so that one

> . . . becomes oneself part of the meaningless
> Rolling and lurching, so hard to read
> Or hear, and never closer
> To the end or to the beginning: the mimesis
> Of death, without the finality.   [*AWK*, 34]

The grammatical discontinuity, the uncertainty of context, and the unpredictability of direction help Ashbery achieve such a precarious stasis within the flow of discourse, granting him a reprieve from the death sentence of a particular meaning or "message."[14]

Circumventing the legalities of discourse and refusing to abide by any consistent set of rules to define a discursive framework,[15] Ashbery achieves a sense of the "dimensionless quality" of life—its "fullness, or, if you wish, the emptiness."[16] The illegality of his method sets him apart from Stevens, whom he echoes in style and tone. Stevens's divagations follow legal procedures and respond to legalistic, interpretational methods based on grammatical consistencies and analogical correspondences. Thus his delays, deferrals, and "errors" finally do "add up" and "make sense," as the poetic imagination returns to accommodate fate. While the relationship between language and life remains a consistent proportion of analogies for Stevens, for Ashbery "there is a very close but oblique connection" between them.[17] Hence his "wacky analogies" (*HD*, 14) divest "the great 'as though'" (*DDS*, 73) of any epistemological value. Like Dickinson's poems, which "Tell all the Truth but tell it slant,"[18] Ashbery's poetry is broadcast on an "unassigned / Frequency" (*SP*, 81). Since neither poet clearly prohibits illicit readings, both offer at once a dearth and a plenitude of meaning. In Ashbery, an excess of randomness generates an excess of meaningfulness, so that his best work contains traces of something spiritual. Yet it is always hard to tell the spiritual from its opposite, a plain everyday "emptiness." Accordingly, a homey note tends to accompany his meditative tone, so that

You know now that it has the form of a string
Quartet. The different parts are always meddling with each other,
Pestering each other, getting in each other's way
So as to withdraw skillfully at the end, leaving—what?
A new kind of emptiness, maybe bathed in freshness,
Maybe not. Maybe just a new kind of emptiness.   [*HD*, 62]

Ashbery's language is an inventory of varieties of emptiness, a "*complete collection*" of "*gaps*" (*AWK*, 19), a palimpsest of lost significances. His verse retains residual echoes of liturgical language and symbolism, critical theorizing, and representational and narrative urges, as well as the forms, rhythms, and tones of "the old poems" (*HD*, 5). Long after the loss of the beliefs and lives authorizing them, "the old poems" echo in the poet's ear and are repeated like sounds without meaning, surviving only as "memorabilia of vision" (*DDS*, 33), in "a weird ether of forgotten dismemberments. Was it / This rosebud? Who said that?" (*HD*, 6). Traces of rhythm, bits of metaphysics, and echoes of a once central meditation persist as reflexes inscribed in poetic language,

  as though Narcissus
Were born blind, and still daily
Haunts the mantled pool, and does not know why.   [*AWK*, 35]

Still, two wrongs might make a right, and we are instructed—another leftover habit—that even though "the future is night,"

> It would probably be best . . .
> To hang on to these words if only
> For the rhyme. [*AWK,* 68]

To put it another way, the surviving forms, associations, and memories remain "strangely rewarding"; they help to place the "random" discourse. For example:

And the whole house was full of people
Having a good time, and though
No one offered you a drink and there were no
Clean glasses and the supper
Never appeared on the table, it was
Strangely rewarding anyway.
It gave one an idea of what they thought of one:
Even the ocean that came crashing almost
Into the back yard did not seem ill-disposed
And that was something. Presently
Out of this near-chaos an unearthly
Radiance stood like a person in the room,
The memory of the host, perhaps. And all
Fell silent, or stayed at their musings, silent
As before, and no one any longer
Offered words of advice or misgiving, but drank
The silence that had been silence before,
On this scant strip of slag,
Basking in the same light as before,
Inhabiting the same thought:
A shelf of breasts and underwear packaging
Rumored in the dark ages. [*AWK,* 21–22]

Such nonpurposeful use of allusion is as characteristic of Ashbery's work as the concluding non sequitur. The past is not so much a point of reference, around which one's visions and revisions might be arranged; it is simply part of the "Haunted Landscape" (*AWK,* 80). Thus, while Ashbery's "narrative" is certainly no gospel, and while it may not be Dickinson's "Word made Flesh" or even Crane's "silken skilled transmemberment of song,"[19] it is "something." Alluding to the central transaction or transubstantiation of letters and spirit that haunts all poetry, it gathers the dispersal. Or, like a convex mirror, it focuses the loss:

> The hand holds no chalk
> And each part of the whole falls off
> And cannot know it knew, except

Here and there, in cold pockets
Of remembrance, whispers out of time.   [*SP*, 83]

If such poetry fails to offer any intimations of immortality, it still resonates
with "whispers out of time." Ashbery's discordant polyphony both dislocates
the center of authority, whether of tradition, poetic ideology, or forms, and
locates its dispersal, which becomes no longer random but "meaningfully
meaningless"—neither all nor nothing but "something," which plays against
both. Thus his "dissection" is not as dramatic as Dickinson's or Crane's; it
renders the drama less than vital and the rending less than Dionysian. In
Ashbery's domesticated, "suburban" Orphism, neither presence nor absence
is absolute, and the poetry that disperses *as* it gathers is "not without its
curious justification / Like the time of a stopped watch—right twice a day"
(*HD*, 24).

The elliptical structure of "Litany" formalizes the ironic play of Ashbery's
two-faced language. "The Great Litany" in *The Book of Common Prayer* may be
the poem's source: here two voices, of the clergy and the congregation, are
also designated by roman and italic type, respectively. In Ashbery, the
arrangement of a leading voice and a responding chorus comes down to two
"simultaneous but independent monologues" (*AWK*, 2). In "The Great
Litany," the sequence of prayers—supplications for "someone" to "come to
take care of us" (*AWK*, 60)—ends with a final appeal, "O Christ hear us,"
repeated by both voices. Much like Dickinson, Ashbery plays in the shadow
of liturgical rhetoric,[20] and the supplication that ends the italic column of
"Litany" and tells "the whole story" of the double poem resonates with
echoes of another supplication:

Some months ago I got an offer
From Columbia Tape Club, Terre
Haute, Ind., where I could buy one
Tape and get another free. I accept-
Ed the deal, paid for one tape and
Chose a free one. But since I've been
Repeatedly billed for my free tape.
I've written them several times but
Can't straighten it out—would you
Try?   [*AWK*, 67–68]

"Litany" not only runs in two columns but draws the line between sacred and
profane language, which is the threshold poetic language delineates. And
between litany as prayer and litany as a list of quotidian irritations falls the
shadow of the Savior, a divine intercessor between the transcendent and the

historical—between the "meaningless" and the "meaningful"—who would heal the diacritical rending of Ashbery's demystified Orphism.

Ashbery's retention in "Litany" of a public prayer form devoid of its metaphysical, theological, and social content repeats Dickinson's strategic use of the hymn form emptied of its content. Her "prayer" also is reduced to rhetoric:

Prayer is the little implement
Through which Men reach
Where Presence—is denied them.
They fling their Speech
By means of it—in God's Ear—
If then He hear—
This sums the Apparatus
Comprised in Prayer—[21]

Just as Dickinson reduces the Logos to a legal apparatus, Ashbery displays in the two columns of "Litany" the apparatus that reinforces and makes official the exile from "Presence." "Our minds" dwell in the interstice or gap at the center of the apparatus, *"someplace between prayers / And the answer to prayers"* (*AWK,* 52). That space "between" is the white page, whose meaning is open to interpretation, depending on how we read the two columns. We can interpret this doubleness any way we like, by analogy to anything we please—to the two sides of the brain, to our two eyes "reading" but focusing only on a blank, to two ears "hearing" but registering only babble, or to two times (objective and subjective, past and future) running concurrently. Ashbery himself suggests, "Perhaps the two columns are like two people whom I am in love with simultaneously," and "I once half-jokingly said that my object was to direct the reader's attention to the white space between the columns. Maybe that's part of it. Reading is a pleasure, but to finish reading, to come to the blank space at the end, is also a pleasure."[22] The poem's divided structure both invites interpretation and denies the possibility of a single or authoritative reading. "Litany" stages the diacritical negotiation that lies behind any unified vision. Thus it exposes the gap that un-grounds any metaphoric equivalence, including the structure of interpretation. The parallel columns question all parallel relationships—whether of metaphor, analogy, or interpretation. All such relationships represent a gap bridging different discourses (literal vs. figurative, textual vs. existential, poetic vs. critical). Ashbery's structure highlights this aporia and shows that, by switching discourses, metaphor or interpretation makes sense but never of *"this thing"*—whether the present or the text.

Ashbery has called Gertrude Stein's *Stanzas in Meditation* a "hymn to possibility"; because it is liberated from context and internal consistencies, it provides a "general, all-purpose model which each reader can adapt to fit his own set of particulars."[23] "Litany" is at once such a model and a hymn, a structure that fosters possibility by sustaining a state of "transcendent" nonmeaning. With an irony comparable to Dickinson's "flights" within the hymnal form, Ashbery's doubling of the authoritative column parodies both closure and "open" form.[24] "Litany" flouts the authority not only of convention but of all "free" forms that are licensed by appeals to nature or an experience surpassing the limits of poetic rhetoric and conventions. Here, "openness"—"And please no talk of openness" (*SP*, 46)—or "freedom" comes down to doubling the closure, repeating the margins. For doubling the structure of closure and meaningfulness, and repeating the margins of inside and outside, also increases randomness, since the content of the two columns appears to be interchangeable. Thus license and transgression increase at the pace of the reinforcement of authority and limits.

As far from a free or open form as from a conventional poem, "Litany" is more like a towpath running alongside such main attractions. Just as paradox parallels the *doxa* and internalizes opposition or difference as a strategy of self-authorization, parody can run alongside paradox and question its authoritative, internalized difference. Ashbery's two-column poem challenges the authority of a single poetic discourse at the same time that it questions its own questioning. The "con-fusing" structure of paradox is taken literally and is presented as in fact two simultaneous discourses.[25] Such a literal confusion parodies the idea of a paradoxical language that separates and joins the spirit and the letter, the Logos and history, language and nature. "Litany" leaves us with two discourses, which only separate and join each other:

Perhaps they were fatal but parallel,
Wounds inflicted on a corpse, footnotes
To the desert.   [*AWK*, 26]

Ashbery's world takes shape as a system of payments and balances, so that to get "*one / Tape*" or one column, one discourse or one time, is always to get another one running alongside and diacritically defining the "original,"

Knowing we wanted to hear it twice,
But knowing also as we knew that speculation
Raves and raves as on a mirror
To the outlandish accompaniment of its own death
That reads as life to the toilers.   [*AWK*, 14]

The center of his discourse would be an end to discourse all right, but not in a sublime apotheosis:

> . . . not everyone can afford the luxury of
> Just being, not alive but being, at the center,
> The perfumed, patterned center.　　　　　　　　　　　　　　[*HD*, 78]

When "the truth becomes a hole" (*HD*, 60), when meaning meanders and demeans, then the center of the divagations of life and art is no longer an apocalyptic union of the human and the natural that would erase difference. Instead, the "sublime" center lies in the antisublime, even in a parody of the sublime, for often Ashbery's descriptions of the "center" sound only like the end of the discourse of "*Gog and Magog*" in the "*fray*" for which they are "*continually preparing*" (*AWK*, 27) with a randomness of their own. In such a center, history exacts payment for one's own story, for "*our chronic reverie (a watch / That is always too slow or too fast)*" (*AWK*, 67).

Our "chronic reverie" is both a delirium and a dream, a sickness and a subversive "erotic double" of the sickness. It designates the "free" times of memory and desire, for which one pays anyway in the currency of the "time [that] is sorting us all out" (*HD*, 73). Thus our "chronic reverie"—or "the chronic inattention / Of our lives" (*AWK*, 88)—and our "passing" may be seen as two simultaneous rhetorics, two coeval discourses, delineating our margins, and Ashbery can say,

> 　　　　. . . our passing is a facade.
> But our understanding of it is justified.　　　　　　　　　　[*HD*, 67]

Our "passing" is only a front, a "facade" (L. *facere*, to do), and our understanding of it, its justification or absolution, is only another surface or a writing, as "justified" (L. *justus*, just + *-ficare*, from *facere*, to do) suggests. Since both facades are of our doing, we could argue that the norm is our understanding, the justified left margin against which we improvise a passing that is ours alone:

> *And so*
> *I say unto you: beware the right margin*
> *Which is unjustified; the left*
> *Is justified and can take care of itself*
> *But what is in between expands and flaps*
> *The end sometimes past the point*
> *Of conscious inquiry, noodling in the near*
> *Infinite, off-limits.*　　　　　　　　　　　　　　　　　　[*AWK*, 42]

"In between" the justified, legal, conventional left margin and the unjustified, negotiable right margin, Ashbery improvises a poem, itself a negotiation between its upright, columnar shape and the speculative "*noodling in the near / Infinite, off-limits.*" It is this negotiation that "Litany" formalizes and illustrates. Accordingly, between the left margin of our understanding and the right margin of our passing, we improvise a parallel discourse and posit margins given and free, legal and illicit. Since both margins and both discourses are coeval, however, our litany remains a continuous parody of both our understanding and our passing.

Notes

INTRODUCTION

1 Harold Bloom, *The Ringers in the Tower: Studies in Romantic Tradition* (Chicago: University of Chicago Press, 1971), p. 302.

2 See Harold Bloom, *Figures of Capable Imagination* (New York: Seabury Press, 1976), p. 71. In *Poetry and Repression* (New Haven: Yale University Press, 1976) Bloom argues that the Emersonian "sublime" was a defensive troping against the "English poetic tradition" in order to present "an American individuality" (p. 254), which Emerson succeeds in doing for the first and last time, since his American followers can only repeat his strategy. Thus, by anchoring on Emerson, Bloom can both acknowledge the "peculiar individuality of post-Emersonian American poetry, when we compare it to the British poetry of the same period, continuing on into our own days" (*Figures,* p. 71), and maintain his theoretical stance on the "anxiety of influence."

3 *Figures,* pp. 76, 75.

4 Bloom writes: "Emerson's Orphism is very much his own, and little is to be apprehended of Emerson by tracking him to any of his precursors, for no other Post-Enlightenment intellect, not even Nietzsche's, has set itself quite so strongly against the idea of influence, and done this so successfully, and without anxiety. Even Emily Dickinson owes more to Emerson than Emerson did to Coleridge, Wordsworth, or any other spiritual father" (*Figures,* p. 69). Emerson represents for Bloom the romantic "humanism" he values, for he gives us all the "immodest hope that we—even we—coming so late in time's injustices can still sing a song of ourselves" (*Figures,* p. 57). In *Wallace Stevens: The Poems of Our Climate* (Ithaca: Cornell University Press, 1976), Bloom acknowledges Coleridge and, especially, Wordsworth as Emerson's "authentic precursors." Emerson, however, evades rather than engages Wordsworth, who "redefined poetry for him, and I think induced a repressive anxiety that prevented him from centering his literary ambitions upon verse" (p. 1).

5 For example, R. A. Yoder in *Emerson and the Orphic Poet in America* (Berkeley and Los Angeles: University of California Press, 1978) traces Whitman, Williams, Pound, and Hart Crane to the early Emerson, and Dickinson, Stephen Crane, Frost, Stevens, and Ammons to the late Emerson (pp. 191–92). This division corresponds to Bloom's alignment of Whitman, Dickinson, Hart Crane, Cummings, and Roethke with the early Emerson—with his dialectic between "the assertion of imagination's autonomy, and a shrewd skepticism of any phenomenon reaching too far into the unconditioned"—and of Robinson and Frost with the "later, resigned Emerson" (*Ringers in the Tower,* p. 292). Elsewhere, Bloom more copiously defines Emerson's progeny in American romantic poetry: "Not the Romantic poem of Bryant or of Poe or of Longfellow, but of Thoreau, Whitman, Dickinson, Melville, Robinson, Frost, Stevens, Williams, Hart Crane, Roethke, and all their followers" (*Figures,* p. 48). David Porter in *Emerson and Literary Change* (Cambridge: Harvard

University Press, 1978) regards Emerson's poetic forms as rigid and restrictive and argues that the essays' "broad reconciliation of art and reality foreshadowed the later formal undertakings of Eliot and Pound, Crane, Olson and Williams, Stevens, Lowell, and others" (p. 5). Finally, Hyatt H. Waggoner in *American Poets* (New York: Dell, 1968) distinguishes a "direct Emersonian line," which includes Whitman, Dickinson, Robinson, and Frost, from an "Emerson-Whitman line" that leads to Hart Crane, Roethke, and "a good many contemporary young poets like Denise Levertov" (pp. 91–92). Albert Gelpi (*The Tenth Muse: The Psyche of the American Poet* [Cambridge: Harvard University Press, 1975]) is an exception to this consensus, for he proposes a dialectical history of American poetry. He divides poets according to the Puritan distinction between "tropes" and "types"—between a conception of "metaphor as figure of speech and metaphor as symbol, between imagination (or fancy) and Imagination" (p. 51)—and offers the following configuration: "On the more tropological side, from Edgar Allan Poe to Wallace Stevens, Robert Frost, and John Crowe Ransom to such contemporaries as Robert Lowell, J. V. Cunningham, and W. D. Snodgrass; on the more typological side, from Taylor through Emerson and Whitman to Pound and Williams to Charles Olson and Denise Levertov, Allen Ginsberg and William Everson" (pp. 53–54).

6 Jacques Derrida, "Structure, Sign and Play in the Discourse of the Human Sciences," *Writing and Difference,* trans. Alan Bass (Chicago: University of Chicago Press, 1978), p. 279. In Derrida's terms, such a center which is itself outside play offers a certitude that masters "anxiety"—"invariably the result of a certain mode of being implicated in the game, of being caught by the game."

7 Bloom, *Figures,* p. 75.

8 Bloom, *Figures,* p. 46; William Shakespeare, *Hamlet,* I. i. 41.

9 Paul de Man distinguishes a syntagmatic-grammatical axis from a paradigmatic-figurative axis—relationships of contiguity from those of similarity, which finally resolve to the axes of grammar and rhetoric—and suggests that these structures might be studied more usefully as points on a continuum (Paul de Man, *Allegories of Reading* [New Haven: Yale University Press, 1979], pp. 6–7). This classification appears to correspond to Jakobson's axes of metonymic and metaphoric organization—organizing by relationships of contiguity and of similarity, respectively—by which he distinguishes prose and poetry (Roman Jakobson and Morris Halle, *Fundamentals of Language* [The Hague: Mouton, 1956], pp. 80–82). Like de Man's, my distinction is intratextual and distinguishes the "rhetoric" and the "grammar" of a poem, which includes its formal "syntax" as well.

10 See Lee A. Sonnino, *A Handbook to Sixteenth-Century Rhetoric* (New York: Barnes and Noble, 1968), p. 11.

11 To illustrate, I will take as examples two critics who have differing understandings of the two faces of rhetoric: Paul de Man and Harold Bloom. De Man writes of Nietzsche's "deconstruction" of metaphysics: "Nietzsche's final insight may well concern rhetoric itself, the discovery that what is called 'rhetoric' is precisely the gap that becomes apparent in the pedagogical and philosophical history of the term. Considered as persuasion, rhetoric is performative but when considered as a system of tropes, it deconstructs its own performance. . . . The aporia between performative and constative language is merely a version of the aporia between trope and persuasion that both generates and paralyzes rhetoric and thus gives it the appearance of a history" (*Allegories of Reading,* p. 131). Bloom objects to "deconstructive" criticism, whether Derrida's or de Man's, and proposes that "what relates one trope to another in a systematic way, and carries each trope from evasion to persuasion, is that trope's function as defense." Citing Vico and Emerson as predecessors, Bloom distinguishes between "signification" or "rhetoric as a system of tropes" and "meaning" or "rhetoric as persuasion," and what holds these together is "the necessity of defense, defense against everything that threatens survival, and a defense whose aptest name is 'meaning'" (*Poetry and Repression,* p. 240). For his reduction of troping to defense, he offers this explanation: "This way of connecting trope and psychic defense . . . to me seems an inevitable aid in the reading of poetry" ("The Breaking of Form," *Deconstruction and Criticism* [New York: Seabury Press, 1979], p. 11). I maintain that the signifying and referential axes of linguistic meaning can only relate as a trope, and

figuration as signification and figuration as persuasion constitute two terms that can be "related" according to one of a limited number of tropological models. Thus, while de Man subscribes to the trope of irony—the structural trope of all deconstructive criticism—and focuses on the aporia or discontinuity between "rhetoric as figuration" and "rhetoric as persuasion," Bloom metonymically tropes that aporia and reads persuasion as the "cause" and figuration as the "effect" that acts out the "cause." The advantage of a deconstructive reading is its intrinsic demystification. But if we take irony as only one trope, the advantage of Bloom's reading is that its commitment is more explicit, as Bloom insists. It is rhetoric as persuasion and thus a function of will: "In part, the explanation for reading trope as defense and defense as trope goes back to my earlier observations on criticism as the rhetoric *of* rhetoric, and so on each critic's individual troping of the concept of trope" ("The Breaking of Form," p. 12).

12 *The Rhetoric and the Poetics of Aristotle,* trans. W. Rhys Roberts and Ingram Bywater (New York: Random House, 1984), *Poetics,* 1457[b]. Aristotle's discussion is brief, but the four tropes—synecdoche, metonymy, metaphor, and irony, respectively—are here in germ, distinguished as different species of "metaphor": "Metaphor consists in giving the thing a name that belongs to something else; the transference being either from genus to species, or from species to genus, or from species to species, or on grounds of analogy. . . . There is also another form of qualified metaphor. Having given the thing the alien name, one may by a negative addition deny of it one of the attributes naturally associated with its new name." I use "trope" for the generic term and reserve "metaphor" for the analogical trope. See Kenneth Burke, "Four Master Tropes," *A Grammar of Motives* (Berkeley: University of California Press, 1969), 503–17.

13 *Princeton Encyclopedia of Poetry and Poetics,* ed. Alex Preminger (Princeton: Princeton University Press, 1965), p. 490.

14 According to Hayden White, in metaphor, literal identification (my love, a rose) signifies or represents a figurative identification (in certain respects my love may be compared with a rose). Metaphor works with analogical relationships and maintains the "adequacy" of the image as a representation of the subject: "The loved one is not *reduced* to a rose, as would be the case if the phrase were read Metonymically, nor is the essence of the loved one taken to be identical with the essence of the rose, as would be the case if the expression were understood as a Synecdoche. Nor, obviously, is the expression to be taken as an implicit negation of what is explicitly affirmed, as in the case of Irony." See Hayden White, *Metahistory: The Historical Imagination in Nineteenth-Century Europe* (Baltimore: Johns Hopkins University Press, 1973), p. 34. In metaphor, then, there is a "free" area—an area of "incongruity," in Kenneth Burke's term—within the equation. Burke writes: "Because the seeing of something in terms of something else involves the 'carrying-over' of a term from one realm into another, [it] . . . necessarily involves varying degrees of incongruity in that the two realms are never identical" (p. 504).

White's *Metahistory* uses a typological framework to argue that nineteenth-century historians and philosophers of history alike have had to "prefigure" their "field" and define what constitutes historical writing on the model of one of these master tropes, each with its proposed correlation of epistemological value and figural style. He maintains that historical writing has a "metahistorical" or tropological "understructure," and following Aristotle, Vico, and modern linguists as well as Burke, he distinguishes "four principal modes of historical consciousness" on the basis of the "prefigurative" (or tropological) strategy that informs them: metaphor, synecdoche, metonymy, and irony. Each of these "modes of consciousness" provides the basis for a distinctive linguistic protocol by which to prefigure the historical field and on the basis of which specific strategies of historical interpretation can be employed to "explain" it. In White's terms, "Irony, Metonymy, and Synecdoche are kinds of Metaphor, but they differ from one another in the kinds of *reductions* or *integrations* they effect on the literal level of their meanings and by the kinds of illuminations they aim at on the figurative level. Metaphor is essentially *representational,* Metonymy is *reductionist,* Synecdoche is *integrative,* and Irony is *negational.*" See *Metahistory,* pp. x, xi, 34.

15 *Rhetoric,* 1411[a]; *Poetics,* 1457[b].

16 *Princeton Encyclopedia,* p. 499.
17 Burke, p. 506. Burke has proposed the following "'literal' or 'realistic' applications" of the four "master tropes:"

> For *metaphor* we could substitute *perspective;*
> For *metonymy* we could substitute *reduction;*
> For *synecdoche* we could substitute *representation;*
> For *irony* we could substitute *dialectic.*

> According to this tropological substitution of the literal applications for the major tropes, we can delineate the "rôle" these figures play "in the discovery and description of 'the truth.'" On metonymy, he elaborates: metonymy's basic "strategy" is "to convey some incorporeal or intangible state in terms of the corporeal or tangible." He writes: "Language develops by metaphorical extension, in borrowing words from the realm of the corporeal, visible, tangible and applying them by analogy to the realm of the incorporeal, invisible, intangible," and "poets regain the original relation, in reverse, by a 'metaphorical extension' back from the intangible into a tangible equivalent (the first 'carrying-over' from the material to the spiritual being compensated by a second 'carrying-over' from the spiritual back into the material); and this 'archaicizing' device we call 'metonymy.'" Moreover, "'Metonymy' is a device of 'poetic realism'—but its partner, 'reduction,' is a device of 'scientific realism.' Here 'poetry' and 'behaviorism' meet." Metonymic figuration works with dramatizations; in drama, this entails the definition of the medium as "the posturing, tonalizing body placed in a material scene," where emotions and relations are known "behavioristically," reducing the mental or emotional state to its "corresponding bodily equivalents." Unlike the scientist, however, the poet knows that "these bodily equivalents are but part of the *idiom of expression* involved in the act. They are 'figures.' They are hardly other than 'symbolizations.'" Thus his reduction is "terminological" rather than "real" (pp. 503, 506, 507). Harold Bloom, who psychologizes the tropes and connects them to psychic defense systems, adds that "metonymy hints at the psychology of compulsion and obsession," and that "regressive behavior expresses itself metonymically" ("The Breaking of Form," p. 11).

18 Burke, *Grammar of Motives,* p. 508. Hence the "noblest synecdoche," the paradigmatic use of this trope, is found in metaphysical doctrines of the identity of the "microcosm" and the "macrocosm," whereby "the whole can represent the part or the part can represent the whole." Although Burke uses the term "representation" (following Leibniz, whose "monadology" is an instance of synecdochic thinking) for the applied form of this trope, he more specifically defines his term: "For 'represent' here we could substitute 'be identified with'" (p. 508). White suggests that "By the trope of Synecdoche . . . it is possible to construe the two parts in the manner of an *integration* within a whole that is *qualitatively* different from the sum of the parts and of which the parts are but *microcosmic* replications" (*Metahistory,* pp. 34, 35).

19 "Romantic irony" as a stylistic device is also different from structural irony; according to the *Princeton Encyclopedia,* here "the writer creates an illusion, especially of beauty, and suddenly destroys it by a change of tone, a personal comment, or a violently contradictory sentiment" (p. 407).

20 Burke, *Grammar of Motives,* p. 512. Burke distinguishes irony from synecdoche: if synecdoche would identify opposite pairs like disease-cure, irony would note the function of the disease in perfecting the cure and the function of the cure in perpetuating the disease. The temptations of irony include, Burke adds, tendencies toward relativism, Pharisaism, and the simplification of literalness. On the relationship between irony and relativism, the *Princeton Encyclopedia* suggests: "Possibly it is a safe generalization to say that periods in which religious and social opinions are relatively homogeneous will feel less need for the skeptical and ironic mind" (p. 408).

21 White writes: "In Irony, figurative language folds back upon itself and brings its own potentialities for distorting perception under question. This is why characterizations of the world cast in the Ironic mode are often regarded as *intrinsically* sophisticated and realistic." The self-critical and

"transideological" trope of irony is "a model of the linguistic protocol in which skepticism in thought and relativism in ethics are conventionally expressed" (*Metahistory*, pp. 37–38).

22 Dante, *Convivio*, trans. William Walrond Jackson (Oxford: Clarendon Press, 1909), pp. 73–74. I am also drawing on the discussion of four levels of interpretation in M. H. Abrams, *A Glossary of Literary Terms* (New York: Holt, 1981), pp. 87–89, and in Northrop Frye, Sheridan Baker, and George Perkins, *The Harper Handbook to Literature* (New York: Harper & Row, 1985), p. 201. In more general terms, the distinction is between literal and spiritual meaning, which in turn is divided into allegorical, tropological, and anagogic levels. In the terms of St. Thomas Aquinas, for instance, the literal sense of the Scripture is the foundation on which the other three senses rest. He distinguishes them thus: "So far as the things of the Old Law signify the things of the New Law, there is the allegorical sense; so far as the things done in Christ, or so far as the things which signify Christ, are signs of what we ought to do, there is the moral sense. But so far as they signify what relates to eternal glory, there is the anagogical sense." Beyond these, Aquinas mentions a "parabolical sense," which he subsumes under the "literal" sense: "When Scripture speaks of God's arm, the literal sense is not that God has such a member, but only what is signified by this member, namely, operative power. Hence it is plain that nothing false can ever underlie the literal sense of Holy Scripture." This "parabolic sense" potentially shades into the paradoxical structure of the literal-ironic trope. See *Summa Theologica, Introduction to St. Thomas Aquinas*, ed. Anton C. Pegis (New York: Random House, 1948), pp. 18–19.

23 Northrop Frye, *Anatomy of Criticism: Four Essays* (Princeton: Princeton University Press, 1957), pp. 78, 79.

24 Ibid., p. 81

25 Ibid., pp. 84, 82.

26 Ibid., pp. 95–96, 97–98.

27 Ibid., p. 119. According to Frye, then, there are four conceptions of the symbol, and the relationship between symbol-units constitutes metaphor: (1) "literal": metaphor in its literal shape of simple juxtaposition—A, B—is literally ironic and paradoxical; (2) "formal": "metaphor as analogy to natural proportion"—A is as B—requires a four-term comparison; (3) "archetypal": metaphor as concrete universal (corresponding to the reduction of metonymy); (4) "anagogical": metaphor as identity—A *is* B (pp. 123, 124–25; see also p. 366).

28 This use is strictly relative and does not imply that the other levels are naive in any sense. I mean only that the literal level constitutes an ironic troping on a prior level, which could be that of metaphor or synecdoche.

29 These relationships define Jakobson's axes of metonymy and metaphor (*Fundamentals of Language*, pp. 80–82), and using his figure helps define how the axes of prose and poetry coincide in anagogic or synecdochic composition.

30 I agree with Northrop Frye that the literalist level links to *Symbolisme* (Frye, *Anatomy of Criticism*, p. 60), for, structurally, Dickinson is the paradigmatic Symbolist in American literature. Such poets as Poe and Eliot, who are historically and tonally connected to the Symbolists, do not work with their diacritical or ironic structures. Kenneth Burke's excellent analysis of why Eliot is not truly an ironic poet is relevant to this point. For Burke, Eliot's irony, with its Pharisaic assumption of superiority to the "enemy," comes under romantic irony—a kind of irony that in fact arose as "an aesthetic opposition to cultural philistinism." "True irony," however, has "humility," according to Burke; it is not superior to the enemy but is "based upon a sense of fundamental kinship with the enemy, as one *needs* him, is *indebted* to him, is not merely outside him as an observer but contains him *within*, being consubstantial with him" (p. 514). As an example, we might think of John Ashbery's "ironic" use of the meaningless, the banal, the "vulgar," as constitutive materials of the poet as "Daffy Duck in Hollywood"; such a use is as different from Eliot's condescending, tonally ironic use of similar material as it is from a romanticized use like William Carlos Williams's.

31 Bloom writes: "Yet the 'achieved dearth of meaning' [the index of a strong poet's mastery of the prior "plenitude of meaning," his predecessors, and the tradition] . . . is accomplished more

powerfully by Wordsworth and Whitman than it is by Eliot and Pound" ("The Breaking of Form,"
p. 13).

32 Marjorie Perloff, "Pound/Stevens: Whose Era?" *New Literary History* 13 (1982): 485–514. Perloff
rightly argues that the split between "Bloom, Hillis Miller, Helen Vendler, Frank Kermode in the
Stevens camp" and "Kenner, Donald Davie, Guy Davenport, Christine Brooke-Rose among
Poundians" is "neither an idle quarrel nor a narrow sectarian war between rival academics"; it
raises central questions, still unresolved, about the "meaning of Modernism—indeed about the
meaning of poetry itself in current literary history and theory" (p. 486). Perloff observes that, for
Bloom, modernism is not a significant movement but a momentary diversion from a dominant and
continuous romanticism.

33 Tzvetan Todorov, *Theories of the Symbol,* trans. Catherine Porter (Ithaca: Cornell University Press,
1982) pp. 146–221. Paul de Man, in "The Rhetoric of Temporality," in *Interpretation: Theory and
Practice,* ed. Charles S. Singleton (Baltimore: Johns Hopkins University Press, 1969), uses the same
dichotomous framework and values "allegory" over the symbol, granting it greater access to truth
and greater cognitive value. Allegory's consciousness of its belatedness is its recognition of "an
authentically temporal destiny"; allegory "renounces the nostalgia and the desire to coincide" and
"establishes its language in the void of this temporal difference" (pp. 190, 191). De Man's
preference for allegory is hard to explain except on the basis of the same kind of prior affinity that
makes some critics of modernism favor metaphor and others synecdoche. The "contradictory"
positions on the priority of subject and/or object, which de Man condemns as mystification on the
part of certain romantic poets and certain critics of romanticism (p. 182), in fact constitutes the
central transaction of the analogical trope, and I am not sure in what sense or on what basis one
trope (allegory) can claim greater access to truth or greater cognitive value than another (symbol),
except on the basis of ideology.

34 *The New Science of Giambattista Vico,* trans. Thomas G. Bergin and Max H. Fisch (Ithaca: Cornell
University Press, 1968), p. 131. Hence, in Schiller's terms, irony is "sentimental," a later re-
creation of an earlier, "naive" mode (Frye, p. 35).

35 De Man notes the "implicit and rather enigmatic link between allegory and irony which runs
through the history of rhetoric" ("The Rhetoric of Temporality," p. 192; see pp. 191–209 for a
discussion of this link). De Man concludes: "Irony is a synchronic structure, while allegory appears
as a successive mode capable of engendering duration as the illusion of a continuity that it knows to
be illusionary. Yet the two modes, for all their profound distinctions in mood and structure, are the
two faces of the same fundamental experience of time. One is tempted to play them off against each
other and to attach value judgments to each, as if one were intrinsically superior to the other. We
mentioned the temptation to confer on allegorical writers a wisdom superior to that of ironic
writers; an equivalent temptation exists to consider ironists as more enlightened than their
assumedly naive counterparts, the allegorists. Both attitudes are in error. The knowledge derived
from both modes is essentially the same. . . . The dialectical play between the two modes, as well
their common interplay with mystified forms of language (such as symbolic or mimetic representation), which it is not in their power to eradicate, make up what is called literary history" (p. 207).
This, I would suggest, is also the basic difference between Poe's or Eliot's irony and Dickinson's
structural irony. Poe's "Israfel" may be the paradigmatic poem of the allegorist's romantic irony,
which registers the discontinuity between language and power. The trope of irony, however, is
intrinsically dialogical and generates its meaning through discontinuity, and this kind of synchronic
irony is not functional in the allegorist's romantic irony, which depends on a diachronic relationship between reality and representation.

36 The term is de Man's ("The Rhetoric of Temporality," p. 190).

CHAPTER ONE

1 Edgar Allan Poe, "Letter to B———," in *The Complete Works of Edgar Allan Poe,* ed. James A. Harrison
(New York: Crowell, 1902), 7:xxxvi. Subsequent references to this edition will be cited in the text
as *CW,* followed by the volume and page numbers.

2 See Roland Barthes, "From Work to Text," in *Image-Music-Text,* trans. Stephen Heath (New York: Hill and Wang, 1977), pp. 155–64; see *S/Z,* trans. Richard Miller (New York: Hill and Wang, 1974), pp. 3–10, for a discussion of texts with plural meanings. See also Edward W. Said's definition of modern works as texts that refer to other works, to reality, or to the reader "by adjacency, not sequentially or dynastically." And because such a text stands "to the side of, next to, or between the bulk of all other works—not in a line with them, nor in a line of descent from them," the "production of meaning within a work has had to proceed in entirely different ways from before"—specifically, without a "central point or central trajectory" (Edward W. Said, *Beginnings: Intention and Method* [New York: Basic Books, 1975], p. 10).

3 See Jacques Derrida, "Plato's Pharmacy," in *Dissemination,* trans. Barbara Johnson (Chicago: University of Chicago Press, 1981), pp. 75–94.

4 See, for example, Joseph N. Riddel, "The 'Crypt' of Edgar Poe," *Boundary 2,* 7, no. 3 (Spring 1979): 117–41.

5 Aldous Huxley, "Vulgarity in Literature," in *The Recognition of Edgar Allan Poe,* ed. Eric W. Carlson (Ann Arbor: University of Michigan Press, 1966), pp. 161, 166.

6 Edwin Fussell, *Lucifer in Harness: American Meter, Metaphor, and Diction* (Princeton: Princeton University Press, 1973), pp. 27, 115.

7 Martin Heidegger, "Hölderlin and the Essence of Poetry," trans. Douglas Scott, in *Existence and Being* (1949; reprint, Chicago: Henry Regnery, 1970), p. 280. Heidegger writes: "The origin of the work of art—that is, the origin of both the creators and the preservers, which is to say of a people's historical existence, is art. This is so because art is by nature an origin: a distinctive way in which truth comes into being, that is, becomes historical" (*Poetry, Language, Thought,* trans. Albert Hofstadter [New York: Harper & Row, 1971], p. 78). Thus "poetry is the foundation which supports history" (*Existence and Being,* p. 283), for history is born in poetry or language, where truth becomes historical. Part of Heidegger's confidence in temporality—the secure surrender to "ravenous time"—is an effect of his confidence in a people's historical being, in a history that preserves. "The innermost essence of home is already the destiny of a Providence, or as we now call it: History" (*Existence and Being,* p. 244), Heidegger affirms, but we must not overlook his context. The subject is Hölderlin's poem about homecoming, and "History" is the history of Germany: "If those 'who are beset with care in the fatherland' are transformed into the careful ones . . . then there is a kinship with the poet. Then there is a homecoming. But this homecoming is the future of the historical being of the German people" (*Existence and Being,* p. 268). I have quoted Heidegger at such length to show how thoroughly social his thinking is; its application to the American poet is at best problematic. Whitman is able to entrust himself to "ravenous time" only by projecting "a history of the future"—by projecting preservers in a cosmic future that enfolds history itself. Poe, however, is deprived of the reassuring coincidence of social/political history with literary history and lacks Whitman's will to write his own coincidences; thus he remains insecure about what he is to preserve and whether he will have hearers and preservers.

8 In Paul de Man's terms, Poe's preference for allegory would render him in good faith in acknowledging the rhetoricity of his rhetoric. While the symbol's nostalgia for a fusion of subject and object is a nostalgia for faith, the allegorical poet acknowledges the impossibility of faith and exposes romantic literary substitutions to be such. See "The Rhetoric of Temporality," in Singleton, ed., *Interpretation: Theory and Practice,* 173–209. De Man's essay is valuable for drawing out some of the links between secular allegory and the recognition that temporality is the subject's peculiar predicament.

9 Edward Davidson, for instance, states Poe's faith that "art is one man's instrument for making some order out of the infinitude of empirical formlessness" (*Poe: A Critical Study* [Cambridge: Harvard University Press, 1957], p. 252). Likewise, Albert Gelpi writes that in Poe "the centripetal pressures of form contain artificially the dispersive and entropic energies which are the law of nature and of the psyche" (*The Tenth Muse,* p. 139). Similarly, Daniel Hoffman proposes that Poe's "straitjacket method enables the poet to deal with his obsessive and inescapable subject by compelling him to think about something else, something other than the woe vibrating within him which to think of would overcome him. So the method of his art enables the madness of his matter

to be spoken" (*Poe Poe Poe Poe Poe Poe Poe* [New York: Doubleday, 1973], p. 92). But we could easily reverse these readings and argue that the priority, arbitrariness, and rigidity of Poe's form exert such unnatural pressure on the forces of "content"—whether natural or psychic—that they become explosive by reaction.

10 Hesiod, "Theogony," in *Hesiod*, trans. Richmond Lattimore (1959; reprint, Ann Arbor: University of Michigan Press, 1972), p. 126.

11 Literary and personal memory, which together weave the poetic text, are at odds not only in Poe but in Eliot; in the opening lines of *The Waste Land*, for example, personal memory is usurped by so many literary allusions that it is rendered incapable of its restorative, re-membering power. Public memory—allusions for Eliot, meters and emblems for Poe—blocks the poet's memory exactly as it builds up his discourse. The same process operates in Sylvia Plath as well, and the public material (the historical guilt, the public hysteria) perverts the psychic force.

12 A survey of the Freudian psychic scape yields a list of the major, recurrent image patterns in Poe, Eliot, and Plath. The following is Jacques Lacan's list of the Freudian metaphors:

The unconscious is that chapter of my history which is marked by a blank or occupied by a falsehood: it is the censored chapter. But the Truth can be found again; it is most often already written down elsewhere. That is to say:

- in monuments: this is my body—that is to say, the hysterical nucleus of the neurosis where the hysterical symptom reveals the structure of a Language and is deciphered like an inscription which, once recovered, can without serious loss be destroyed;
- in archival documents also: these are my childhood memories, just as impenetrable as are such documents when I do not know their source;
- in semantic evolution: this corresponds to the stock of words and acceptations of my own particular vocabulary, as it does to my style of life and to my character;
- in traditions as well, and not only in them but also in the legends which, in a heroicized form, transport my history;
- and lastly, in the traces which are inevitably preserved by the distortions necessitated by the linking of the adulterated chapter to the chapters surrounding it, and whose meaning will be re-established by my exegesis. (*The Language of the Self*, trans. Anthony Wilden [New York: Dell, 1968], p. 21.)

13 Allen Tate discusses Poe's "angelic" imagination in these terms and cites Jacques Maritain's *The Dream of Descartes:* "Cartesian dualism breaks man up into two complete substances, joined to one another none knows how: on the one hand, the body which is only geometrical extension; on the other, the soul which is only thought—an angel inhabiting a machine and directing it by means of the pineal gland" ("The Angelic Imagination," in Carlson, *Poe*, p. 245). Stephen L. Mooney discusses the ramifications of Poe's Cartesian dualism in "Poe's Gothic Waste Land" (in Carlson, *Poe*, pp. 278–97).

14 In Julia Kristeva's designation, this axis stands in distinction to the signifying, paternal axis of language and characterizes the "*heterogeneousness* to meaning and signification" of poetic language. See *Desire in Language*, trans. Thomas Gora, Alice Jardine, and Leon S. Roudiez (New York: Columbia University Press, 1980), pp. 132–34.

15 Roman Jakobson and Linda Waugh, *The Sound Shape of Language* (Bloomington: Indiana University Press, 1979), pp. 177–231.

16 See C. G. Jung, *Mysterium Coniunctionis*, trans. R. F. C. Hull (Princeton: Princeton University Press, 1970), p. 510.

17 Roman Jakobson observes this near-anagram: the "raven" appears "as an embodied mirror image of this 'never': /n.v.r/-/r.v.n/. Salient paronomasias interconnect both emblems of the everlasting despair." See "Linguistics and Poetics," in *The Structuralists from Marx to Lévi-Strauss*, ed. Richard and Fernande DeGeorge (New York: Doubleday, 1972), p. 113.

18 The "legended tomb" of "Ulalume" is similar:

And we passed to the end of the vista,
But were stopped by the door of a tomb—

By the door of a legended tomb;
And I said—"What is written, sweet sister,
On the door of this legended tomb?"
She replied: "Ulalume—Ulalume—
'T is the vault of thy lost Ulalume!"   [*CW*, 7:104]

The "tomb"-"Ulalume" rhyme has already spelled the legend that closes the future, that marks "the end of the vista."

19 Ovid, *The Metamorphoses,* trans. Horace Gregory (New York: New American Library, 1960), pp. 146–59.

20 Derrida, *Dissemination,* p. 135.

21 Critics have leveled this charge against Sylvia Plath as well, but they have tended to reduce her sensationalism to a psychological rather than literary despair.

22 Barton Levi St. Armand's reading of "The Raven" is valuable here. He argues that emblems are "natural objects" "designed to convey a certain rigid meaning": "Is the Raven angel or devil, saint or demon, divine messenger or satanic trickster? Poe suggests that it is madness to so speculate because, as *pars pro toto* or 'capital' thing, the Raven on the bust of Pallas forbids deeper inquiries and cautions a mute acceptance of the finality of not knowing and of not being able to know—the finality of 'Nevermore.' The Raven is a hedge around meaning rather than an expansion of it; for, to take the bird as a symbol, as a material object representing something alien or invisible, is to open up the possibility of cosmically threatening and uncontrollable meanings." See "Poe's Emblematic Raven: A Pictorial Approach," *Emerson Society Quarterly* 22 (1976): 191, 197.

23 See, for example, Marie Bonaparte, who bases her argument for Poe's necrophilia on the fact that he witnessed his mother's death and repeated the trauma with the death of Mrs. Allan (*The Life and Works of Edgar Allan Poe: A Psycho-Analytic Interpretation,* trans. John Rodker [London: Imago, 1949], p. 45). Kenneth Burke estheticizes Poe's necrophilia, characteristically reversing such theories that explain the art in terms of psychological causation. According to Kenneth Burke, Poe's esthetic motivation for perfection led to necrophiliac fantasies, since death is a state of "finish" and "perfection" ("The Principle of Composition," *Poetry* 99 [1961]: 53). I would cross these two readings: Poe's formalism, for example, leads to a special kind of perfectionism, which exaggerates and freezes the maternal function of language. The mother-worship, necrophilia, and worship of artistic perfection dovetail in Poe's letter-worship.

24 Burke, "The Principle of Composition," pp. 46–53.

25 See, for example, Vincent Buranelli, who considers Poe "the first of the New Critics," in *Edgar Allan Poe* (Boston: Twayne, 1977), p. 113.

CHAPTER TWO

1 T. S. Eliot, "From Poe to Valéry," in Carlson, *Poe,* pp. 205–19.

2 Ibid., p. 207.

3 In a telling comparison with Henry James, Eliot adds: "It is almost too difficult even for H.J. who for that matter wasn't an American at all, in that sense." See Herbert Read, "T. S. E.—A Memoir," in *T. S. Eliot, The Man and His Work,* ed. Allen Tate (New York: Delacorte Press, 1966), p. 15.

4 Review of *After Strange Gods, New English Weekly* (1934); quoted in Lyndall Gordon, *Eliot's Early Years* (New York: Oxford University Press, 1977), p. 69.

5 Canto 81, *The Cantos of Ezra Pound* (New York: New Directions, 1981), p. 522.

6 T. S. Eliot, *Collected Poems, 1909–1962* (New York: Harcourt, 1963), p. 5. Subsequent references to this volume will be cited in the text as *CP,* followed by the page number.

7 T. S. Eliot, "Tradition and the Individual Talent," in *The Sacred Wood: Essays on Poetry and Criticism* (London: Methuen, 1960), p. 56. Subsequent references to this volume will be cited in the text as *SW,* followed by the page number.

8 T. S. Eliot, "The Three Voices of Poetry," in *On Poetry and Poets* (New York: Farrar, Straus, 1957), p. 110.

9 Ibid., p. 102.

10 See, for example, Poe, *The Complete Works,* 9: 73. In "Johnson as Critic and Poet," Eliot more confidently announces that "originality does not require the rejection of convention" (*On Poetry and Poets,* p. 209).

11 The facsimile edition of *The Waste Land* notes that the source for "He Do the Police in Different Voices" is Charles Dickens's *Our Mutual Friend,* chapter 16, "Minders and Reminders": Sloppy is a foundling adopted by old Betty Higden, a poor widow. "'I do love a newspaper' she says. 'You mightn't think it, but Sloppy is a beautiful reader of a newspaper. He do the Police in different voices.'" See *The Waste Land: A Facsimile and Transcript of the Original Drafts,* ed. Valerie Eliot (New York: Harcourt, 1971), p. 125.

12 Ibid., p. 81; emphasis mine. The closing lines of *The Waste Land,* coming after the delivery of a moral message, are the most disjunctive in the poem. All of the allusions refer to the still unresolved problem of the poet, and the line from Nerval—"*Le Prince d'Aquitaine à la tour abolie*"—links poetic dispossession and imagery of archaeological ruins.

13 For a contrasting point of view, see William V. Spanos's "Repetition in *The Waste Land:* A Phenomenological De-struction," *Boundary 2,* 7, no. 3 (Spring 1979): 225–85. Spanos makes use of Heidegger's concept of tradition as a forgetfulness and a concealment of being and argues that *The Waste Land* is a Heideggerian "de-structive" poem of open form and a precursor of the postmodern poetics of Pound, late Stevens, Olson, and Creeley. Against this reading, we might consider the "esthetic" closure Eliot provides for his poem. The poet who dismembers such central texts of the tradition as Homer, the Bible, Dante, and Shakespeare gives the last word to the critic, who undertakes, in the notes, to reinstitute the smashed authorities. Eliot's remark that "criticism is as inevitable as breathing" (*SW,* 48) helps us see why criticism infiltrates *The Waste Land,* the poem in greatest need of the "breather" of criticism. The notes, which propose a "philosophy" for the "composition" (or "de-composition") of the poem, deliver the poet from the "hushing" enclosure of forms, the tyranny of the past, and obsessive feelings and compulsive repetitions. Only in the notes does Eliot speak in a voice we recognize as his own, without the masks and mediation of other poets, characters, lines. Eliot's half-joking explanation that the notes were offered "with a view to spiking the guns of critics of my earlier poems who had accused me of plagiarism" (*On Poetry and Poets,* p. 121) is probably not too far off the mark. The radically displaced poet finds his true voice in criticism, a retrospective activity for which the poem already belongs to the past. And the critic's task is the opposite of the poet's: he is to show just how, and how tightly, the poem fits into the tradition. Thus the notes make peace and reassure us that the poet has a "method," that he is "manipulating a continuous parallel between contemporaneity and antiquity," that his method is "simply a way of controlling, of ordering, of giving a shape and a significance to the immense panorama of futility and anarchy which is contemporary history" ("'Ulysses,' Order, and Myth," *The Dial,* Nov. 1923, reprinted in *Criticism: The Foundations of Modern Literary Judgment,* ed. Mark Shorer et al. [New York: Harcourt, 1948], p. 270). In the notes, Eliot repairs the damage done by the poem and provides yet another alien closure by imposing traditional kinds of thematic and narrative order and continuity on the poem. The notes offer an authoritative and therefore limited way of reading the poem and restore it to the tradition; their belatedness, however, should pose as much of a problem as the problem of belatedness that they would mask. In attempting to cover up the poem's discontinuities, they in effect unmask them, showing the text to be in need of an authority, an author, a story line. I have analyzed the effect of the notes in "*The Waste Land:* Gloss and Glossary," *Essays in Literature* 9, no. 1 (Spring 1982): 97–105.

14 *The Waste Land: A Facsimile and Transcript of the Original Drafts,* p. 17.

15 Walt Whitman, *Leaves of Grass,* ed. Sculley Bradley and Harold W. Blodgett (New York: Norton, 1973), p. 87.

16 *John Keats: Complete Poems,* ed. Jack Stillinger (Cambridge: Harvard University Press, 1982), pp. 439, 173–74.

17 Later, in "The Function of Criticism," Eliot revises himself: "I thought of literature then, as I think

of it now, of the literature of the world, of the literature of Europe, of the literature of a single country" (*Selected Essays* [New York: Harcourt, 1960], p. 12).

18 "From Poe to Valéry," p. 209. Eliot writes: "Poetry, of different kinds, may be said to range from that in which the attention of the reader is directed primarily to the sound, to that in which it is directed primarily to the sense. With the former kind, the sense may be apprehended almost unconsciously; with the latter kind—at these two extremes—it is the sound, of the operation of which upon us we are unconscious. But, with either type, sound and sense must cooperate; in even the most purely incantatory poem, the dictionary meaning of words cannot be disregarded with impunity" (p. 210). This, Eliot charges, Poe tended to do.

19 William Harmon, in "T. S. Eliot's Raids on the Inarticulate," *PMLA* 91, no. 3 (1976): 450–59, studies Eliot's use of inarticulate language. In the early work, Harmon suggests, inarticulate language signifies a horrifying "impoverishment." In the later poems, silence is considered not as a loss but a gain—an ascent above speech. In other terms, the early poems explore the inarticulate particulars—or the Exoteric Inarticulate—and the latter poems contemplate the inarticulate universal—the Esoteric Inarticulate. But throughout this development, language remains "a mid-region, and misty indeed" (p. 455).

20 Jean Starobinski, *The Invention of Liberty, 1700–1789,* trans. Bernard C. Swift (Geneva: Skira, 1964), p. 180.

21 Allen Tate, "The Angelic Imagination," in Carlson, *Poe,* p. 237. Lyndall Gordon's *Eliot's Early Years* supports this reading.

22 "From Poe to Valéry," p. 213.

23 Poe's "To Helen" appears to be the source of the entire passage ("The Burial of the Dead," 11. 31–42); Poe's figure beckons home, to his "own native shore," the "weary, way-worn wanderer" long roaming "desperate seas."

24 In "The Hollow Men" the spiritual condition of those unable to believe becomes the explicit correlative of the poet without faith in the incarnational Word. Only faith in the Incarnation would deliver the poet from the mechanisms of nature and language. Eliot uses poetic devices—alliteration, assonance and consonance, rhyme, repetition and refrain, anaphora, regular rhythm—with a vengeance but without reference to a recognizable form. Much like Poe's "novel combinations" of bits and pieces of traditional forms or the improvised formalism of Plath's later poems, Eliot's novel combination of conventional devices makes a mockery of the traditional function of poetic forms. The formal husk is hollow—a ruined site, an "empty chapel," a scarecrow's chatter—and correlates with the "hollow men," who have human shape but lack an inhering and informing spirit. Thus

Shape without form, shade without colour,
Paralysed force, gesture without motion   [*CP,* 79]

are all symptomatic of the sickness of both the subjects and the physician. Formal gestures that neither are authorized and hallowed by tradition nor help the poet climb to "paradise" are dead letters, killing the spirit and severing lines of communication.

CHAPTER THREE

1 Sylvia Plath, "*ocean 1212-W,*" in *The Art of Sylvia Plath,* ed. Charles Newman (Bloomington: Indiana University Press, 1971), pp. 266, 267.

2 Ibid., pp. 268, 269.

3 Sylvia Plath, *The Collected Poems,* ed. Ted Hughes (New York: Harper & Row, 1981), pp. 156–57. Subsequent references will be cited in the text as *CP,* followed by the page number.

4 "*ocean 1212-W,*" p. 272.

5 Sylvia Plath, *The Bell Jar* (New York: Bantam, 1972), p. 129.

6 Ibid., p. 199.

7 Pamela Smith, "Architectonics: Sylvia Plath's Colossus," in *Sylvia Plath: The Woman and the Work,* ed. Edward Butscher (New York: Dodd, Mead, 1977), p. 114. Plath's formalism has been much discussed, and the consensus is that the formal poet of *The Colossus* broke loose in *Ariel* into a demonic poet. For example, John F. Nims praises Plath's early work for its control and notes the variety of meters, including the iambic, that she uses in *The Colossus.* Metricists, he argues, would consider Plath's later work severely regressive: the poems in *Ariel* vary only between loose and strict iambic ("The Poetry of Sylvia Plath—A Technical Analysis," in Newman, *Sylvia Plath,* pp. 136–52). Hugh Kenner shares the same view of Plath's career: he deplores the "voodoo encouragement" of the heuristic rhymes in *Ariel* and argues that the later work represents not a development but a regression to simpler, even archaic patterns and techniques ("Sincerity Kills," in *Sylvia Plath: New Views on the Poetry,* ed. Gary Lane [Baltimore: Johns Hopkins University Press, 1979], p. 43). In her essay on Plath's metrics, Pamela Smith challenges this schizophrenic reading of Plath's career. Although Plath shares Nims's convinction that "iambic is the *lubdubb* of the heartbeat, perhaps the first sensation that we, months before our birth, are aware of" (p. 146), Smith argues that Plath uses the iambic meter with deliberate irony in *The Colossus* (p. 114).

8 David Shapiro ("Sylvia Plath: Drama and Melodrama," in Lane, *Sylvia Plath: New Views,* pp. 45–56) proposes that the Aristotelian notion of dramatic poetry, where structure dominates diction, does not explain Plath's poetry: in Plath, we have melodrama, where "the whole tendency is to a diction-dominated formlessness punctuated by hyperbole appealing to the emotions" (p. 53). Shapiro is right that Plath's is a poetry of "diction and spectacle" rather than of structure—that it is melodrama rather than drama; he fails to register, however, Plath's full consciousness of and complicity in such language.

9 This is the reading A. Alvarez offers in "Sylvia Plath," in Newman, *Sylvia Plath,* p. 66.

10 Vowels "rise" in Plath; consonants "check" and "barb." See, for example, "Morning Song" (*CP,* 157). In "Ariel," a rare poem of transcendence, it is the vowel "I" through which the liberation courses (*CP,* 239).Vowels sound the breath; consonant stops make articulation and syntax possible but may also rob one of breath.

11 Jacques Derrida, *Of Grammatology,* trans. Gayatri Chakravorty Spivak (Baltimore: Johns Hopkins University Press, 1974), pp. 141–64.

12 "*OCEAN 1212-W,*" p. 267.

13 T. S. Eliot, "The Hollow Men," *Collected Poems,* p. 82.

14 Alan Williamson's review of *The Collected Poems,* "Confession and Tragedy" (*Poetry* 142, no. 3 [June 1983]: 170–78), offers a good reading of this aspect of Plath's work.

15 See J. D. O'Hara, "Plath's Comedy," in Lane, *Sylvia Plath: New Views,* p. 94.

16 Richard Allen Blessing ("The Shape of the Psyche: Vision and Technique in the Late Poems of Sylvia Plath," in Lane, *Sylvia Plath: New Views,* pp. 57–73) observes Plath's willingness "to flirt with tastelessness shamelessly" (p. 66).

17 "Sincerity Kills," pp. 42, 39.

18 Eliot, *The Sacred Wood,* p. 102.

19 "*OCEAN 1212-W,*" p. 266.

20 The raven is one of Apollo's birds, and Plath also uses croaking black birds as emblems of failed poetry. "Conversation Among the Ruins," which properly opens *The Collected Poems,* provides one example of a scene where the "net" of "decorum" is rent, the "rich order of walls is fallen; rooks croak / Above the appalling ruin," and no "ceremony of words can patch the havoc" (p. 21).

21 Gary Lane ("Influence and Originality in Plath's Poems," in Lane, *Sylvia Plath: New Views,* pp. 116–37) suggests that this poem is about liteary influence and that the threat of nature veils the real threat of poetic predecessors—in this instance, the threat of Dylan Thomas's voice (p. 120). Plath's impasse becomes clearer, however, when we see the threats of nature and tradition as real, equal forces.

22 Ted Hughes reports that Plath composed "thesaurus open on her knee" ("Notes on the Chronological Order of Sylvia Plath's Poems," in Newman, *Sylvia Plath,* p. 188). Murray M. Schwartz and Christopher Bollas, in "The Absence at the Center: Sylvia Plath and Suicide," report that the thesaurus belonged to her father (Lane, *Sylvia Plath: New Views,* p. 187).

23 "Sylvia Plath's 'Sivvy' Poems," in Lane, *Sylvia Plath: New Views,* pp. 163–69. In this respect, Plath's career is not unlike Eliot's, whose stage is also overcrowded. Theirs are scenes of collective "influence," and the voices of others are masks and allusions the poets use and drop.

24 Quoted by A. Alvarez, in Newman, *Sylvia Plath,* p. 59.

25 This phrase is about a writerly language and how it robs one of breath: "The word, defining, muzzles; the drawn line / Ousts mistier peers and thrives, murderous, / In establishments which imagined lines // Can only haunt" (*CP,* 106).

26 Blessing aptly discusses the poem as a strip-tease act (Lane, *Sylvia Plath: New Views,* p. 67).

27 See, for example, "Widow" (*CP,* 164), "Crossing the Water" (*CP,* 190), and "Tulips" (*CP,* 161).

28 John Berryman, *The Dream Songs* (New York: Farrar, Straus, 1969), DS 16, 53.

29 DS 8; in Berryman, the "prying" of the stylus compares to a surgical operation (DS 67) and can lead to death (via Hemingway, in DS 34).

30 Judith Kroll borrows this term from ethnology to describe how Plath's images function: they do not mediate but automatically trigger or release "predetermined" meanings. They serve to discharge preexisting configurations that lie within the psyche, already complete. See *Chapters in a Mythology: The Poetry of Sylvia Plath* (New York: Harper & Row, 1978), pp. 16–20.

CHAPTER FOUR

1 *The Collected Works of Ralph Waldo Emerson* (Cambridge: Harvard University Press, Belknap Press. 1971–), 1:19. Subsequent references to this edition will be cited in the text as *CW,* followed by volume and page numbers.

2 *The Complete Works of Ralph Waldo Emerson,* ed. Edward Waldo Emerson (Boston: Houghton Mifflin, 1904), 8: 9–10. Subsequent references to this edition will be cited in the text as *W,* followed by volume and page numbers.

3 See Yoder, *Emerson and the Orphic Poet in America,* p. 10.

4 *The Journals and Miscellaneous Notebooks of Ralph Waldo Emerson,* ed. William H. Gilman et al. (Cambridge: Harvard University Press, Belknap Press, 1960–1978), 5: 9. Subsequent references will be cited in the text as *JMN,* followed by volume and page numbers.

5 Quoted in *Selections from Ralph Waldo Emerson,* ed. Stephen E. Whicher (Boston: Houghton Mifflin, 1960), p. 146.

6 *Plato's Timaeus,* trans. Francis M. Cornford (Indianapolis: Bobbs-Merrill, 1959), pp. 17–18.

7 M. H. Abrams, *The Mirror and the Lamp: Romantic Theory and the Critical Tradition* (New York: Norton, 1958), p. 42.

8 Wallace Stevens, *The Collected Poems* (New York: Knopf, 1954), p. 250.

9 *The Correspondence of Emerson and Carlyle,* ed. Joseph Slater (New York: Columbia University Press, 1964), p. 482.

10 Porter, *Emerson and Literary Change,* p. 90.

11 Stevens, *Collected Poems,* p. 250.

12 Georg Lukács, *Soul and Form,* trans. Anna Bostock (Cambridge: MIT Press, 1974), pp. 16–17.

13 Ibid., p. 17.

14 Ibid., pp. 20–21.

15 Bloom, "Bacchus and Merlin: The Dialectic of Romantic Poetry in America," *The Ringers in the Tower,* p. 299.

16 Fussell, *Lucifer in Harness,* p. 28.

17 Hyatt H. Waggoner, *Emerson as Poet* (Princeton: Princeton University Press, 1974), p. 30. Waggoner's analysis of "Merlin," for example, reveals that the poem contains many irregularly stressed segments, the number of stresses varying between two and five per line, and irregular rhyme units—some couplets, some triplets, and some quatrains. "But," Waggoner rightly concludes, "the poem made from all these irregular pieces does not seem 'formless'; its movement does not seem arbitrary but inevitable" (p. 142).

18 Paul Ricoeur, "The Metaphorical Process as Cognition, Imagination, and Feeling," in *On Metaphor,* ed. Sheldon Sacks (Chicago: University of Chicago Press, 1979), p. 144.

19 Stevens, *Collected Poems,* p. 88.

20 Porter contends that in "Merlin" Emerson "stresses liberation from constraints of form": "Merlin says the primal word because he is unencumbered by the courtly restraints of artifice" (p. 89). Since the poem is highly structured, however, it seems that the "liberated" art of Merlin ends up coinciding with formal artifice.

21 Stephen E. Whicher, *Freedom and Fate: An Inner Life of Ralph Waldo Emerson* (Philadelphia: University of Pennsylvania Press, 1971), p. 75.

22 Thus, for Emerson, organic form does not mean free form: "Rightly, poetry is organic. We cannot know things by words and writing, but only by taking a central position in the universe and living in its forms. We sink to rise:—

'None any work can frame,
Unless himself become the same.'"   [*W,* 8: 42–43]

23 Emerson's prose resists the deadly implications of language-as-fate, the face of language poetry wears. Nietzsche's analysis of the relation between prose and poetry touches on this conflict: "Good prose is written only face to face with poetry. For it is an uninterrupted, well-mannered war with poetry: all of its attractions depend on the way in which poetry is continually avoided and contradicted. Everything abstract wants to be read as a prank against poetry and as with a mocking voice." See Friedrich Nietzsche, *The Gay Science,* trans. Walter Kaufmann (New York: Random House, 1974), p. 145.

24 Waggoner, *Emerson as Poet,* pp. 192–93.

CHAPTER FIVE

1 Wallace Stevens, *The Necessary Angel: Essays on Reality and the Imagination* (New York: Random House, 1951), p. 81. Subsequent references will be cited in the text as *NA,* followed by the page number.

2 Wallace Stevens, *Opus Posthumous* (New York: Knopf, 1957), p. 104. Subsequent references will be cited in the text as *OP,* followed by the page number.

3 *The Collected Poems of Wallace Stevens* (New York: Knopf, 1954), p. 382. Subsequent references will be cited in the text as *CP,* followed by the page number.

4 Stevens's view of W. C. Williams as a "romantic poet" (*OP,* 251) is understandable in this context. The faith that subject and object can be fused in poetry underlies Williams's idea that there is a poem absolute to any given subject, experience, or fact. Ezra Pound's faith in a poetic rhythm absolute to every thought and perception marks another phase of this faith. Williams's Objectivist poems and Pound's Imagist/Vorticist poems both aim to achieve a fusion of the subjective and the objective that is more substantial than rhetorical. In Stevens's terms, this, too, would have to be added to "rhetoric" (*CP,* 198–99). A poem like "Thirteen Ways of Looking at a Blackbird" shows the difference between Stevens's modernism, which is based on deconstructing rhetorics of transcendence or fusions of the mind and nature, and Pound's and Williams's modernism, which is based on technically adequate reconstructions of fusions that are more or less than metaphoric.

5 My reading of Stevens's idea of metaphor diverges both from a synchronic reading like Joseph N. Riddel's ("Metaphoric Staging: Stevens' Beginning Again of the 'End of the Book'" in *Wallace Stevens: A Celebration,* ed. Frank Doggett and Robert Buttel [Princeton: Princeton University Press, 1980], pp. 308–37) and from Harold Bloom's diachronic reading of a trope as "a cut or gap made in or into the anteriority of language, itself an anteriority in which 'language' acts as a figurative substitution for time" (Harold Bloom, *Wallace Stevens: The Poems of Our Climate* [Ithaca: Cornell University Press, 1977], p. 393). I suggest that the temporal structure of syntax and poetic form renders time and rhetoric coeval centers of poetic language.

6 Emerson foreshadows Stevens's complex vision only in rare moments like "The Snow-Storm." Here an exoteric blank verse tells of an art and nature equally eccentric, each mimicking the other and centering in the metaphoric language of a resemblance-making mind, which can *see* the wind *as* a mason and stone *as* snow, negotiating between art and nature, form and force. Yet the metaphor

that carries these mutual resemblances hinges on architecture, a structure that separates humans from nature and acknowledges our need for protection from nature in order to live at all. Stevens strikes just such a balance, which remained largely beyond Emerson.

7 Thus, while Emerson proposes a fated poetic language as his center, Stevens reclaims the freedom of rhetoric without reducing it to an illusion or relinquishing claims to its centrality.

8 Helen Vendler suggests that the "ravishing but inherited harmonies" of the poem mourn the death not only of the gods but of the possibility of poetry in the High Romantic mode. See *On Extended Wings: Wallace Stevens' Longer Poems* (Cambridge: Harvard University Press, 1969), pp. 64, 54–55. For a discussion of the romantic contexts of "Sunday Morning," see Bloom, *Wallace Stevens,* pp. 27–35.

9 Isabel G. MacCaffrey, "The Ways of Truth in 'Le Monocle de Mon Oncle,'" in Doggett and Buttel, *Wallace Stevens: A Celebration,* pp. 213–214, 201, 204.

10 Bloom, *Wallace Stevens,* p. 43.

11 For example, Crispin is a "clown," which derives from the French word for "farmer," *colon* (originally a colonist or settler). But even when Crispin rejects poetic conventions, founds his colony in North America, and becomes a cultivator of the earth, his relation to the land remains peripheral: "colony" stems from *colere* ("cultivate"), with a probable Indo-European base in *kwel* ("turn," "dwell," "care for"). Dwelling, then, is a turning. The word "verse" is itself related to agriculture, and "versus" also signifies the turn of the plow at the end of a row. The roots of "verse" go back to "warp"—and to "worm" ("twist") with its Indo-European root *wer. Wer* means "to turn" and "to speak"; it is also the root of "word."

12 Stevens's remarks about the title are well known. He wrote to Hi Simons that "The Comedian as the Sounds of the Letter C" would more accurately convey what he meant by using the letter C as "cypher" for Crispin. *Letters of Wallace Stevens,* ed. Holly Stevens (New York: Knopf, 1966), p. 351.

13 *Letters,* pp. 351–52, 778.

14 Emerson, *The Complete Works,* pp. 30–31.

15 Martin Heidegger, *An Introduction to Metaphysics,* trans. Ralph Manheim (New York: Doubleday, 1961), pp. 69, 50, 49. J. Hillis Miller offers a Heideggerian reading of Stevens's "being" in *Poets of Reality* (Cambridge: Harvard University Press, 1965), pp. 279–84.

16 Whitman, "Song of Myself," in *Leaves of Grass,* p. 74.

17 A comparison of "Metaphor as Degeneration" with Frost's "West-Running Brook" brings Stevens's poem into focus. Frost's interest in "naming" (ll. 3, 74) and "saying" (ll. 73, 75) remains thematic. Naming and saying represent human resistance to "The Westwardness of Everything" (Stevens, *CP,* 455), the "backward motion toward the source" (*The Poetry of Robert Frost: The Collected Poems* [New York: Holt, 1979], p. 260). Stevens's distinction is to see poetic creation *itself* as both entropic and troping from entropy. Poetry tropes away from entropy; since that troping is a temporal turn, however, it is also entropic.

18 Quoted in Whicher, *Freedom and Fate,* p. 98.

19 Marie Borroff, *Language and the Poet: Verbal Artistry in Frost, Stevens, and Moore* (Chicago: University of Chicago Press, 1979), p. 61; Vendler, *Extended Wings,* p. 13–37.

20 Borroff, pp. 54–56, 45, 71.

21 Quoted in Whicher, p. 155.

22 Emerson, "The Poet," *The Collected Works,* 3:5–6.

CHAPTER SIX

1 An overview of Bishop criticism reveals a wide range of readings. Anne Stevenson and Jan B. Gordon note the formality and the impersonal manner of Bishop's work. See, respectively, *Elizabeth Bishop* (Boston: Twayne, 1966) and "Days and Distances: The Cartographic Imagination of Elizabeth Bishop," in *Contemporary Poetry in America,* ed. Robert Boyers (New York: Schocken, 1974), pp. 348–59. David Kalstone and Jerome Mazzaro, however, read her poems as personal, emotional, and, indeed, autobiographical. See, respectively, *Five Temperaments* (New York: Oxford

University Press, 1977) and *Postmodern American Poetry* (Urbana: University of Illinois Press, 1980). Lloyd Schwartz reads *Geography III* as autobiographical and argues that the book reveals Bishop's earlier work as well to be "more 'felt,' less 'objective,' more 'serious.' " See "One Art: The Poetry of Elizabeth Bishop, 1971–1976," *Ploughshares* 3, nos. 3–4: 30.

Stevenson describes Bishop as in part a "traditional New England Realist" and in part "modernist or Surrealist-like (not Surrealist)" (pp. 57, 58). Richard Mullen points out some of the Surrealist techniques Bishop uses. In his view, while Bishop shares the Surrealists' interest in the unconscious, she differs from them in approach: instead of subverting everyday or "natural" realities, she blurs the distinction between them and the oneiric, between "objective" and "subjective" perception. See Richard Mullen, "Elizabeth Bishop's Surrealist Inheritance," *American Literature* 54, no. 1 (March 1982): 63–80. According to Helen Vendler, Bishop's work vibrates between "two frequencies—the domestic and the strange"; for Bishop, however, "it is not only the exotic that is strange and not only the local that is domestic." See Helen Vendler, "Domestication, Domesticity and the Otherworldly," *World Literature Today* 51, no. 1 (Winter 1977): 23. Finally, Kalstone (p. 14) and Mazzaro (p. 184) both judge Bishop's observations "uncommitted," for they are not chosen or ordered according to the thematic requirements of a poem. Both defend such "useless," nonprofessional observations against Stephen Stepanchev's attack on the same mode. See Stephen Stepanchev, *American Poetry since 1945* (New York: Harper & Row, 1965), p. 74.

2 Stevens, *The Collected Poems*, pp. 179–80.

3 Elizabeth Bishop, *The Complete Poems 1927–1979* (New York: Farrar, Straus, 1983), p. 4. Subsequent references to this volume will be cited in the text as *CP*, followed by the page number.

4 Alfred, Lord Tennyson, "The Lady of Shalott," *The Poems of Tennyson*, ed. Christopher Ricks (New York: Longman, 1969; reprint, Norton, 1972), pp. 355–61.

5 See William Carlos Williams, "The Poem as a Field of Action," in *Selected Essays* (New York: New Directions, 1954), pp. 280–91, and Charles Olson, "Projective Verse," in *Selected Writings* (New York: New Directions, 1966), pp. 15–26.

6 Whitman, "A Song of the Rolling Earth," in *Leaves of Grass*, p. 219.

7 "The Art of Poetry, XXVII: Interview with Elizabeth Bishop," *The Paris Review* 23, no. 80 (Summer 1981): 69.

8 *The Complete Poems of Emily Dickinson*, ed. Thomas H. Johnson (Boston: Little, Brown, 1960), no. 1638.

9 This "adequacy" of the "sheltering" form to what it may or may not contain gives Bishop's work its "classical" poise. The classical spirit, Fritz Strich writes, "did not seek to reach behind language any more than it sought to reach behind the appearances—illusory for the Romantics—of the phenomenal world." See Fritz Strich, "From *Language*," in *Essays in Stylistic Analysis*, ed. Howard S. Babb (New York: Harcourt, Brace, 1972), p. 140.

10 T. S. Eliot, "Burnt Norton," *Collected Poems 1909–1962* (New York: Harcourt, Brace, 1963), p. 177.

11 Bonnie Costello observes the prevalence of the interrogative form in Bishop's verse and relates it to the theme of travel: both resist closure, displacing us from the original certainties of home and preventing us from reaching the final certainties of answers and destinations. See "The Impersonal and the Interrogative in the Poetry of Elizabeth Bishop," in *Elizabeth Bishop and Her Art*, ed. Lloyd Schwartz and Sybil P. Estess (Ann Arbor: University of Michigan Press, 1983), pp. 109–53.

CHAPTER SEVEN

1 Walt Whitman, "Song of Myself," in *Leaves of Grass*, ed. Sculley Bradley and Harold W. Blodgett (New York: Norton, 1973), p. 30. Subsequent references to this edition will be cited in the text as *LG*, followed by the page number.

2 "Slang in America," *Prose Works 1892*, 2 vols., ed. Floyd Stovall, *The Collected Writings of Walt Whitman* ed. Gay Wilson Allen and Sculley Bradley (New York: New York University Press, 1963–1964), p. 577. Subsequent references will be cited in the text as *PW*, followed by the page number.

3 Frye, *Anatomy of Criticism,* p. 119.

4 Ibid., pp. 119, 120, 121.

5 Ibid., p. 124.

6 Harold Bloom, *Agon: Towards a Theory of Revisionism* (New York: Oxford University Press, 1982), pp. 182, 195.

7 In "Plato's Pharmacy," Jacques Derrida discusses writing as a democratic and patricidal challenge to the Logos. In disseminating and dispersing the authority of the living word, writing challenges the legitimate succession of kingship, the authorized speakers of the living word. See *Dissemination,* pp. 142–46.

8 *Collected Writings of Walt Whitman,* vol. 3, *Daybooks and Notebooks,* ed. William White (New York: New York University Press, 1978), p. 669. Subsequent references will be cited in the text as *DN,* followed by the page number.

9 Whitman prophesies: "In the future of these States must arise poets immenser far, and make great poems of death" (*PW,* 420).

10 *Leaves of Grass,* pp. 121, 120, 39.

11 In an interesting reading, Edwin Fussell suggests that this line tolls the death knell of the pentameter. See *Lucifer in Harness,* pp. 133–34.

12 Sigmund Freud, in *The Interpretation of Dreams,* trans. James Strachey (New York: Avon, 1965), notes the point in a dream where there is a "tangle of dream-thoughts which cannot be unravelled." He calls this point, which remains outside the interpretive framework, the "dream's navel, the spot where it reaches down into the unknown" (p. 564).

13 Derrida's distinction between the Logos and writing is Whitman's distinction as well, although Whitman claims to be writing the Logos. See Derrida, *Dissemination,* pp. 143, 159.

14 Jakobson and Halle, *Fundamentals of Language,* The Hague, pp. 80–82.

15 This is the judgment of an otherwise sympathetic English critic, George Saintsbury, who also considers Whitman's "ugly trick of using foreign words" to be his "chief blemish" (*LG,* 785, 789).

16 Whitman writes: "All that immense volumes, and more than volumes, can tell, are conveyed in the right name" (*DN,* 756). His concern with names is evident throughout his notebooks. See, especially, *DN,* pp. 682, 684, 693, 695, 696, 705, 743, 753–57.

17 Pound's figure for transparent layers of isomorphic metamorphoses and patterns is an isomorph of Whitman's "leaf over leaf." See *The Cantos of Ezra Pound* (New York: New Directions, 1981), cantos 4, 17.

18 Northrop Frye, *The Great Code: The Bible and Literature* (New York: Harcourt Brace, 1983), p. 21.

19 This is how he appears to Denis Donoghue, for example, who sees Whitman as evading such romantic oppositions as appearance and reality, subject and object, life and death, and good and evil "simply by declaring their identity." See *Connoisseurs of Chaos: Ideas of Order in Modern American Poetry* (New York: Macmillan, 1965), pp. 28–29. Yet the word "declare" is the crux: Whitman's system is always acknowledged to be a verbal construct, a faith, a "declaration," "just words." American politics, which underwrites his poetry, itself rests on both a "natural" truth and a document that affirms certain truths to be "self-evident." The gap between natural and self-evident truths is spanned by a declaration, which attests to the political power of language *and* acknowledges its limits.

20 If we follow Georg Lukács's theory of the epic, Whitman's unclassifiable work would qualify as epic. In the age of the epic—and the Homeric world provides Lukács's example—"the world is wide and yet it is like a home, for the fire that burns in the soul is of the same essential nature as the stars"; "There is not yet any interiority, for there is not yet any exterior, any 'otherness' for the soul." In such a world, "being and destiny, adventure and accomplishment, life and essence are . . . identical concepts. For the question which engenders the formal answers of the epic is: how can life become essence? . . . before the progress of the human mind through history had allowed the question to be asked." See *The Theory of the Novel*, trans. Anna Bostock (Cambridge: MIT Press, 1971), pp. 29, 30. Lukács considers dramatic and other teleological forms to be historically later

products; they appear when eternal essence becomes removed from the visible world and esthetic and formal unities increasingly come to substitute for the lost, empirical totality of the metaphysical spheres that the epic records. Whitman, in his "turbulent" nineteenth century, stands at the end of a history of ever-widening separation between the visible world and eternal essences and, correspondingly, between outer nature or form and inner soul or force. Despite this Western philosophical history, however, and in the very vocabulary of dualism that is its legacy, he declares himself equal to the epic poet's task. And the fact that genre classifications blur in his work is a gauge of his success in writing an "epic of Democracy" (*LG*, 741).

21 Sculley Bradley has argued that Whitman's verse indeed has metrical regularity: "In the majority of the lines of Whitman, which are not brought into equivalence by repetition of substance and phrases, there is still the equivalence of a rhythm regulated by a periodicity of stress so uniformly measured as to constitute a true 'meter.'" See "The Fundamental Metrical Principle in Whitman's Poetry," *American Literature* 10 (Mar. 1938–Jan. 1939): 447. The difficulty with this position becomes clear when it comes to determining the stresses in a given line without a metrical "frame" or "contract," in John Hollander's terms (*Vision and Resonance: Two Senses of Poetic Form* [New York: Oxford University Press, 1975], pp. 135–64). For example, Bradley scans the following lines by making use of what he calls a "gliding stress," which helps him throughout with Whitman:

Which of the young men does she like the best?
Ah the homeliest of them is beautiful to her.

Bradley explains: "If one reads that second line without the 'glide,' and with strong vocalic accent on the words 'them' and 'her' the quality and emotional sense are changed, and the line, indeed, becomes jocose instead of pathetic" (p. 445). But, if the correct placement of stress is bound to and follows from context, sense, and correct interpretation, it cannot constitute a meter, for its very periodicity is contingent on extraformal matters. In metrical poetry, the stress pattern guides the correct interpretation and may be used to modify and undercut meaning; Whitman, however, cannot tap such rhetorical resources, which are made available by an interplay of sense and a metrical "frame." In Whitman, it is less the sense and more the pattern of stress that is open to debate. Indeed, my reading of any given line is likely to differ from someone else's. Bradley proposes:

The young men float on their backs, their white bellies
    bulge to the sun, they do not ask who seizes fast to
    them   [p. 457]

Why, for example, is "young" unstressed while the second "their" receives a stress, if not because of a certain reading or interpretation of the lines? Moreover, while some of Whitman's lines may be scannable, such patterns exist alongside semantic and syntactic patterning and cannot be isolated as strictly quantitative measures.

22 Another statement of this position is found in "A Backward Glance O'er Travel'd Roads": "No one will get at my verses who insists upon viewing them as a literary performance, or attempt at such performance, or as aiming mainly toward art or aestheticism" (*LG*, 574).

23 Paul Fussell, *Poetic Meter and Poetic Form* (New York: Random House, 1979), p. 84.

24 Whitman cites the "Hebrew Bible" among the "autochthonic bequests of Asia" (*PW*, 545).

25 See Gay Wilson Allen, *American Prosody* (New York: American Book Co., 1935), pp. 217–43.

26 James L. Kugel, *The Idea of Biblical Poetry: Parallelism and Its History* (New Haven: Yale University Press, 1981), pp. 1–95. In "The Bible As Poetry," Whitman cites De Sola Mendes, who writes that "'rhyming was not a characteristic of Hebrew poetry at all. Metre was not a necessary mark of poetry. Great poets discarded it; the early Jewish poets knew it not'" (*PW*, 546).

27 See, for example, "By Blue Ontario's Shore," which recycles lines from the 1855 preface. It appeared in the 1856 edition, and one fourth of the poem consisted of material from the preface.

28 Whitman writes that "while England is among the greatest of lands in political freedom, or the idea of it, and in stalwart personal character, &c.—the spirit of English literature is not great, at least is

not greatest—and its products are no models for us." He suggests overrefinement as one problem (*PW*, 522). The Bible, "through its divine and *primal poetic structure*" (*PW*, 549; emphasis mine), provided a model for a use of the English language that could not be found in English literature.

29 Northrop Frye, "Verse and Prose," in the *Princeton Encyclopedia*, p. 886.

CHAPTER EIGHT

1 Ezra Pound, *Selected Prose 1909–1965*, ed. William Cookson (New York: New Directions, 1975), pp. 389, 390. Subsequent references to Pound's work will be abbreviated in the text as follows:
Guide to Kulchur (New York: New Directions, 1970): *GK*
Literary Essays (New York: New Directions, 1968): *LE*
Personae (New York: New Directions, 1971): *P*
Selected Prose: *SP*
The Spirit of Romance (New York: New Directions, 1968): *SR*
References to *The Cantos of Ezra Pound* (New York: New Directions, 1981) will cite the canto number, followed by the page number in this edition.

2 Pound's derogatory comments about Whitman are well known (see, for example, *SR*, 168–69); less noted are his homages to Whitman. For a discussion of Pound's relationship to Whitman, see James E. Miller, Jr., *The American Quest for a Supreme Fiction* (Chicago: University of Chicago Press, 1979), pp. 68–98.

3 Whitman, *Leaves of Grass*, p. 544. Subsequent references to Whitman will be cited in the text as *LG*, followed by the page number.

4 See Pound's attack on the mimetic (*SP*, 41–42).

5 *LG*, 58. Whitman's thought derives support from the evolutionary theories that were "in the air" before the publication of Charles Darwin's *Origin of Species* (1859). Similarly, Pound's thought is influenced by the evolutionary theories of Louis Agassiz, which Guy Davenport has discussed (see "Louis Agassiz," *The Geography of the Imagination* [San Francisco: North Point, 1981], pp. 230–49).

6 On Pound's "method" of translation on the tongue, breath, and throat, see Hugh Kenner, *The Pound Era* (Berkeley and Los Angeles: University of California Press, 1971). Kenner suggests that Pound mimes the "gestures of tongue and expulsions of breath" that mime, in their original language, a given emotion-subject (p. 484).

7 Pound's use of the English meter in canto 81 compares with Whitman's occasional allusions to the same rhythm: it both invokes the authority of the English lyric tradition and justifies his deviation from it.

8 James E. Miller points out that Whitman's "Long, Long Hence" is an important poem for Pound. While Whitman does not command Pound's knowledge of the "ages," he certainly subscribes to the idea of diachronic and synchronic layerings of leaves, "ply over ply." Process in both runs diachronically, connecting the past and the present, and synchronically, connecting isomorphic revelations of the life energy in myriad forms.

9 As Hugh Kenner describes this diachronic/synchronic isomorphism, the "principle is very general. Poems cohere, as do fish, and yet are derivable from other poems, as *Lycidas*, via Vergil, out of Moschus and Theocritus. 'Influence' is no longer the relevant metaphor: we are dealing not with inflow but homeomorphism, the domain of topology, systems of identical interconnectedness" (Kenner, *The Pound Era*, p. 169).

10 "An Essay on CHINESE WRITTEN CHARACTER by the late ERNEST FENOLLOSA," ed. Ezra Pound, in *Instigations of Ezra Pound* (New York: Boni and Liveright, 1920), pp. 378, 366, 364, 377. Discussing Arnaut Daniel, Pound calls his "picture making" neither "simile" nor "metaphor" but a "language beyond metaphor . . . the use of the picturesque verb with an exact meaning" (*SR*, 33).

11 Kenner, *The Pound Era*, p. 145.

12 Laszlo Géfin, *Ideogram* (Austin: University of Texas Press, 1982), pp. xiii, xvi. On this basis, he distinguishes Pound's terms from Fenollosa's: Pound desired to move "beyond metaphoric con-

struction," even though such a stance may seem to go "against the grain of Fenollosa's assertions about the links between metaphor and ideogram" (p. xiii). Géfin correctly states that "ideograms point to a reality and an order which is not human"; the "ideogrammic form is coextensive with [a] pre-logical and posthumanist outlook" (p. 140). Hence he can claim that "it is the most important methodological achievement of modernist poetics" (p. xi) and trace to it the poetics of William Carlos Williams, Charles Olson, Louis Zukofsky, Charles Reznikoff, Robert Duncan, Robert Creeley, Allen Ginsberg, and Gary Snyder.

13 Herbert Schneidau, "Pound's Book of Cross-cuts," *Genre* 11 (Winter 1978): 511. For Pound's distinction between *zeitgeist* and *paideuma*, see *GK*, 58.

14 Hugh Kenner writes, "No poem is an end product. Each is a controlled transformational process. As the cables of a suspension bridge graph a system of stresses, the words on the page plot stabilized energies" (Kenner, *The Pound Era*, p. 171).

15 Pound, *Instigations*, p. 361. Whitman also associates clarity and sanity with more and less than metaphoric language (*LG*, 764).

16 Pound, *Instigations*, pp. 367, 361, 380, 379.

17 For Pound, even architecture can be part of the process. Canto 17 presents such an architecture, which embodies the obverse of the metamorphosis in canto 2. Zagreus presides over both of these metamorphoses of water and stone. The source of Pound's architectural descriptions in canto 17 has been identified as Adrian Stokes on Venice, and "Venice" appropriately puns on "Venus," the wind-borne, foam-born goddess. She represents the opposite of the stony Medusa (15:66), who is the ancestor of Geryon, the figure of usury. Indeed, the genealogy of Geryon itself is curiously mixed: Medusa and Poseidon beget both Pegasus and Chrysaor, who begets Geryon in turn. See H. J. Rose, *A Handbook of Greek Mythology* (New York: Dutton, 1959), p. 30.

18 Pound, *Instigations*, pp. 366, 371, 365, 387.

19 Grosseteste is Pound's source for these recurrent phrases. See *LE*, 160–61, where he cites "Lux enim per se [83:528] in omnem partem [55:298] se ipsam diffundit" and "transitus . . . per . . . plura diaphana." For other sources of "ply over ply," see Carroll F. Terrell, *A Companion to the Cantos of Ezra Pound*, (Berkeley and Los Angeles: University of California Press, 1980), 13.

20 *Confucius: The Unwobbling Pivot & The Great Digest*, trans. Ezra Pound, *Pharos* (Winter 1947): 34. Pound adds to this definition, "Refer to Scotus Erigena, Grosseteste and the notes on light in my *Cavalcanti*," thus linking the *ming* ideogram with the Neoplatonists' light.

21 The *cheng ming* ideogram combines the *ming* ideogram with the *cheng* ideogram (honesty, sincerity) and means "the precise definition of the word, pictorially the sun's lance coming to rest on the precise spot verbally" (*Confucius*, p. 34)

22 Dante, *Inferno*, trans. Allen Mandelbaum (New York: Bantam, 1982), pp. 155, 151, 271, 281.

23 Kenner, *The Pound Era*, p. 488.

24 One index of Pound's distance from Stevens's poetic is in the difference between their respective poetic economies. "Money is a kind of poetry," Wallace Stevens wrote (*Opus Posthumous*, p. 165). An elegiac poet, Stevens begins by accepting the "fraud" of language—its abstraction, its "poverty," its lack of "equity" or "collateral" in "real estate." Pound, however, is an ecstatic, elemental, immanentist poet, for whom the root of all evil is abstraction. He attempts to make the signifier and signified coincide in order to prevent the reduction of the living body/universe to a signifier, whose "breath" is "stolen" by the unseen referent or the signified. To identify the two terms of the linguistic sign—and hence of the "vehicle" and "tenor" of metaphor, the seen and unseen worlds—denies the logical and temporal difference between them; it attempts in language, "on the barb of time" (5:17), to undo difference and time ("Time is not, Time is the evil") so that the "hours" can be "beloved" again (74:444).

25 Wendy Flory (*Ezra Pound and the* Cantos [New Haven: Yale University Press, 1980], p. 287) points out that these lines were not intended to be the last canto. Yet the passage is appropriate as such, showing the drift of the cantos to be a drift or passage.

26 See Rose, *Handbook of Greek Mythology*, p. 61.

CHAPTER NINE

1   Frank O'Hara, "Nature and New Painting," in *Standing Still and Walking in New York*, ed. Donald Allen (Bolinas, Calif.: Grey Fox Press, 1975), pp. 41–42. Subsequent references will be cited in the text as *SS*, followed by the page number.

2   Pound, "Affirmations," *Selected Prose 1909-1965*, pp. 374–375.

3   "A Retrospect," *Literary Essays of Ezra Pound*, ed. T. S. Eliot (New York: New Directions, 1968), p. 4.

4   Frank O'Hara, *Art Chronicles 1954–1966* (New York: Braziller, 1975), p. 35. Subsequent references will be cited in the text as *AC*, followed by the page number.

5   Charles Olson, whose essay "Projective Verse" propounds the same poetic values, may have influenced O'Hara more than O'Hara admits. While O'Hara was irreverent toward what Olson himself calls "the usual 'poetics' biz," his thought closely parallels Olson's (Charles Olson, *Selected Writings* [New York: New Directions, 1966], p. 28). His assessment of Olson's poetry touches on a crucial difference between the two poets: "I think that Olson is—a great spirit. I don't think that he is willing to be as delicate as his sensibility may be emotionally and he's extremely conscious of the Pound heritage and of saying the important utterance, which one cannot always summon up and indeed is not particularly desirable most of the time" (*SS*, 13). O'Hara, however, is able in his work to revitalize the Whitmanic tradition of a poetry responsive to the poet's physiology, where the important and the casual utterance, as well as form and force, in fact coincide.

6   Pound, *Cantos*, pp. 17, 797.

7   *The Collected Poems of Frank O'Hara* (New York: Knopf, 1971), p. 554. Subsequent references will be cited in the text as *CP*, followed by the page number.

8   Pound would agree with O'Hara's judgment and choice of image:

> The fair Greek saw himself only. *He* petrified his own semblance.
> *His sculpture was derivative*, his feeling for form secondary. The absence of direct energy lasted for a thousand years. (*Guide to Kulchur*, p. 64.)

While Pound allows for a resurgence of "direct energy" in the medieval period, O'Hara would concur with Olson that "humanism is (homer) coming in, and (melville) going out" (Olson, *Selected Writings*, p. 112).

9   See, respectively, sections 41, 44 and 31–33, of "Song of Myself," in *Leaves of Grass*.

10   "Biotherm," *CP*, p. 438. Unless otherwise noted, all subsequent quotations from O'Hara will be from "Biotherm."

11   Sigmund Freud, *Three Essays on the Theory of Sexuality*, trans. James Strachey (New York: Basic Books, 1962), pp. 48, 47.

12   Sigmund Freud, *Jokes and Their Relation to the Unconscious*, trans. James Strachey (New York: Norton, 1963), p. 160. In the Freudian method of analysis, the ambiguities of the text clarify as a text behind the text, although Freud admits, "There is no possibility of *explaining* dreams as a psychical process, since to explain a thing means to trace it back to something already known" (*Interpretation of Dreams*, p. 549). Thus the metatext that "explains" the dream is in fact a rational transcript of the psychic experience of the dream and can only exist after the dream.

13   Freud, *Interpretation of Dreams*, p. 332. Such word use is an important element in O'Hara's work as a whole. An interesting example is the much-admired final stanza of "The Day Lady Died": the sequence of events here may have been chosen for effect or may seem to be based on chance, but the text is also firmly rooted in the literal chemistry of anagrams, moving from "NEW YORK POST" to "5 SPOT" to "I *stopped* breathing" (*CP*, 325; emphasis mine).

14   Edward Sapir, *Culture, Language, and Personality* (Berkeley and Los Angeles: University of California Press, 1956), p. 3.

15   Derrida, "La Parole Soufflée," in *Writing and Difference*, p. 194.

16   Ibid., pp. 174–75.

17   In Artaud's words, "All Writing is Pig-Shit." Quoted in Gilles Deleuze, "The Schizophrenic and

Language: Surface and Depth in Lewis Carroll and Antonin Artaud," in *Textual Strategies: Perspectives in Post-Structuralist Criticism*, ed. Josué Harari (Ithaca: Cornell University Press, 1979), p. 287.

18 Again, O'Hara's understanding of poetic form as a physiological process dovetails with Olson's. Just as O'Hara attempts to guard his poem from "mess and measure" (*CP*, 444), Olson also calls for an "organization" that "resists" at once the "Beast" (nature/death) and the "fraud": "This organism"—the "organized ground" of human physiology—is not chaos, and it "never was cathedral, draughty tenement of soul" (Olson, *Selected Writings*, pp. 13-14). If poetic organization has its basis in the body, O'Hara's remark "the slightest loss of attention leads to death" is both a physiological imperative and an aesthetic charge (quoted by Bill Berkson, "Frank O'Hara and his Poems," *Art and Literature* 12 [Spring 1967]: 53). Literally, the organism's life depends on attention, which replaces the tensions of form and irony as a way of energizing the poem without structuring it. This conception is shared by Olson, for whom attention determines the "push" of a line and of history at large; thus he objects to "similes," "adjectives," "slow things," "*any* slackness [that] takes off attention" and saps "the going energy of the content toward its form" (Olson, *Selected Writings*, pp. 19–20, 169).

Moreover, in his call for a poetic process of selection and organization without generalization or abstraction from experience, Olson appeals to scientific discoveries for support: "And it has gone so far, that is, science has, as to wonder if the fingertips, are not very knowing knots in their own rights, little brains (little photo-electric cells, I think they now call the skin) which, immediately, responding to external stimuli, make decisions" (ibid., p. 60). This idea of a decentered organization is useful for understanding the imagery and form of "Biotherm." Olson goes on to suggest that "this metaphor of the senses—of the literal speed of light by which a man absorbs, instant on instant, all that phenomenon presents to him—is a fair image as well . . . of the ways of his inner energy, of . . . his dreams, for example, his thoughts (to speak as the predecessors spoke), his desires, sins, hopes, fears, faiths, loves" (ibid.). "Biotherm" processes stimuli on this model and, as such, is isomorphic with a biological organism. Ultimately, however, O'Hara's precedent here is Walt Whitman, who processes external and internal stimuli all over but especially on the skin and converts them into the organization/organism of the poem. Such kinetic conversions, which restore language to the human organism, are antithetical to metaphoric or symbolic conversions, which work by substitution and displacement.

Interestingly, Olson appears to have admired "Biotherm." O'Hara, he writes, was "*the* other poet for all of us to have lived out the rest of this century by, simply that his tone and pitch was to be the lyre of this too, he was so capable of footing the measure once his feet were on the way. (The long poem in fine print to Bill Berkson . . . so established his priority amongst us that it is lonely here." In *Homage to Frank O'Hara*, ed. Bill Berkson and Joe LeSueur, *Big Sky* 11–12 (1978): 178.

19 Quoted in Derrida, *Writing and Difference*, p. 179.

20 This is Jacques Lacan's wording; see *The Language of the Self: The Function of Language in Psychoanalysis*, trans. Anthony Wilden (New York: Dell, 1968), p. 84.

21 William Carlos Williams, *Paterson* (New York: New Directions, 1963), pp. 108, 111; *The Collected Earlier Poems* (New York: New Directions, 1966), p. 271. "Stealing" is Artaud's term, and Derrida's analysis of its range of implications is relevant to the economy of "Biotherm" as well.

22 Anthony Wilden in Lacan, *The Language of the Self*, pp. 129–130.

23 The term "sliding" is Lacan's. See "The Insistence of the Letter in the Unconscious," in *The Structuralists from Marx to Levi-Strauss*, ed. Richard and Fernande DeGeorge (Garden City, N.Y.: Doubleday, 1972), p. 297.

24 Deleuze, "The Schizophrenic and Language," pp. 286, 287, 285, 290–92. Here, O'Hara presents Olson's "muthologos" in action; while Olson does not go beyond using food imagery, O'Hara does "eat" the "book."

25 Deleuze, "The Schizophrenic and Language," p. 287.

26 Lacan, *The Language of the Self*, p. 85.

CHAPTER TEN

1 *The Complete Poems of Emily Dickinson*, ed. Thomas H. Johnson (Boston: Little, Brown, 1960), no. 285. Subsequent references to Dickinson's poems will be cited in the text as P–, followed by the poem's number.

2 Elsewhere, in P–18, Dickinson juxtaposes the Christian version of immortality with the Transcendentalist vision and uses one to dissect the other, giving a mock-Christian burial to dying nature and paying mock-Transcendentalist homage to the dying Christian hope for Heaven. Dickinson parodies both versions of an atemporal "heaven" by playing her writerly alliterations (Summer-Sister-Seraph and Bee-Butterfly-Breeze) and, as Harold Bloom has pointed out, her allusions to Bryant and Emerson against each other. Bloom writes, "Parody of a natural or analogical hope could hardly be taken farther. . . . She is distrustful of finding sermons in gentians, even as she is of Bacchic possession." Bloom, "Bacchus and Merlin: The Dialectic of Romantic Poetry in America," *Ringers in the Tower*, pp. 309–10.

3 In P–1072, Dickinson refers to herself as "Empress of Calvary," in a more explicit comparison with Christ.

4 See Sharon Cameron's discussion of this subject in *Lyric Time: Dickinson and the Limits of Genre* (Baltimore: Johns Hopkins University Press, 1979).

5 Julia Kristeva's parallel but slightly different analysis of the contemporary dilemma of women offers an interesting perspective on Dickinson. Both the symbolic (semantic) and functional (syntactic) classifications of words constitute systems of creating meaning by positing an absent signified and a material signifier that is absented in order to signify or mean. The role of women in this system is to be an absence—the symbolic or the signified—for the categories of absence and presence, as they are established in the socialization of actual families, originate with the distinction between female and male, with the absence or presence of the iconic signifier, the penis, as the focal point. Thus the woman who consents to enter into the system by which cultural meanings are generated in fact enters into a sacrificial sociocultural contract and agrees to represent a lack, which explains her concurrent placement in supportive roles and backup professions like motherhood, nursing, and teaching. Kristeva urges that women politically oppose the symbolic operations of language by resisting semantic and syntactic transparency, by resisting the absence-presence dichotomy ("Women's Time," trans. Alice Jardine and Harry Blake, *Signs* 7, no. 1 [Autumn 1981]: 13–35). But to carry the argument a step further and apply it to Dickinson's concerns, emphasizing the signifier and partaking of its power by insisting on literal presence places the language user in another dichotomous system and locks her into mortality, cutting her off from the power of the signified—the absent Divinity or, in more Dickinsonian terms, the Divinity of Absence. Thus Dickinson gains the power of writing at the expense of losing heaven. These associations inform P–789:

> On a Columnar Self—
> How ample to rely
> In Tumult—or Extremity—
> How good the Certainty
>
> That Lever cannot pry—
> And Wedge cannot divide
> Conviction—That Granitic Base—
> Though None be on our Side—
>
> Suffice Us—for a Crowd—
> Ourself—and Rectitude—
> And that Assembly—not far off
> From furthest Spirit—God—

Albert Gelpi notes the "male connotations" of "columnar" and reads the poem as celebrating the strength of the poet who has assimilated her animus (*The Tenth Muse*, p. 267–68). His gloss on line 7 above supports such a reading: in a letter, Dickinson called Emerson's *Representative Men* "a little Granite Book you can lean upon" (*The Letters of Emily Dickinson*, ed. Thomas H. Johnson [Cambridge: Harvard University Press, 1958], no. 481. Subsequent references will be cited as L–, followed by the letter number). Leaning on the male self, this reading goes, the poet enlists the support of a pantheon of father figures. Approached in my terms, however, the poem becomes ironic. "Columnar" also suggests columns of print, especially the "columnar" shape of poems; the "Columnar Self," then, is the self in print, rectified by the male power of the signifier that it has erected. But the "Granitic" column is also a gravestone, the signifier that blocks "Assembly" and permanently defers access to God—who remains beyond the "furthest Spirit."

6 In P–214 as well, Dickinson parodies Emerson's "Bacchus," lightly dismissing such inspiration by exposing its basis in natural law. Her "Inebriate of Air" is evicted from the "inn" when the "endless summer days" end, and is not admitted into the company of the saved. Dickinson has no more use for such a "sublime" than she has for the "saved."

7 Dickinson's hymn stanza works with this basic form: $a_4b_3c_4b_3$. Useful studies of her metric form are Allen, *American Prosody*; Brita Lindberg-Seyersted, *The Voice of the Poet: Aspects of Style in the Poetry of Emily Dickinson* (Cambridge: Harvard University Press, 1968); and David Porter, *Emily Dickinson and the Modern Idiom* (Cambridge: Harvard University Press, 1981).

8 Dickinson's "off" or "slant" rhymes—given the trouble she takes to rhyme—are, again, subversive; like her use of Christian vocabulary, her rhyming questions the Emersonian assumption that the universe rhymes. Her practice suggests that only poems rhyme—and then not without considerable pains. For a detailed and discerning analysis of Dickinson's idiosyncratic style, see Porter, *Emily Dickinson and the Modern Idiom*.

9 A pertinent example of how grammatical deviance undermines statement is in P–290, where a comma insinuates itself into an otherwise reasonable statement and bisects a primary presence— the link of the grammatical subject ("I") to the actor-speaker ("I am") of the sentence—that is the basis of articulation:

But their Competeless Show
Will entertain the Centuries
When I, am long ago,
An Island in dishonored Grass—
Whom none but Beetles—know.

Of course, the comma that isolates the "I" also separates the lasting "Show" of her poems from the passing of her. Thus the punctuation mark that points up "mere" writing—that introduces periodization, subordination, and temporality into the authoritative identity of "I am"—also saves the "I" from identity with nature and dissolution into it, thereby mastering what threatens to master a "mere" writer. The dialectic Dickinson works with here is discussed by Jacques Derrida in "Plato's Pharmacy," where he shows how the Logos, in order to sustain itself as the Word, requires its opposite, a writing, a mimesis of the living word; but writing is the "dangerous supplement" that usurps the power of the Logos it would substitute for (*Dissemination*, pp. 80, 90–93).

10 Dickinson writes to Thomas Wentworth Higginson (L–271): "I had no Monarch in my life, and cannot rule myself, and when I try to organize—my little Force explodes—and leaves me bare and charred." To read this "admission" as a plea for help to learn "control" is to seriously misread it. Dickinson knows that "organization" and "rule" are monarchical prerogatives, and giving one up she must give up the other. Indeed, such "explosion" defines her subversive poetry, which skews organized categories and indulges in an excess of meaning that is erotic and potentially destructive. For example, one of Dickinson's most explicitly erotic poems, "Wild Nights," lingers between the two different readings that it entertains: Eden may be a heaven-haven, where she might moor and find relief from the wild nights of earthly passions; it may also be an earthly paradise, the fulfillment of erotic desires. It is impossible to say whether heaven is the subject of her metaphor and love the

analogue, or vice versa. And this promiscuity or excess of meaning is both erotic and "heavenly." Dickinson's layering of the semantic axis of her poems slows down a poem's movement and the reader's pace to create an erotic language that resists diachrony. Yet the source of such a multiplicity of meanings is diachrony itself, which Dickinson explores in P–1498:

Glass was the Street—in tinsel Peril
Tree and Traveler stood—
Filled was the Air with merry venture
Hearty with Boys the Road—

Shot the lithe Sleds like shod vibrations
Emphasized and gone
It is the Past's supreme italic
Makes this Present mean—

The contract of meaning by absenting the literal present, by making the "Present" "Past," diminishes the present even as it endows it with significance. At the same time, the multiplicity of meanings—the polysemy—of "mean" endows the word with a presence that belies the argument of the poem, which locates value (import or "italic") in the past. Dickinson's poetic truth is not incarnational; it is not even a legitimate reproduction, repetition, or mimesis. It is a diacritical truth that draws the line between presence and loss in representation: "Night is the morning's Canvas / Larceny—legacy—" (P–7). And in this representational breach, which is Dickinson's concern, the Logos yields, and yields to logic.

11 L–470. In Dickinson, the pen has more inflections than the voice, precisely because writerly features call into doubt the context of the written word.

12 The syllable, the grammatical threshold between articulation and disarticulation, sense and non-sense, has thematic analogues in the threshold between the temporal and the timeless that pain and, ultimately, death mark. Dickinson writes: "I hesitate which word to take, as I can take but few and each must be the chiefest, but recall that Earth's most graphic transaction is placed within a syllable, nay, even a gaze" (L–873). Between a multiple choice of words and a silent gaze lies the transactional line of syllable-death. This equation is reiterated in:

The Living—tell—
The Dying—but a Syllable—
The Coy Dead—None—   [P–408]

It also informs P–1409:

Could mortal lip divine
The undeveloped Freight
Of a delivered syllable
'Twould crumble with the weight.

Divining the "Freight" of a "delivered syllable" would simultaneously deliver the "mortal lip" into the status of divinity and kill it, for "crumble," connoting the breakdown of stone or clay, evokes Dickinson's many images of gravestones—the "granite lip" of P–182, for example. "Undeveloped Freight," of course, is the temporal displacement and death projected by the syllable. When the syllables combine, we have the *developed fright*, the temporal march of the poem paralleling other decay:

Crumbling is not an instant's Act
A fundamental pause
Dilapidation's processes
Are organized Decays.

. . . .

Ruin is formal—Devil's work
Consecutive and slow—

Fail in an instant, no man did
Slipping—is Crash's law   [P–997]

CHAPTER ELEVEN

1 James E. Miller, Jr., sees Crane's career as straddling two literary groups in the 1920's: "Crane's emotions were with one camp, his style (in some aspects) with another. There were the Whitmanites . . . Gorham Munson and Waldo Frank, with eclectic mystic P. D. Ouspensky assuming the role of a kind of culture hero. And there were the classicist anti-Whitmanites, Allen Tate and Yvor Winters, with eclectic pessimist T. S. Eliot as culture hero." (*American Quest for a Supreme Fiction*, p. 164).

2 Sherman Paul, *Hart's Bridge* (Urbana: University of Illinois Press, 1972), p. 290.

3 Dickinson, *The Complete Poems*, nos. 689, 650, 644.

4 Heidegger, *Poetry, Language, Thought*, pp. 202, 204, 152–53, 205–09.

5 "Voyages," *The Complete Poems and Selected Letters and Prose of Hart Crane*, ed. Brom Weber (New York: Liveright, 1966), p. 37. References to this edition will hereafter be cited in the text as *CP*, followed by the page number.

6 Joseph N. Riddel, "Hart Crane's Poetics of Failure," in *Modern American Poetry: Essays in Criticism*, ed. Jerome Mazzaro (New York: McKay, 1970), pp. 273, 274. Given this strategy, Riddel suggests, "Crane's poetry is less Whitmanesque than Poesque" (p. 274).

7 "To Emily Dickinson" (*CP*, 170), who concurs:

He joins me in my Ramble—
Divides abode with me—
No Friend have I that so persists
As this Eternity.   [P–1684]

8 The source of this concept appears to be Mallarmé: "Poetry fashions a single new word which is total in itself" (Paul, *Hart's Bridge*, p. 297). And the poetic goal of achieving a stasis within motion appears to be formulated by Valéry: "The poem is a prolonged hesitation between sound and meaning." Valéry also writes that metaphor "marks in its naive principle a *groping*, a hesitation between several different expressions of one thought, an explosive incapacity that surpasses the *necessary* and *sufficient* capacity" (*The Art of Poetry*, trans. Denise Folliot [New York: Random House, 1961], p. 177). Crane, as well as John Ashbery, is influenced by the French Symbolists, following not the tonal strains that Eliot echoes but the various models of fashioning a language that "hesitates" between possible readings to give us an erotic/transcendent excess of meaning that points to a single, unspeakable word. This unspeakable word also has a precedent in Dickinson's "One" missing word that would authorize the whole system of representational substitutions. See, for example, Dickinson, *The Complete Poems*, no. 581.

9 Allen Tate charges Crane with the failure to subdue "sensation to a symbolic form"; Crane, however, is interested precisely in the "sensation" of the "threshold" that symbolic form marks. See Tate, *Reactionary Essays on Poetry and Ideas* (New York: Scribner's 1936), p. 36.

10 Roland Barthes, *Writing Degree Zero*, trans. Annette Lavers and Colin Smith (New York: Hill and Wang, 1968), pp. 46–47.

11 Dickinson, *The Complete Poems*, no. 505.

12 Ibid., no. 721.

13 Crane associates bones and shells with dead letters, a crypt-script, in other poems. "At Melville's Tomb" has the "calyx of death's bounty" give back "the dice of drowned men's bones" with "obscured" numbers, "a scattered chapter, livid hieroglyph" (*CP*, 34). In "O Carib Isle!" the shells spell "death's brittle crypt"—"Brutal necklaces . . . around each grave"—and form the shards or splinters of the poet's exploded Word (*CP*, 156–57).

14 This is Allen Tate's view: the poem, unlike the great epic poems of "our tradition," lacks an

intellectual "groundwork"; its center is the bridge—which is "variously metaphor, symbol, and analogy"—surrounded with a "periphery of sensation" (Tate, *Reactionary Essays*, pp. 32–33).

15 Thus John Rowe's reading of *The Bridge*, which is based on the Heideggerian notion of a rift-design, takes the most balanced view: "Crane's 'primordial One' is the energy of differences, never a synthesis that would destroy those tensive and productive relations." Crane's Logos is "defined both by fusion and dispersion," for his "intrinsic Myth" is "a figure for that energy of creation and destruction in which life itself is preserved as a system of differences. Everything converges only ironically." See John Rowe, "The 'Super-Historical' Sense of Hart Crane's *The Bridge*," *Genre* 11 (Winter 1978): 610–11.

16 For a discussion of Crane on the introduction of history into the American continent, see Paul, *Hart's Bridge*, pp. 190–91.

17 See Heidegger, *Poetry, Language, Thought*, pp. 152–54. For example, "Always and ever differently the bridge escorts the lingering and hastening ways of men to and fro, so that they may get to other banks and in the end, as mortals, to the other side. . . . The bridge *gathers* to itself in *its own* way earth and sky, divinities and mortals."

18 Crane's epic trappings signify only "conceptually"; he is not writing an epic but questioning the very possibility of an epic—of immanent significance, of a charged history—by playing up the ironic, paradoxical structure of his medium. *The Bridge* projects a "truth" to the extent that it undermines the generic bases of its claim to truth—whether epic or lyric, narrative or formal.

19 Whitman, *Leaves of Grass*, p. 692. In fact, Crane is at his weakest in *The Bridge* when he tries to sound like Whitman, writing in a freer verse form and a more expansive voice. Crane is most successful when the Whitmanic vision is scanned in iambic pentameter and compressed in syntax.

20 According to R. P. Blackmur, Crane confused the two idioms: "He used the private lyric to write the cultural epic; used the mode of intensive contemplation, which secures ends, to present the mind's actions, which have no ends." Blackmur judges this confusion a "profound duplicity—a deception in the very will of things—in Crane's fundamental attitudes toward his work." The confusion also leads to his mistaking his true predecessor: "Crane had the sensibility typical of Baudelaire and so misunderstood himself that he attempted to write *The Bridge* as if he had the sensibility typical of Whitman"; more specifically, "Baudelaire aimed at control, Whitman at release." See "New Thresholds, New Anatomies," *Form and Value in Modern Poetry* (Garden City, N.Y.: Doubleday, 1957), pp. 274, 273, 272. Blackmur's standard of judgment is consistency, and Crane's diacritical logic eludes this standard.

21 Dickinson, *The Complete Poems*, no. 1411.

CHAPTER TWELVE

1 John Ashbery, *Self-Portrait in a Convex Mirror* (New York: Viking, 1975), p. 77. Subsequent references to Ashbery's work will be abbreviated in the text thus:

AWK   *As We Know* (New York: Viking, 1979)
HD   *Houseboat Days* (New York: Viking, 1977)
SP   *Self-Portrait in a Convex Mirror*
DDS   *The Double Dream of Spring* (New York: Dutton, 1970)
TP   *Three Poems* (New York: Viking, 1972)

2 Charles Altieri, in "Motives in Metaphor: John Ashbery and the Modernist Long Poem" (*Genre* 11 [Winter 1978]: 653–87), discusses Ashbery's work in the context of the "historical, stylistic, and epistemological" "betweenness" of the modernist long poem, which registers an "oppressive dichotomy between the impulse to lucidity and the impulse to lyricism" (pp. 655–56). These impulses represent, for Altieri, the Enlightenment and post-Enlightenment models of the long poem. Yet Ashbery also places himself "between" his modernist predecessors in this mode. "Daffy Duck in Hollywood" reads:

> . . . to be ambling on's
> The tradition more than the safekeeping of it. This mulch for
> Play keeps them interested and busy while the big,
> Vaguer stuff can decide what it wants—what maps, what
> Model cities, how much waste space. Life, our
> Life anyway, is between.   [*HD*, 34]

It is possible to hear in the last lines references to Charles Olson, Ezra Pound, W. C. Williams, and T. S. Eliot. Ashbery situates himself "between" the concerns of these poets—much as Crane placed himself between his predecessors—but without even the ironic promise to "bridge" them.

3 "Craft Interview with John Ashbery," in *The Craft of Poetry: Interviews from* The New York Quarterly, ed. William Packard (Garden City, N.Y.: Doubleday, 1974), pp. 112, 121, 123. "Litany," in its deconstruction of prayer, seems to formalize the last divestiture.

4 John Ashbery, "The Invisible Avant-Garde," in *Avant-Garde Art*, ed. Thomas B. Hess and John Ashbery (New York: Collier, 1967), p. 184. Ashbery appears to regard his work in these terms: "I think there's something quite reckless about my poetry in general; I think for many people it's quite debatable whether it is poetry or not, and it is for me too. And I can never be certain that I'm doing the right thing by writing this way which nevertheless seems the only right way of writing to me. I think the poignancy of this position gets into the poetry too and intensifies it" (Packard, *The Craft of Poetry*, p. 128).

5 Packard, *The Craft of Poetry*, p. 121. This remark appears to be the source of a number of readings. Charles Molesworth, for example, describes Ashbery's style as a play between prose syntax and a figurative excess: "Much of the feel of Ashbery's poetry comes from the tension between its proselike discursiveness and the random, sometimes elliptical tenuousness of its associative gatherings" (*The Fierce Embrace* [Columbia, Mo.: University of Missouri Press, 1979], p. 170). Marjorie Perloff's reading works on the same model but with a Heideggerian vocabulary: Ashbery's is a dialectic "of opening and closing, of revelation and re-veiling, of simultaneous disclosure and concealment" (*The Poetics of Indeterminacy: Rimbaud to Cage* [Princeton: Princeton University Press, 1981], p. 262). In David Kalstone's terms, Ashbery attempts "to keep the poem's accounting powers even with the pace of inner and outer events," balancing "our experience of particulars" with the "generalizing and pattern-making powers." Thus he also observes a tension between meaningfulness and randomness, but he tends to situate this dialectic in the meeting of art (concision, "to leave all out") and life (copiousness, "to put it all down" [*TP*, 3]). See David Kalstone, *Five Temperaments* (New York: Oxford University Press, 1977), pp. 194, 195, 188–193. In Ashbery's "all-embracing" (Packard, *The Craft of Poetry*, p. 122) or "environmental" kind of poetry, however, the art-life dialectic is internalized in the crossing of the opposing axes of language and compositional dynamics. Charles Altieri's reading touches on this issue: Ashbery's "decreation" of the lyric (the "host" norm Ashbery sets up only to "decreate") proceeds by subjecting the "concentrative focus of the lyric imagination to a series of self-conscious dispersals over apparently diverse associations." Ashbery plays pattern and contingency off each other, because for him "a lyrical stance not aware of its own dispersal among contingent anti-lyric elements traps the mind in nostalgia and self-deceit" (Altieri, "Motives in Metaphor," pp. 659–61).

6 Ashbery suggests that his compositional strategy reflects how "experience happens" to him. He tells an interviewer: "I can concentrate on the things in this room and our talking together, but what the context is is mysterious to me." See "The Art of Poetry 33," *Paris Review* 90 (1983): 43.

7 Packard, *The Craft of Poetry*, p. 123.

8 Ibid., p. 124.

9 "The Art of Poetry 33," p. 56.

10 Quoted in Richard Kostelanetz, "How to Be a Difficult Poet," *New York Times*, 23 May 1976, Magazine section.

11 Crane, *The Complete Poems*, p. 221. I suspect that Crane was, in fact, an early influence on Ashbery; if there is a precedent in American poetry for *The Tennis Court Oath*, it would be Crane. And Crane's

mixing of Orphic language with the profane idiom of the "tribe" in, for example, the "River" section of *The Bridge* is a precedent for Ashbery's characteristic ironic juxtapositions of the diction of "the old poems" with the verbal debris of pop culture.

12 Ibid., p. 98.

13 "The Art of Poetry 33," p. 57. This effect characterizes not only Ashbery's syntax but his form. For example, his "long" line allows him—in his words—an "expanded means of utterance": "Saying a very long thing in place of what might originally have been a much shorter and more concise one is an overflowing of the meaning. It often seems to me to have almost a sexual quality to it in the sense that the sexual act is a kind of prolongation of and improvisation on time in a very deep personal way which is like music, and there's something of the expansiveness of eroticism in these lines very frequently for me, although that's by no means a conscious thing that I undertake in writing them" (Packard, *The Craft of Poetry*, p. 124–25). The idea of a long line that overflows with meaning as opposed to a short, witholding line implies a norm line, a coincidence of meaning and length, quality and quantity, against which these improvisations are sounded. Such a norm is present only as a ghost in Ashbery, a conventional residue of blank verse. Yet Ashbery's long line does not resemble Whitman's, either, for his, too, is a natural base that grounds the rhetoric. Ashbery writes:

> *There is no soothsaying*
> *Yet it happens in rows, windrows*
> *You call them in your far country*   [*AWK*, 67]

The allusion here to Whitman's "loose windrows"—the "natural" writing of a "far country"— suggests that Ashbery's concept of a line is not of a natural unit.

14 Ashbery distinguishes "meaning" from "message": "Meaning yes, but message no. I think my poems mean what they say, and whatever might be implicit within a particular passage, but there is no message" ("The Art of Poetry 33," p. 44).

15 Leslie Wolf observes that Ashbery detaches language "from any *consistent* referential process" ("The Brushstroke's Integrity," *Beyond Amazement: New Essays on John Ashbery*, ed. David Lehman [Ithaca: Cornell University Press, 1980], p. 246). He evokes a multiplicity of referential codes, engages a multiplicity of interpretive codes, but resists reduction to any one, consistent code. Hence, as Jonathan Culler observes about Ashbery, "connections are multiple and tenuous, especially since the plethora of deictics prevents us from constructing a discursive situation and determining which are its prime constituents"; thus we become aware of and question our procedures of ordering and "naturalizing" texts according to a teleological procedure, making the elements of the text answer to "a sense of totality" (*Structuralist Poetics* [Ithaca: Cornell University Press, 1975], pp. 169, 171).

16 "The Art of Poetry 33," p. 46–47.

17 Ibid., p. 43.

18 Dickinson, *The Complete Poems*, no. 1129.

19 Dickinson, *The Complete Poems*, no. 1651; Crane, *The Complete Poems*, p. 37. Crane's note of crisis, also heard in Dickinson's "precarious Gait" (no. 875), is not available to Ashbery, among whose predecessors or foils are Dickinson and Crane themselves.

20 If Dickinson tends to be misread as a Christian poet, Ashbery is misread as an entirely secular poet. Both are situated between knowing and not knowing; they are agnostic gnostics. Marjorie Perloff notes that "however we splice the parts, 'Litany' is, first and foremost, a penitential poem, playing on the conventions of intercession, supplication, and deprecation. Thus religious vocabulary . . . floats to the surface of the text repeatedly only to disappear once more as if the presence of these words were accidental" (*Poetics of Indeterminacy*, p. 283).

21 Dickinson, *The Complete Poems*, no. 437.

22 "The Art of Poetry 33," p. 50.

23 John Ashbery, "The Impossible," *Poetry* 90, no. 4 (July 1957): 251.

24 Marjorie Perloff reads the poem as an "open field of narrative possibilities" (*Poetics of Indeterminacy*, pp. 280–81). The idea of an open field challenges the convention of the single column and implies

that the page as field offers a truer and more "central" role for poetic language. Yet Ashbery's is a subversive technique, which challenges at once the authority of convention (the single column) and the authority of experience (the page as a force field).

25 If we take Crane's gloss in *The Bridge* as one of Ashbery's models, we see how he revises Crane. Crane's dialogical poem stands on the threshold between two kinds of mutually defining discourses: the lyrical fragmentation into momentary stases is countered by the epical (grammatical and narrative) regathering of the story line. Ashbery levels this qualitative distinction, so that not even the deconstructionist's diacritical path is "central," and beginning with "Litany," Ashbery explicitly questions his own authority. Since his project is to "dismantle" authorizing rhetorics and procedures, his becoming all but canonized as an authority on our times is something of an unintentional parody of the rhetoric of his work. Certain passages in "Litany" suggest he desires to divest himself of such early "stellification"—though no doubt "secretly satisfied with the result" (*SP, 80*):

> In the occupied countries
> You are raised to the statute of a god, no one
> Questions your work, its validity, all
> Are eager only to support it. . . .   [*AWK,* 46]

Ashbery's increased flirting—in *As We Know, Shadow Train*, and *A Wave*—with the "bad line" and even the bad poem may also be seen as resisting his own authority.

Index

Abrams, M. H., 70
Allegory, 5, 13, 14, 218; and metonymy, 6;
  retrospective structure of, 6, 7, 8, 13; and
  dualism, 8; reductive formalism of, 8
Allen, Gay Wilson, 136
Altieri, Charles, 239, 240
American poetry: and literary authority, 1–3,
  7, 12, 17–22, 133; and tradition, 1–3, 12–
  14; and romanticism, 2, 12, 13; types of, 3,
  7–12
Ammons, A. R., 1, 213
Anagogy, 5, 6, 7, 9, 14, 121–23, 156–57, 168;
  and synecdoche, 6, 9; and poetic form, 9;
  and metamorphic figuration, 9, 120–23,
  145–49; and time, 14
Analogical meaning. See Tropological meaning
Analogy, 4, 6, 8, 13, 156, 218; and resemblances, 4, 6, 8; and poetic form, 8. See
  also Emerson and analogy; Stevens and
  analogy
Anomaly, 9–10
Aristotle, 4, 215
Artaud, Antonin, 165–66, 168, 233
Ashbery, John, 1, 11, 12, 217; and irony, 9, 10;
  and Crane, 9–10, 200, 201, 204, 205, 207,
  240–41, 242; and Dickinson, 9–10, 200,
  201, 205–10 passim, 241; deconstructive
  rhetoric of, 10, 200–01, 209; and Stevens,
  10, 201, 205–06; and tradition, 200, 206,
  207, 208, 239–40; diacritical language of,
  201, 204, 208–09, 241, 242; "Litany," 201,
  208–12, 240, 241, 242; randomness and
  meaningfulness in, 201–02, 205–10 passim,
  240; "Self-Portrait in a Convex Mirror,"
  202; subversive techniques of, 202, 205,
  240, 241; and Orphic poetry, 203, 204,

208, 241; and Emerson, 203, 205; and time,
  203, 205, 211; and romantic sublime, 203–
  04, 211; illegality of discourse of, 205–06;
  and liturgical rhetoric, 208, 241; and paradox, 210; and parody, 210–12; and Whitman, 241; poetic line of, 241. See also Crane
  and Ashbery

Barthes, Roland, 194
Baudelaire, Charles, 36, 37, 239
Benn, Gottfried, 62
Berryman, John, 11, 17, 62, 225
Bishop, Elizabeth: and analogy, 8; and Emerson,
  8, 82, 101, 102; and representation, 101,
  103–08, 109; interpretations of, 101, 227–
  28; and Stevens, 101–02; "Santarém," 102;
  reality and imagination in, 102–04; "The
  Gentleman of Shalott," 102–05; "Poem,"
  105, 106; "The Monument," 106, 112;
  "The Map," 106–08; emotion in, 107, 108;
  and metaphysics, 107, 109; "Filling Station," 107–08; "12 O'Clock News," 108;
  "Insomnia," 109; and the reverses of art,
  109, 110, 111; "Anaphora," 110; "Sonnet,"
  110–11; "One Art," 111–12; and history,
  112, 113; "Paris, 7 A.M.," 112, 113; "Over
  2,000 Illustrations and a Complete Concordance," 113; "Faustina, or Rock Roses,"
  113–14; "At the Fishhouses," 114; "In the
  Waiting Room," 114–15
Blackmur, R. P., 239
Blessing, Richard Allen, 224
Bloom, Harold, 12, 60, 90, 124, 215, 226, 235;
  on Emerson, 1, 2, 74–75, 213; on rhetoric,
  4, 214–15; on the "American sublime," 24;
  on metonymy, 216

243

Bonaparte, Marie, 221

Borroff, Marie, 98

Bradley, Sculley, 230

Burke, Kenneth: on the four master tropes, 4, 5, 215, 216; on criticism, 34; on Poe, 34, 221; on irony, 217

Byron, George Gordon, Lord, 37

Cameron, Sharon, 235

Carroll, Lewis, 168

Confessional poetry, 40–41

Costello, Bonnie, 228

Crane, Hart, 1, 12, 213, 214; and irony, 9, 10, 188–92 passim; and Dickinson, 9–10, 188–99 passim, 238; and Eliot, 10, 188, 193, 238; and anomalous forms, 10, 189–94 passim; and the Word, 10, 189–99 passim, 238; and Whitman, 188, 191, 195–99 passim, 238, 239; and metaphor, 188, 193, 194, 195; and Symbolism, 188, 197, 238; "The Bridge," 188, 197–99, 238–39; and the epic, 188–89, 197–99, 239; diacritical language of, 188–94, 198–99, 239; and pain, 189; "Voyages," 189, 192, 194–96, 205; as mythic poet, 190–91; "Lachrymae Christi," 190–91; and poetic form, 191–92; "Paraphrase," 191–92; and time, 191–92, 195, 197–99; "The Broken Tower," 192–93; and Emerson, 193; and Poe, 193, 238; "At Melville's Tomb," 193, 238; and Ashbery, 194, 195, 238; "A Name for All," 196; and writing, 196, 238; "O Carib Isle!" 196–97; and the lyric, 197–99, 239. *See also* Ashbery and Crane

Culler, Jonathan, 241

Dante Alighieri, 5, 151–52

Davidson, Edward, 219

Deleuze, Gilles, 168

de Man, Paul: on allegory and symbol, 24, 218, 219; on syntagmatic and paradigmatic relations, 214; on rhetoric, 214–15; as ironic critic, 215; on allegory and irony, 218

Derrida, Jacques: on the metaphysics of centrality, 2, 214; on literary authority, 18; on writing, 32, 229, 236; on the dangerous supplement, 54; on Artaud, 165

Dickinson, Emily, 1, 3, 7, 12, 13, 14, 112, 213, 214, 217, 218; and irony, 9, 10, 173, 174, 189, 235; and anomalous forms, 9–10; formal subversiveness of, 10, 173, 174, 175, 179, 235, 236; and Christianity, 10, 174–75, 181, 209, 235; and the hymnal form, 10, 179, 236; and tradition, 13–14; "One day is there of the Series," 173; "Who were 'the Father and the Son,'" 173; and authority, 173, 174–76, 179, 181, 238; and writing, 173–79 passim, 185–87, 235, 236, 237; "Behind Me—dips Eternity—," 174; "God is a distant—stately Lover—," 174; "I dreaded that first Robin, so," 174; and gender, 174–75, 177, 235–36; and the Logos, 174–76, 179, 180, 236, 237, 238; "Upon the gallows hung a wretch," 175; and inspiration, 175–76, 195; "Let Us play Yesterday—," 176; "To pile like Thunder to its close," 176; "I would not paint—a picture—," 176, 195; and Emerson, 176, 235, 236; "It was given to me by the Gods—," 176–77; "To fill a Gap," 177; and letters, 177, 179, 184–87; "To tell the Beauty would decrease," 177, 182; diacritical language of, 177–79, 180–81, 186, 237; "I dwell in Possibility—," 178; "They shut me up in Prose—," 178; and illicit meanings, 178, 179–80, 185–86, 236–37; and poetic form, 178–80; and syllables, 179, 181–83, 237; and punctuation, 179, 236; and violations of grammar, 179, 236; literalizing imagination of, 181; "Those—dying then," 181; "If my Bark sink," 182; "More than the Grave is closed to me—," 182; "The Veins of other Flowers," 182; "Forever at His side to walk—," 183; "Of Paradise' existence," 183; "One Joy of so much anguish," 183; "The Brain—is wider than the Sky—," 183; "Apparently with no surprise," 184–85; "'Sic transit gloria mundi,'" 185; "There is a word," 185; "The Zeroes—taught us—Phosphorous," 186; "Without a smile—Without a Throe," 186; "By homely gift and hindered Words," 187; "'Tis One by One—the Father counts—," 187; and pain, 189, 194, 237; "Wild Nights," 205, 236–37; "Prayer is the little implement," 209; "The Gentian weaves her fringes—," 235; "On a Columnar Self—," 235–36; "Of Bronze—and Blaze—," 236; and death, 237; "Could mortal lip divine," 237; "Glass was the Street—in tinsel Peril," 237; "Unit, like Death, for Whom?" 237; "Crumbling is not an instant's Act," 238. *See also* Ashbery and Dickinson; Crane and Dickinson

Donoghue, Denis, 229
Dramatic poetry, 7, 38–39, 41, 61–62
Duncan, Robert, 11, 232

Eliot, T. S., 1, 10, 214, 217, 218; and allegory,
7, 8, 40; and Poe, 7–8, 36–47 passim, 223;
The Waste Land, 20, 37, 41–46, 220, 222;
"Tradition and the Individual Talent," 20,
41, 42, 45; and Symbolism, 36, 238; and
Whitman, 36, 44, 45; displacement of, 37;
early personae of, 37; historical belatedness
of, 37, 38, 39, 42, 44, 47, 48, 222; and tradition, 37, 38–39, 41–43, 45, 48, 222, 223;
and Pound, 37, 42, 222; "The Love Song of
J. Alfred Prufrock," 37–40; and poetic
form, 38, 39–40, 46, 223; as expressionist,
38, 40, 41, 46; and dramatic verse, 38, 41;
and the dramatic monologue, 38–39; use of
epigraphs, 38–39; and textuality, 38–41
passim, 44; *Prufrock and Other Observations,*
39; and the objective correlative, 40;
"Rhapsody on a Windy Night," 40; and nature, 40, 44–47 passim; and Plath, 41, 223;
and literary authority, 42, 46; archaeological imagery of, 42, 46, 222; and originality,
42, 222; modernism of, 42–43; parodic language of, 43, 46; and the Word, 46, 47–48,
223; "Mr. Eliot's Sunday Morning Service,"
47–48; *Four Quartets,* 48–49; and criticism,
222; "The Hollow Men," 223. *See also*
Crane and Eliot; Plath and Eliot; Poe and
Eliot; Pound and Eliot
Emerson, Ralph Waldo, 7, 10, 13, 14; and literary influence, 1, 2, 213; and American
poetry, 1–3, 67, 82–83, 213, 214; and tradition, 8, 13–14, 213; and analogy, 8, 67–
68, 71–72, 82; "Uriel," 24, 72, 80, 81; theory of language of, 67–69, 81; on the poet,
68–75 passim, 81; poetry and fate in, 69,
72–75 passim, 76–82, 83; as essayist, 69–
71, 72–74, 75, 81, 82; poetry and prose in,
69–77 passim, 81–82, 226; and Stevens,
70, 71, 72, 80, 82; "Circles," 71, 81; "Bacchus," 74, 76; "The Poet," 75; and poetic
form, 75–76, 78–82 passim, 134–35;
"Terminus," 76; on rhyme, 76–80, 81, 82;
"Merlin," 76–80, 81, 226; "Art," 77;
"Hamatreya," 78–79; "Blight," 80; and
open form, 80, 82, 226; and Whitman, 82;
"The Snow-Storm," 92, 226–27. *See also*
Ashbery and Emerson; Bishop and Emerson; Crane and Emerson; Dickinson and

Emerson; Poe and Emerson; Stevens and
Emerson; Whitman and Emerson
Epic poetry, 7, 9, 198–99, 229–30
Expressionism, 8, 40–41, 62–63

Fenollosa, Ernest, 147, 148, 231–32
Flory, Wendy, 232
Free verse, 134–39 passim
Freud, Sigmund, 26, 53, 162, 163, 168, 220,
229, 233
Frobenius, Leo, 140–41
Frost, Robert, 1, 11, 82, 94–95, 193, 213, 214,
227
Frye, Northrop: on the four phases of symbol-
ism, 6, 217; on anagogy, 122–23; on the
"subject," 133; on oracular rhythm, 139
Fussell, Edwin, 21, 76, 229
Fussell, Paul, 135

Géfin, Laszlo, 147, 231–32
Gelpi, Albert, 214, 219, 236
Ginsberg, Allen, 11, 214, 232
Gordon, Jan B., 227

Harmon, William, 223
H.D., 11
Heidegger, Martin, 239; on poetry and history,
21, 219; on the copula, 93; on "dif-ference,"
189; on symbolic structure, 197; and open
form, 222
Hoffman, Daniel, 219–20
Homer, 12, 144–46
Huxley, Aldous, 20–21

Imagist poetry, 147–49, 156–57, 226
Interpretation, four levels of, 5, 6, 217
Irony, 5, 6, 7, 14, 215–18 passim; polyphony
of, 5; dialogical structure of, 5, 218; and literalism, 6; and anomalous forms, 7, 9, 10;
subversive strategies of, 9, 10; deconstructive rhetoric of, 10; and time, 14

Jakobson, Roman: on metonymic and meta-
phoric organization, 131, 214, 217; on "The
Raven," 220
Jeffers, Robinson, 11

Kalstone, David, 227, 228, 240
Keats, John, 26, 44–45, 156
Kenner, Hugh, 56, 147, 153, 224, 231, 232
Kristeva, Julia, 220, 235
Kroll, Judith, 225
Kugel, James L., 137

Lacan, Jacques, 167, 169, 220
Lane, Gary, 224
Levertov, Denise, 11, 214
Literal meaning, 5, 6, 7–8, 217
Longfellow, Henry Wadsworth, 20, 141, 213
Lowell, Robert, 1, 11, 17, 214
Lukács, Georg, 72–73, 229–30

MacCaffrey, Isabel, 90
Mallarmé, Stéphane, 36, 238
Mazzaro, Jerome, 227, 228
Merrill, James, 82
Metaphor, 4, 6, 7, 13, 215, 216; and poetic
    form, 7. *See also* Analogy; Crane and meta-
    phor; Stevens and metaphor
Metonymy, 4, 6, 7, 215, 216
Miller, James E., Jr., 231, 238
Miller, J. Hillis, 227
Molesworth, Charles, 240
Moore, Marianne, 11, 82, 110
Mullen, Richard, 228

Nietzsche, Friedrich, 214, 226
Nims, John F., 224

Objective correlative, 33, 40, 63
O'Hara, Frank, 10, 11, 12; and anagogy, 9,
    156–57, 168; and Whitman, 9, 156–60
    passim, 234; on Keats, 156; on nature,
    156–57; and Pound, 156–57, 158, 165,
    167, 233; and transcendence in art, 157,
    158; on Jackson Pollock, 157, 158, 161;
    "Second Avenue," 157, 160; and referential
    language, 157, 163, 166–69; and Olson,
    157, 233, 234; and poetry as process, 157–
    58, 165–66; and the physiology of speech,
    157–69 passim, 233, 234; "Biotherm," 158,
    161–68, 234; and history, 158–59; on
    sculpture, 158–59, 233; "In Memory of My
    Feelings," 158–60, 161; and time, 159,
    166–69; and humanism, 159, 233; the self
    in, 159–60; deep surface of, 160, 161–63,
    168; and interpretation, 160, 162–63; and
    grace, 160–61; and names, 160–61; "Poem
    (Khrushchev is coming on the right day!)"
    160–61; and the Logos, 161; "Essay on
    Style," 161; intimate language of, 161, 162,
    163, 168; syllabic chemistry in, 163, 233;
    alimentary imagery in, 163–65; "Personism:
    A Manifesto," 165; and poetic form, 165–
    66; and Williams, 166–67; "Poetry,"168–
    69; "A Step Away from Them," 169; "The
    Day Lady Died," 233

Olson, Charles, 1, 11, 108, 214, 222, 232. *See
    also* O'Hara and Olson
Ovid, 31, 44, 145

Paul, Sherman, 188, 239
Perloff, Marjorie, 12, 60, 218, 240, 241
Plath, Sylvia, 11, 12; and allegory, 7, 8, 56, 59;
    and Poe, 7–8, 50, 52–53, 55, 58, 224; and
    poetic form, 41, 51–56 passim, 62, 63, 224;
    "OCEAN 1212-W," 50, 54; and the origin,
    50–51, 57, 58; archaeological imagery in,
    51; "Morning Song," 51; as Gothic writer,
    51, 55; and Eliot, 51, 56, 57, 58, 62, 63,
    225; *The Bell Jar,* 51–52; and drama, 51–56
    passim, 61, 63, 224; and textuality, 51–59
    passim; "Suicide off Egg Rock," 52; suicidal
    strategies of, 52, 53, 55; and meter, 52, 54,
    224; "Cut," 53; "Daddy," 53, 54; repetition
    in, 53, 54, 55; and literary authority, 53–61
    passim; and metonymy, 54; "The Spider,"
    55; "Two Sisters of Persephone," 56; *Ariel,*
    56, 224; *The Colossus,* 56, 224; and tradition,
    57–58, 59, 60, 224; "On the Decline of
    Oracles," 58; "The Colossus," 58, 59;
    "Hardcastle Crags," 59; and nature, 59, 60,
    63; "Barren Women," 60; "Heavy Wom-
    en," 60; "Spinster," 60; masks of, 60–61,
    225; "Lady Lazarus," 61, 62; "The Eye-
    Mote," 61–62; as expressionist, 61–63;
    "Words," 63; figuration of, 63, 225;
    "Ariel," 224. *See also* Eliot and Plath; Poe
    and Plath

Plato, 69–70
Poe, Edgar Allan, 3, 13, 14, 213, 214, 217, 218;
    and allegory, 7, 8, 24, 33, 219, 221; and
    tradition, 13–14, 18–22 passim, 25, 26,
    30–35 passim; in France, 17, 18; and Eliot,
    17, 20, 25, 34, 35, 220; and poetic failure,
    17, 20–21, 30–31; and Symbolism, 17, 25;
    and Plath, 17, 220, 221; displacement of,
    17–21 passim; and literary authority, 17–
    21 passim, 31–35 passim; and textuality,
    18, 19; and modernism, 18, 219; "William
    Wilson," 19–20; and originality, 20; and
    plagiarism, 20; and English meters, 20, 21;
    parodic language of, 20, 21, 22, 26, 27, 32;
    and poetic form, 20–33 passim; and Emer-
    son, 21, 24, 25, 30; "Ulalume," 21, 26,
    220–21; and Whitman, 21–22, 26, 219;
    "The Raven," 22, 26, 27–33, 34, 38, 40,
    52–53, 221; on poetry, 22–23; form and
    force in, 22–26 passim; and time, 22–27

passim, 219; "The Bells," 23; "Israfel," 23–24, 218; formalism of, 24, 25, 26, 33, 221; and memory, 25, 26, 31–32, 220; "Loss of Breath," 25–26; archaeological imagery of, 26; and formal closure in, 27–30, 32–33, 40, 220–21; repetition in, 28, 29, 32; and "Lenore," 28–29, 30; and letter fetishism, 28–33 passim, 221; and literary criticism, 34–35; "The Philosophy of Composition," 34–35; "The Haunted House," 40; "To Helen," 47, 223. *See also* Crane and Poe; Eliot and Poe; Plath and Poe; Whitman and Poe

Poetic language: formal and referential axes of, 3–4; and letters, 28–30

Porter, David, 213–14, 226, 236

Pound, Ezra, 1, 10, 11, 12, 213, 214, 218; and anagogy, 9, 123, 142, 232; and Whitman, 9, 141–48 passim, 231, 232; and Stevens, 12, 218, 232; and tradition, 37, 140–46 passim; and Eliot, 140; and Plotinus, 141–42; natural and textual patterns in, 141–47; and isomorphism, 142, 146, 147, 231; and the Theos, 142, 150; as mythic poet, 142–43, 148, 152, 232; and translation, 142–43, 231; canto *81*, 143, 231; and breath, 143–44, 153–55; canto *1*, 144, 145; and Homer, 144–46; canto *83*, 145, 149; canto *2*, 145–47; and ideogrammic figuration, 145–50 passim, 231–32; metamorphic language of, 145–50 passim, 232; and analogy, 146, 147, 150–52; and process, 146–48, 153–55, 232; on metaphor, 147, 148, 150, 226, 231–32; Imagism of, 147–49; "In a Station of the Metro," 149; canto *51*, 151; on names, 150, 232; and usury, 151; on Greek philosophy, 152; on Confucianism, 152–53. *See also* Eliot and Pound; O'Hara and Pound; Stevens and Pound; Whitman and Pound

Rhetoric, 2, 3, 4, 214–15
Rhyme, 30, 76–80
Ricoeur, Paul, 79
Riddel, Joseph N., 191, 226, 238
Rowe, John, 239

Said, Edward W., 219
St. Armand, Barton Levi, 221
Sandburg, Carl, 11
Sapir, Edward, 163
Scaliger, Julius Caesar, 4

Schiller, Friedrich, 7
Schneidau, Herbert, 147–48
Schwartz, Lloyd, 228
Sexton, Anne, 13
Shakespeare, William, 38, 44, 57, 70, 141
Shapiro, David, 224
Shelley, Percy Bysshe, 97
Smith, Pamela, 52, 224
Snodgrass, W. D., 11, 214
Snyder, Gary, 11, 146, 232
Spanos, William V., 223
Starobinski, Jean, 46
Stein, Gertrude, 210
Stevens, Wallace, 1, 10, 11, 12, 213, 214, 218, 222; and analogy, 8, 86, 87; and Emerson, 8, 84–93 passim, 96, 99, 226–27; and Pound, 12, 87, 218, 226; and philosophy and poetry, 84–85, 91, 93, 94, 97–98; and rhetoric, 84–91 passim, 99; "Notes Toward a Supreme Fiction," 85, 97; and time, 85–89 passim, 93–97; eccentric truth of, 85–91 passim, 96, 97, 99; and metaphor, 86, 87, 92, 93–95; and Whitman, 87, 94; and death, 88–89; freedom and fate in, 88–89; and meditation, 88–89, 96; "Sunday Morning," 88–90, 91, 227; style of, 89, 97–98; "Le Monocle de Mon Oncle," 90; "The Comedian as the Letter C," 91, 227; "The Idea of Order at Key West," 91–93; "Sea Surface Full of Clouds," 92; and the critic as poet, 92–93; "The Auroras of Autumn," 94; and Frost, 94–95, 227; "Metaphor as Degeneration," 94–95, 227; "A Primitive Like an Orb," 96; "Men Made Out of Words," 96; and poetic form, 97, 99; and Williams, 226; "Thirteen Ways of Looking at a Blackbird," 226. *See also* Ashbery and Stevens; Bishop and Stevens; Emerson and Stevens; Pound and Stevens

Stevenson, Anne, 227–28
Symbol, conceptions of, 5, 6, 13, 217
Symbolism, 25, 217
Synecdoche, 4–5, 6, 7, 14, 215, 216; integrative structure of, 4; and poetic form, 7

Tate, Allen, 46, 220, 238–39
Tennyson, Alfred, Lord, 103, 105
Thomas Aquinas, Saint, 217
Todorov, Tzvetan, 13
Tradition: metaphysics of, 2, 18; and American poetry, 12–14. *See also* Ashbery and tradition; Eliot and tradition; Plath and tradi-

Tradition (*continued*)
tion; Poe and tradition; Pound and
tradition; Whitman and tradition
Tropes, 3–4, 215; structural, 3–4, 6–7; the
four master tropes, 4–5; and time, 13–14,
218
Tropological meaning, 5, 6, 217

Valéry, Paul, 36, 238
Vendler, Helen, 98, 227, 228
Vico, Giambattista, 14, 214, 215

Waggoner, Hyatt H., 76, 82, 214, 225
Whicher, Stephen E., 80
White, Hayden, 5, 215, 216, 217
Whitman, Walt, 1, 3, 7, 10–14 passim, 213,
214, 218; and anagogy, 9, 122–23, 127; and
tradition, 13–14, 141, 143; and Poe, 119;
and the origin, 119, 121; and Emerson,
119, 122, 124, 134–35; and identity, 119–
20, 122, 125, 126, 127, 130, 139; on language, 120, 123, 131; "Crossing Brooklyn
Ferry," 120, 127, 158; and evolution, 120,
231; natural and textual patterns in, 120–
21, 124, 125; hieroglyphic language of,
120–25 passim, 129, 139; "Song of Myself,"
121, 122, 123, 126, 130, 133–34, 135, 137,
159; and "leaves of grass," 121–25 passim;
and the Logos, 122, 125; and breath, 124;
"My Legacy," 124; "There Was a Child
Went Forth," 125; "On the Beach at Night
Alone," 125, 127; "kosmos" of, 125–26;
"Kosmos," 126; "The Sleepers," 126;
"Democratic Vistas," 126, 133; and death,
126–28, 229; "Scented Herbage of My
Breast," 127; "Out of the Cradle Endlessly
Rocking," 127–28, 137; "As I Ebb'd with
the Ocean of Life," 128–29; and Pound,
129, 229; on Hegel, 130–31; and poetic
form, 130–31, 134–39; style of, 131; and
the epic, 131, 134, 229–30; prose and po-
etry in, 131, 137–39; "Mannahatta," 132;
and names, 132, 229; "One's Self I Sing,"
133; political language of, 133–34, 135,
137; prosody of, 134–36, 230; and English
meters, 135, 136, 138, 229, 230–31;
"When I Heard the Learn'd Astronomer,"
135–36; use of parallelism, 136–38; and
Biblical verse, 136–39, 230, 231; "When
Lilacs Last in the Dooryard Bloom'd," 137;
"Shakespere-Bacon's Cipher," 141. *See also*
Ashbery and Whitman; Crane and Whit-
man; Eliot and Whitman; Emerson and
Whitman; O'Hara and Whitman; Poe and
Whitman; Pound and Whitman; Stevens
and Whitman
Williams, William Carlos, 11, 37, 108, 213,
214, 217, 226, 232
Williamson, Alan, 224
Wolf, Leslie, 241
Wordsworth, William, 12, 213, 218

Yoder, R. A., 213

Zukofsky, Louis, 11, 232